OLD BOTTLES OF MACON

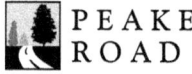 PEAKE
ROAD

Peake Road Press
6316 Peake Road
Macon, Georgia 31210-3960
1-800-747-3016
©2016 by Thomas Lowrell Pierce

Library of Congress Cataloging-in-Publication Data

Names: Pierce, Thomas Lowrell, 1929-2013, artist.
Title: Old bottles of Macon / by Thomas Lowrell Pierce.
Description: Macon, GA : Peake Road Press, 2016. | Includes bibliographical
references and index.
Identifiers: LCCN 2016000865 | ISBN 9780991574452 (pbk. : alk. paper)
Subjects: LCSH: Pierce, Thomas Lowrell, 1929-2013--Themes, motives. | Pen
drawing, American--Themes, motives. | Bottles in art. | Pitchers in art. |
Macon (Ga.)--Antiquities--Pictorial works.
Classification: LCC NC139.P53 A4 2016 | DDC 741.973--dc23
LC record available at http://lccn.loc.gov/2016000865

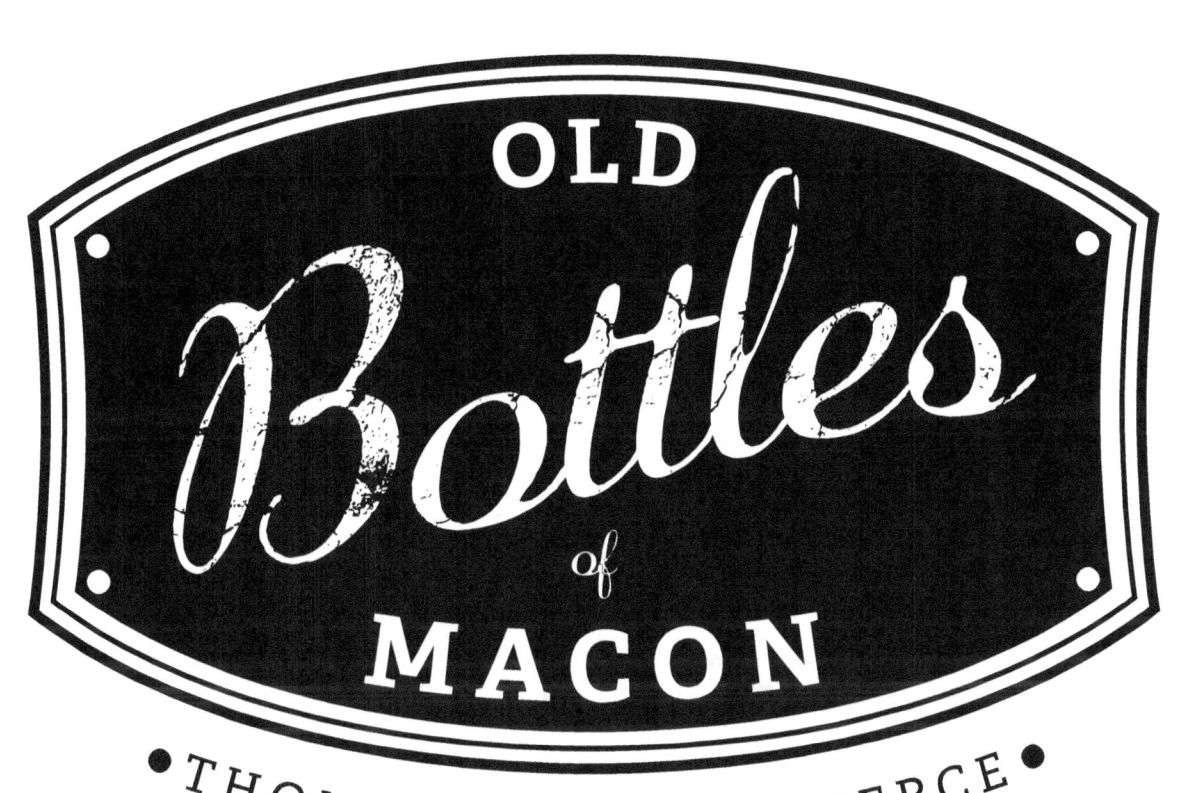

OLD

Bottles

of

MACON

• THOMAS LOWRELL PIERCE •

Introduction

Beginning around 1965, a relatively new craze spread rapidly across the U.S. Collecting antique bottles had been mostly the province of more affluent northern collectors, who had been buying and trading for decades. These bottles were selling relatively inexpensively, but the average collector thought even $5.00 was out of reach.

Times were about to change. The government began a somewhat questionable program known as "urban renewal", where the oldest, poorest, most dilapidated, and often most historic sections of towns were bulldozed flat. Then came the diggers: rich and poor, young and old, male and female. After picking through the rubble and once-foundations of these historic districts, many people began exploring other sites, such as old city dumps.

Diggers discovered thousands of bottles no one had ever heard of, their purposes and origins inscrutable. Bottle clubs formed, holding regular meetings at which members would show their most recent finds. One of these diggers and collectors was Lowrell Pierce, though Lowrell was not the average collector. He was an illustrator inspired to put every known variation of a Macon bottle to paper.

What an amazing and thrilling sight to watch Lowrell hold a bottle in one hand, to see it appear by the skill of his other hand on a blank sheet of white paper. He recorded all the known Macon bottles, many being one of a kind, many passing from his hand back to their owners, perhaps never to be seen again. Lowrell pursued this project with great passion and pride, producing the only book devoted entirely to Macon, Georgia bottles and jugs.

Of great interest to bottle collectors, historians, researchers, and anyone who has an interest in the city of Macon, Georgia, this book preserves what urban renewal unearthed. Thanks to the diligence of Lowrell, and now to this book, these bottles will never be lost again.

Thank you, Lowrell, a quiet, multitalented, unassuming man. You left your mark.

James T. Hicks
October 15, 2015

Book 1

Sodas & Household

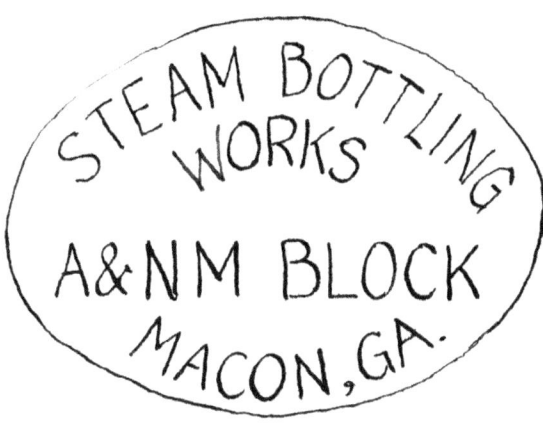

STEAM BOTTLING WORKS

A&NM BLOCK

MACON, GA.

REVERSE

THIS BOTTLE
NOT TO
BE SOLD

ALSO WITH THE EMBOSSING
IN A ROUND CIRCLE AND
THE TOP IS A CLUB LIKE.
NO EMBOSSING ON THE
REVERSE —

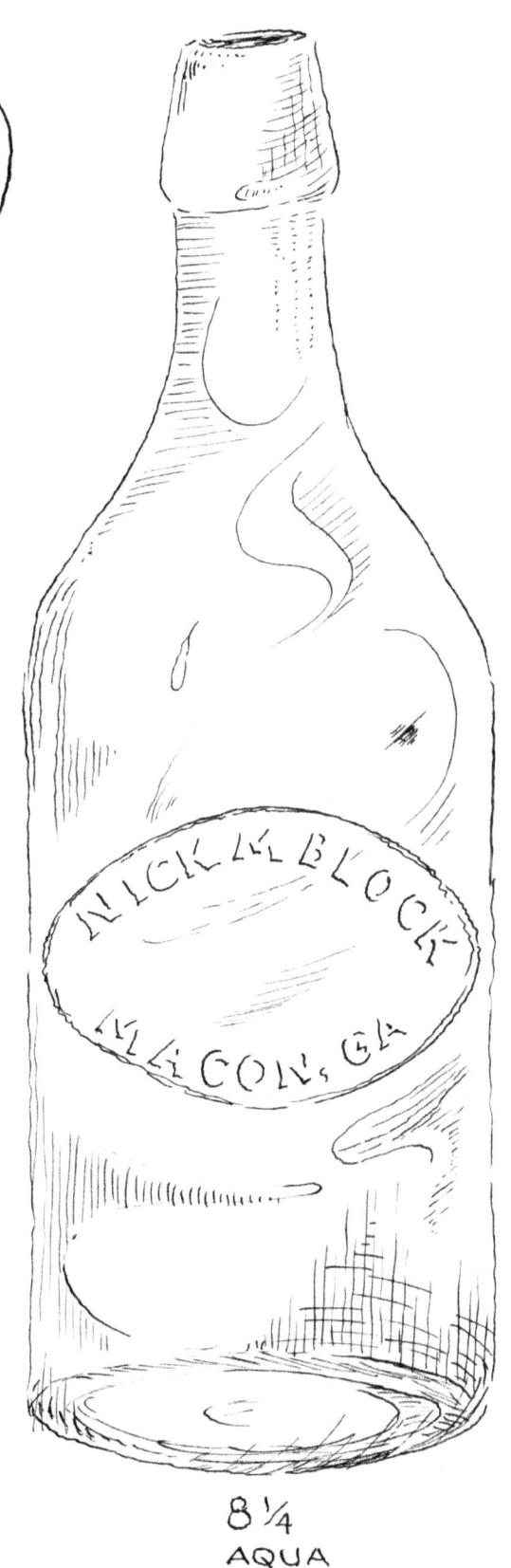

8 ¼
AQUA

7½ INCHES LIGHT GREEN
BACK SIDE - PROPERTY OF
THE ACME ICE & BOTTLING
CO.

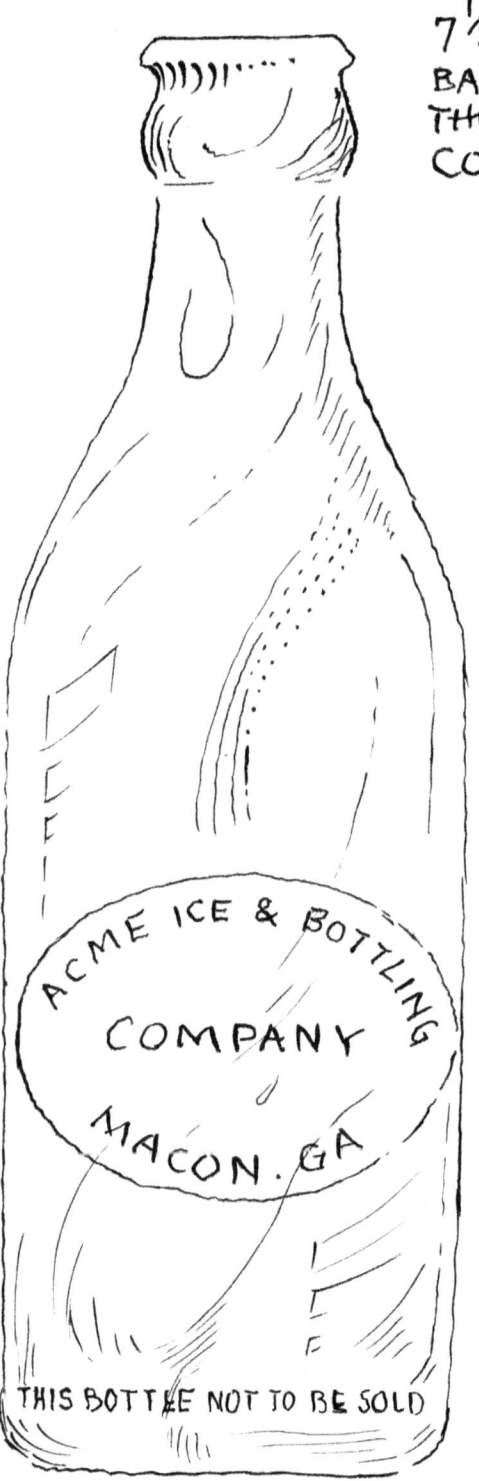

ACME ICE & BOTTLING
COMPANY
MACON. GA

THIS BOTTLE NOT TO BE SOLD

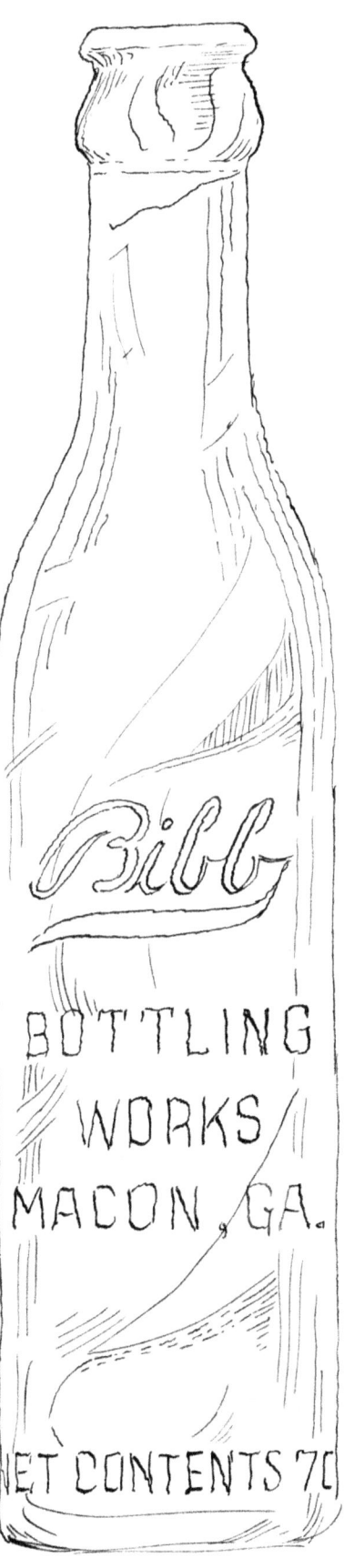

8 ¾ GREEN

Bibb

BOTTLING
WORKS
MACON, GA.

NET CONTENTS 7O

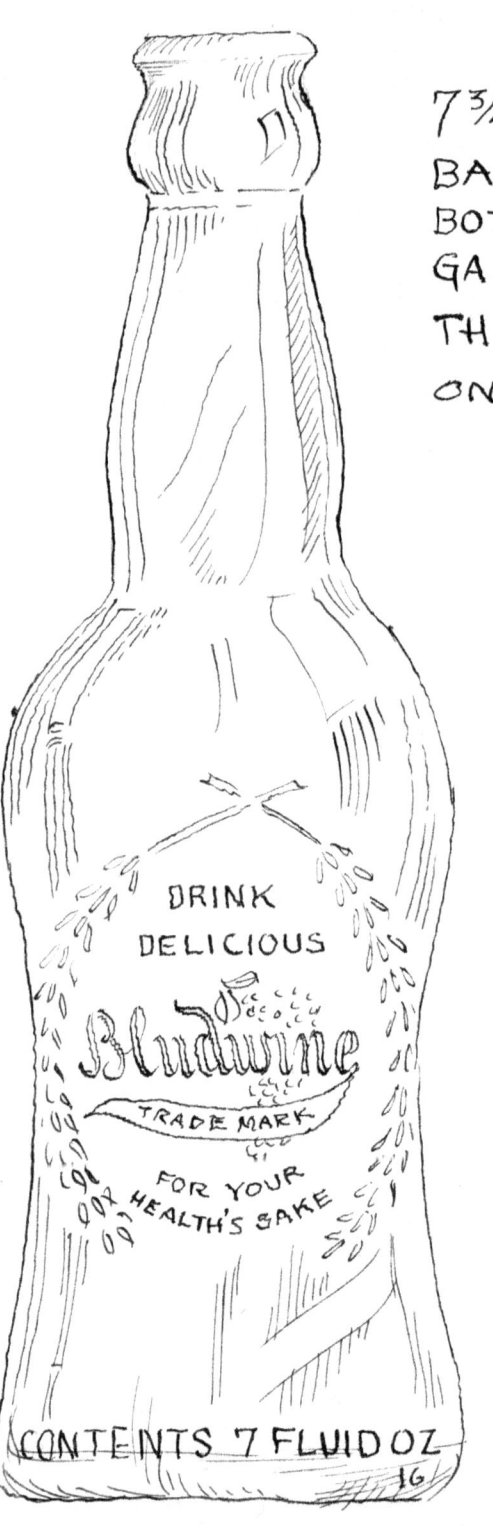

7¾ GREEN ON THE BACK, BLUDWINE BOTTLING CO. MACON GA. BY A SLUG PLATE. THEY ARE SO CLEAR ONES

DRINK DELICIOUS

Bludwine

TRADE MARK

FOR YOUR HEALTH'S SAKE

CONTENTS 7 FLUID OZ

16

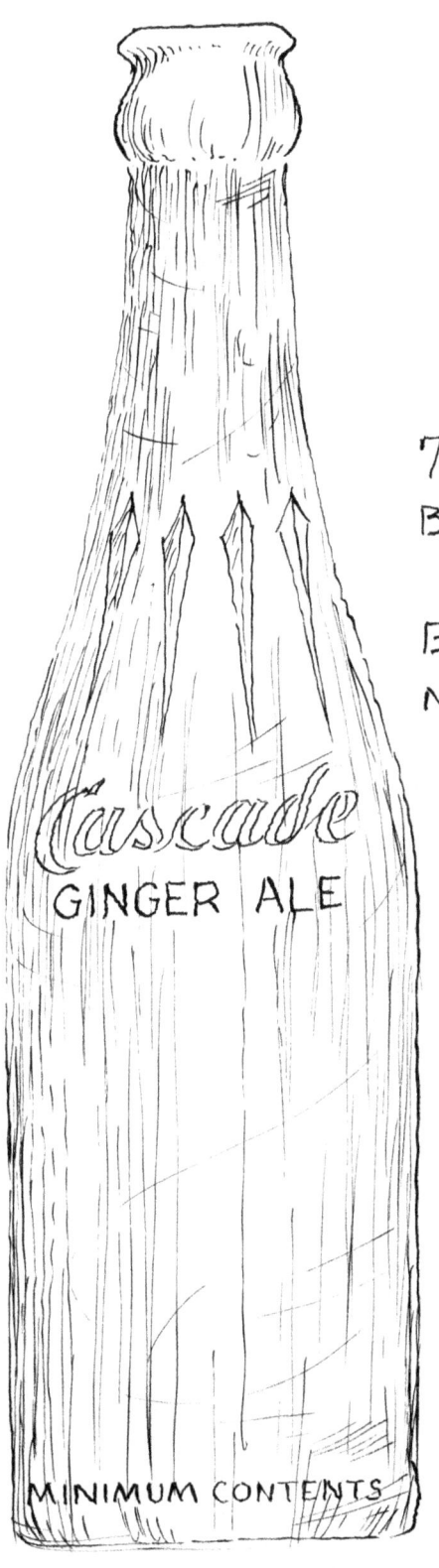

7 UP GREEN
BOTTOM - MACON, GA.
50S

BACK - 7 FLUID OZS.
MACHINE MADE

CLEAR

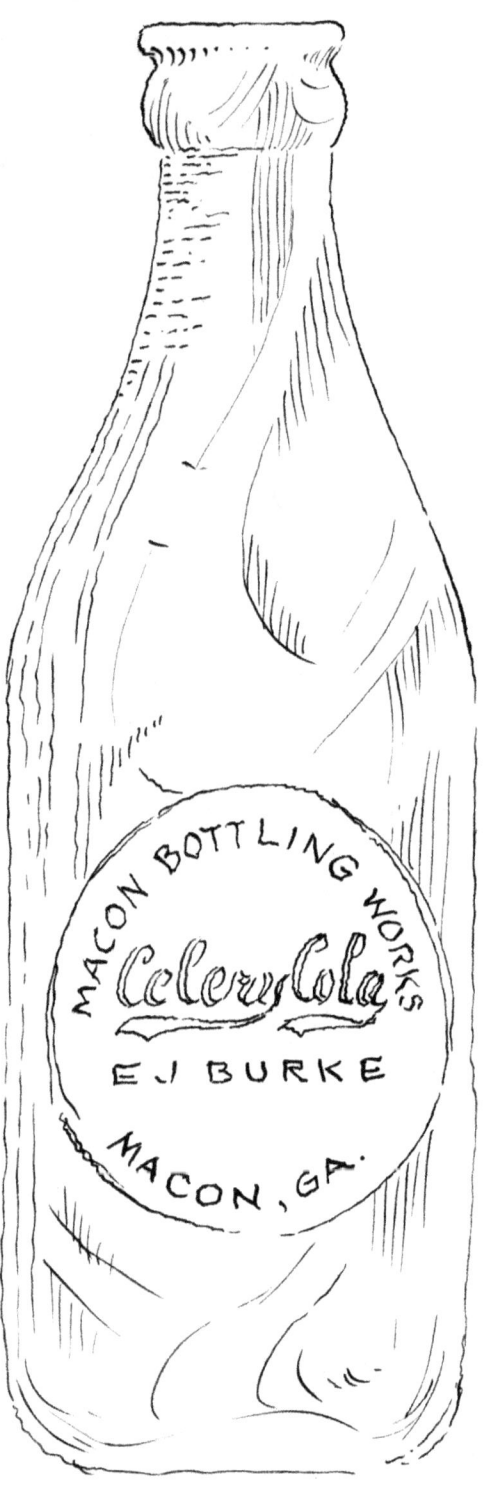

MACON BOTTLING WORKS

Celery Cola

E J BURKE

MACON, GA.

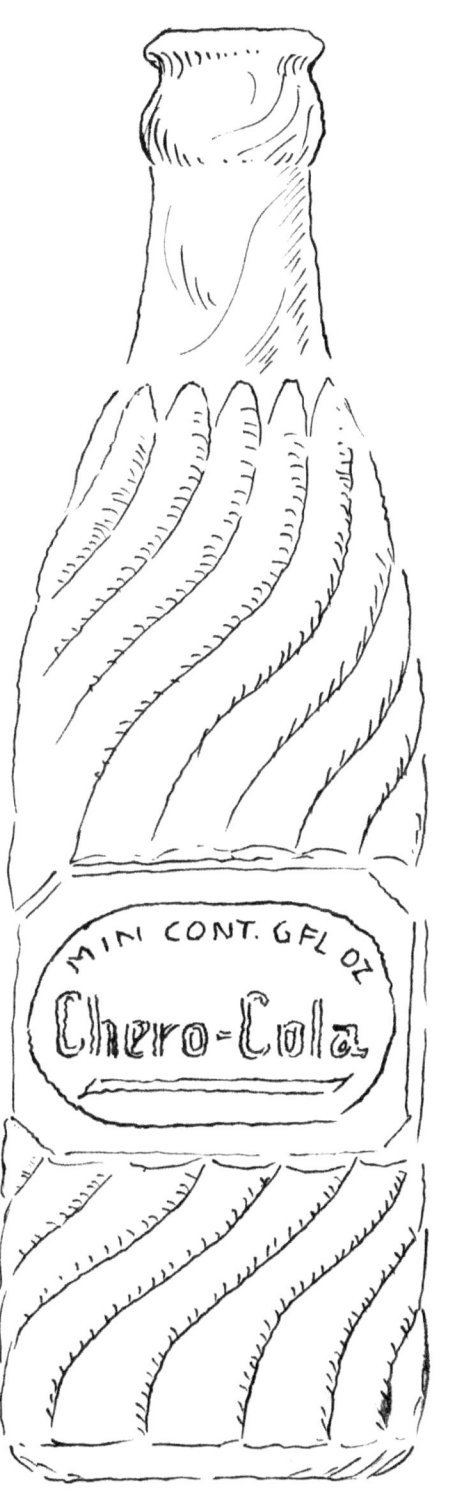

MIN CONT. 6FL OZ

Chero-Cola

CLEAR
BACK – (IN SLUG PLATE)
MACON, GA.
BOTTOM – PATENT
PENDING 22
MACHINE MADE

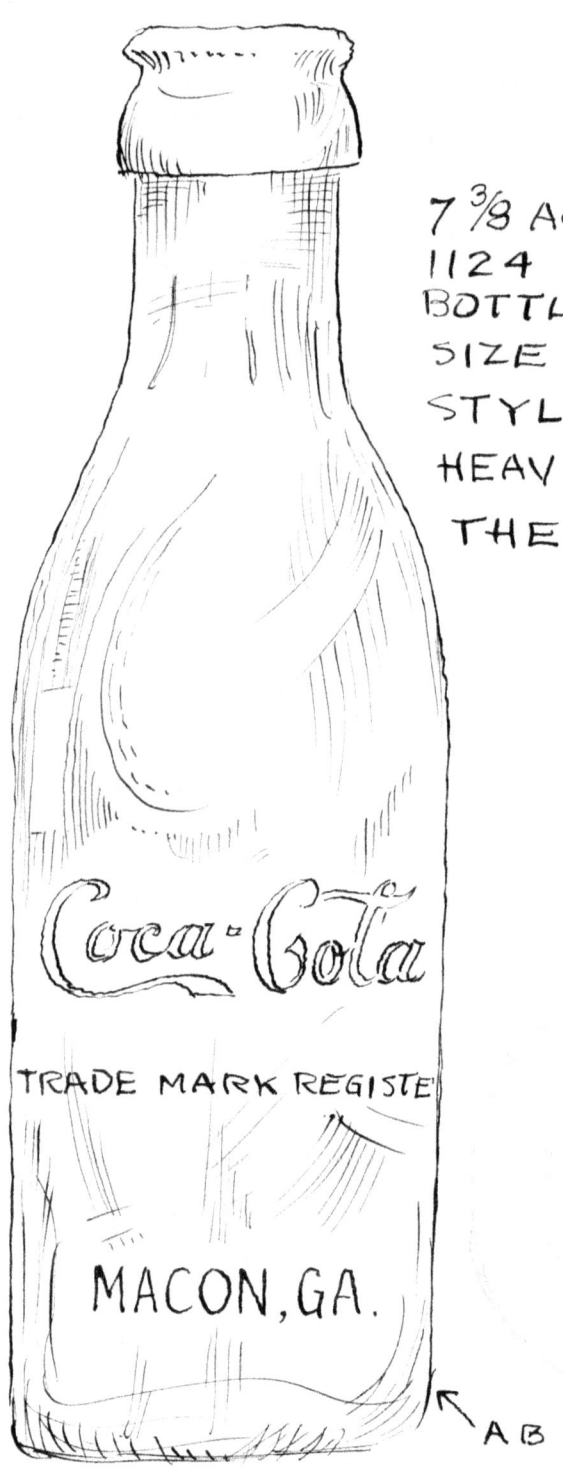

Coca-Cola

TRADE MARK REGISTE

MACON, GA.

A B CO.

7 3/8 AQUA - BOTTOM
1124 B - ANOTHER
BOTTLE THE SAME
SIZE BUT THE
STYLE WRITING IS
HEAVER AND ON
THE BOTTOM IS
R & CO
4

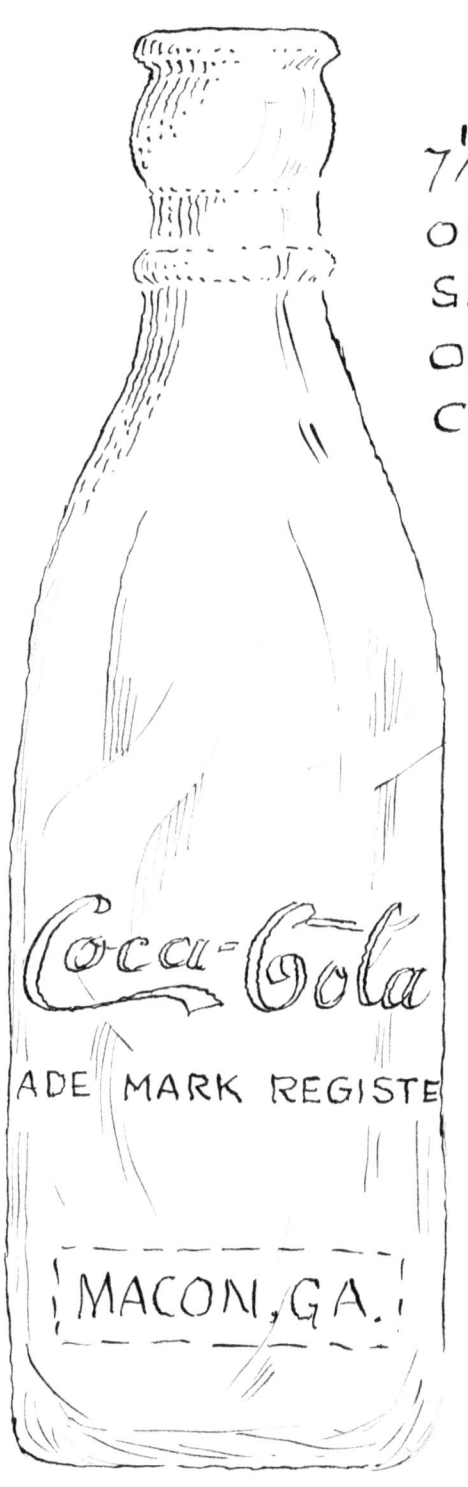

7½ L.GREEN
ON THE REVERSE
SIDE - PROPERTY
OF COCA COLA BOTTLING
CO.

2 ON THE BOTTOM

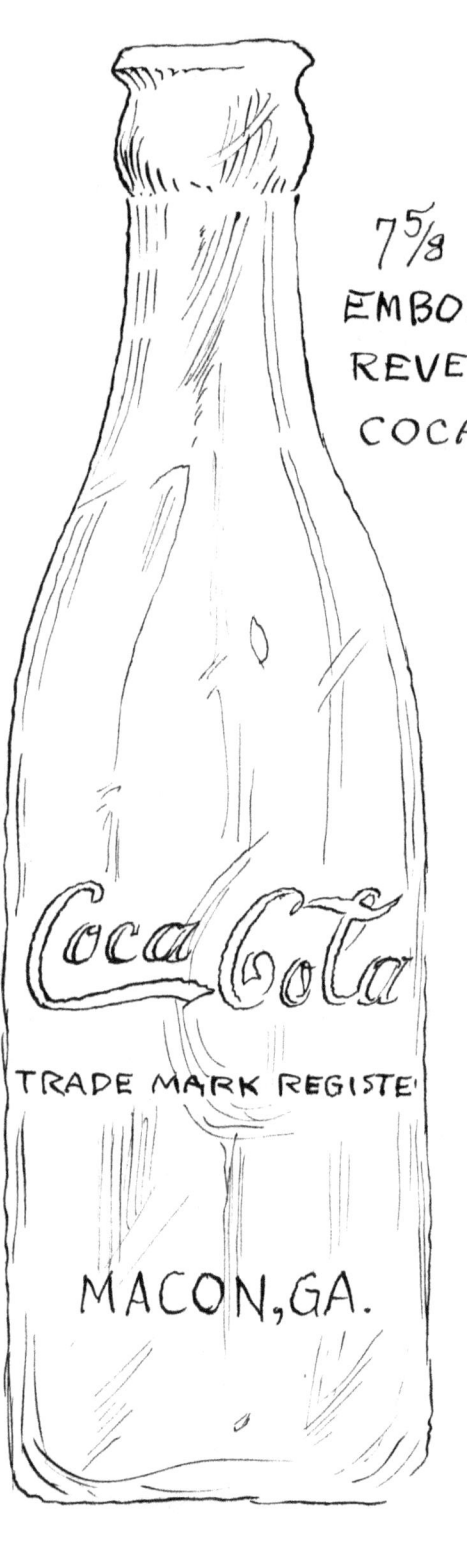

7⅝ LI. GREEN - BOTTOM
EMBOSSED WITH COCA COLA
REVERSE - PROPERTY OF
COCA COLA BOTTLING CO.

Coca Cola

TRADE MARK REGISTE

MACON, GA.

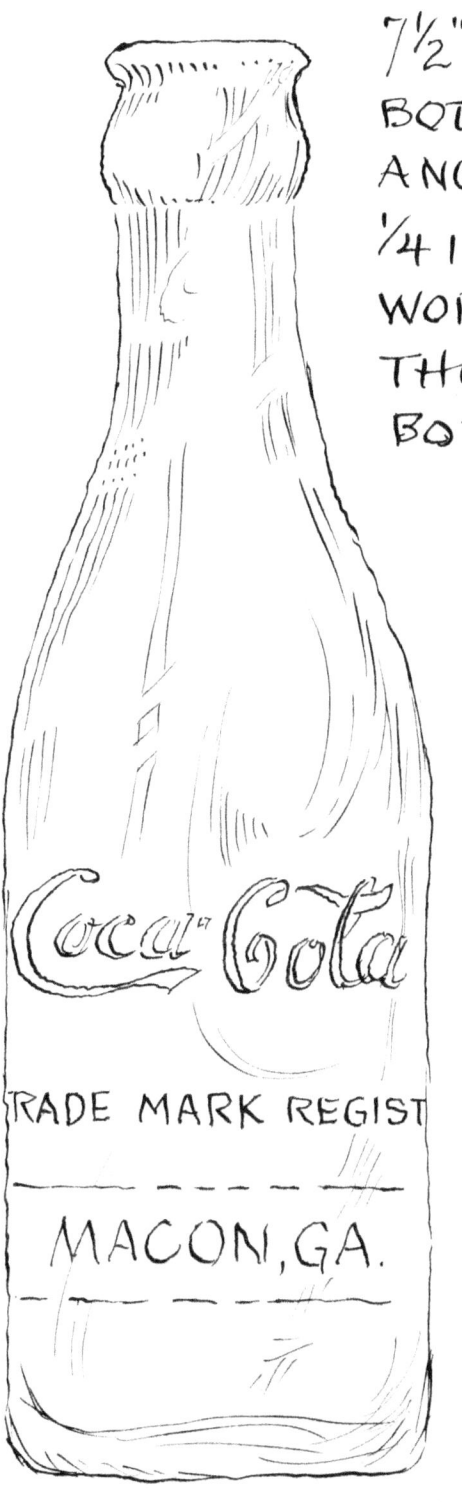

7½" CLEAR NOTHING ON THE BOTTOM.. THERE IS ANOTHER CLEAR ONE AND ¼ INCH SHORTER AND THE WORD Coca Cola IS NOT THE SAME AND ON THE BOTTOM IT HAS COCA COLA

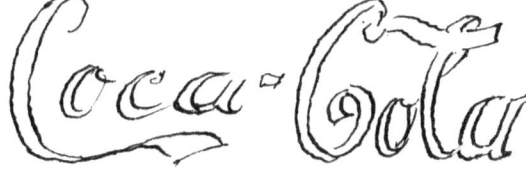

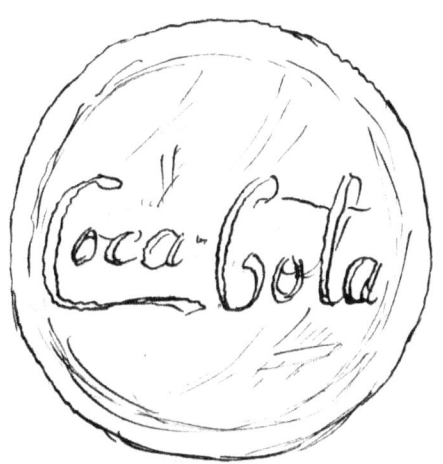

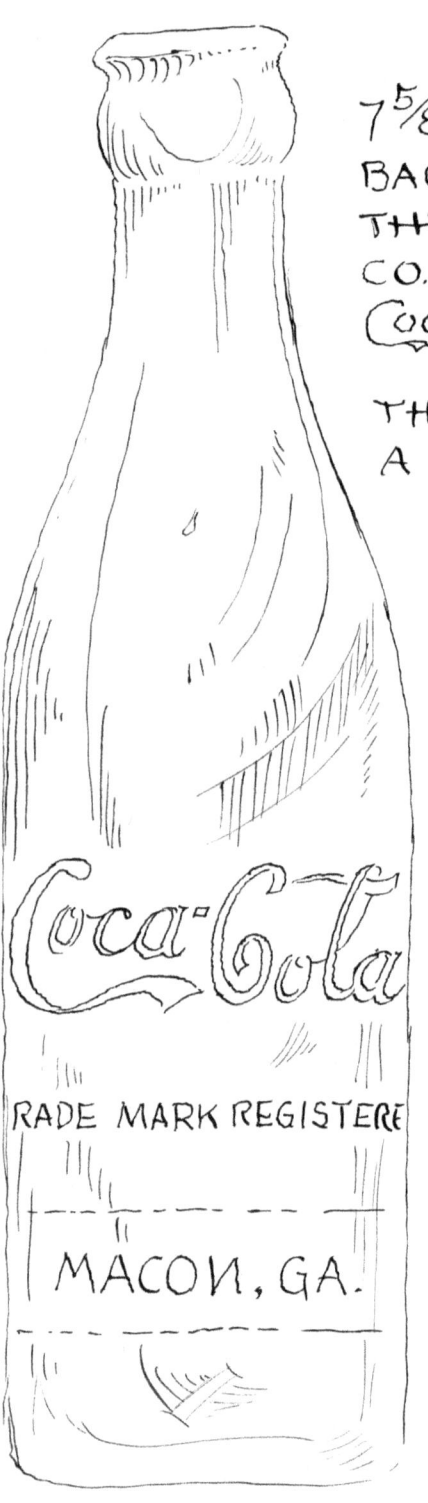

7⅝ CLEAR – ON THE
BACK PROPERTY OF
THE *Coca Cola* BOTTLING
CO. ON THE BOTTOM IS
Coca Cola

THEY ARE SOME WITH
A STRIGHT "N"

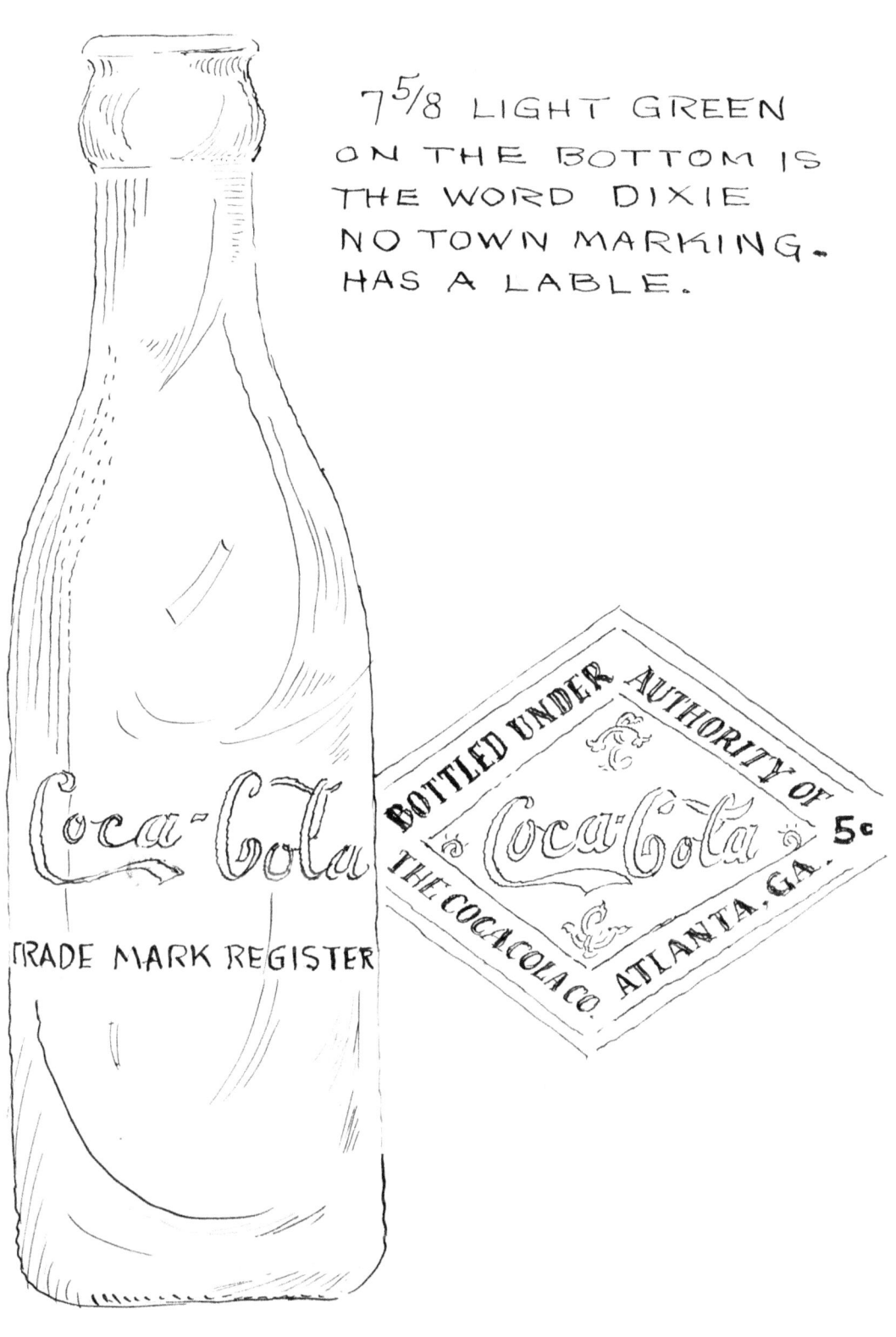

7 5/8 LIGHT GREEN
ON THE BOTTOM IS
THE WORD DIXIE
NO TOWN MARKING.
HAS A LABLE.

Coca-Cola
TRADE MARK REGISTER

BOTTLED UNDER AUTHORITY OF
Coca-Cola
THE COCA COLA CO.   ATLANTA, GA.   5¢

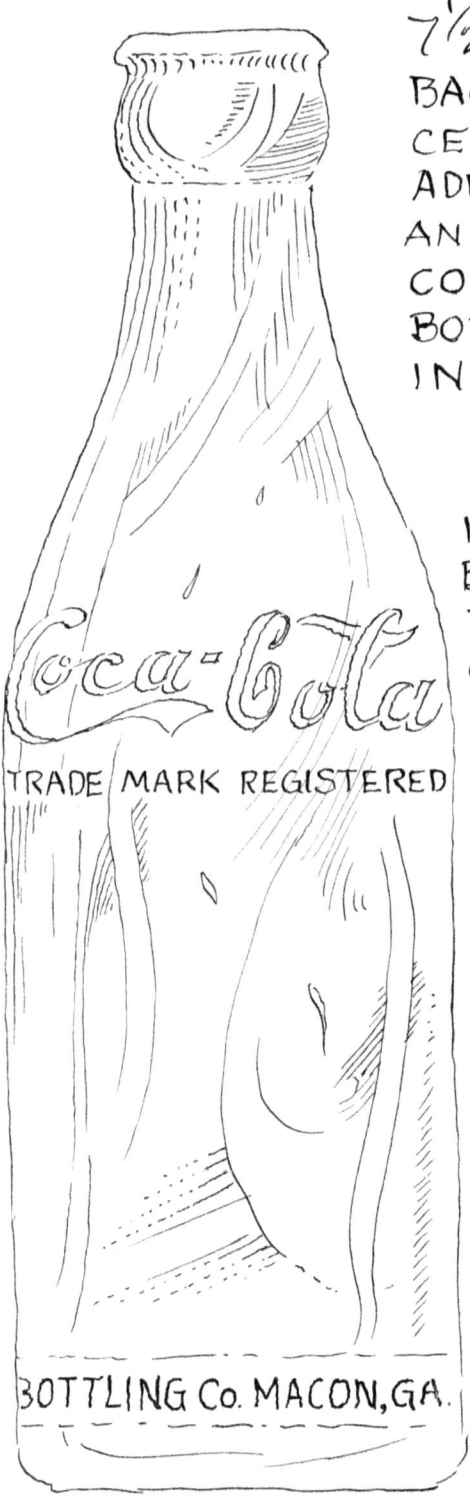

7½ AQUA , ON THE BACK THE SAME EXCEPT AT THE TOP THEY ADDED - CONTENTS 7 OZ. AND PPOPERTY OF COCA COLA AND ON THE BOTTOM COCA COLA IN COCA COLA SCRPT.

THIS STYLE COMES IN CLEAR, AQUA, LI BLUE, LI GREEN AND 7 OZ - 6½ OZ & 6 OZ. THE ENBOSSING IS THE SAME ON MOST, BUT IN DIFFERENT PLACES -

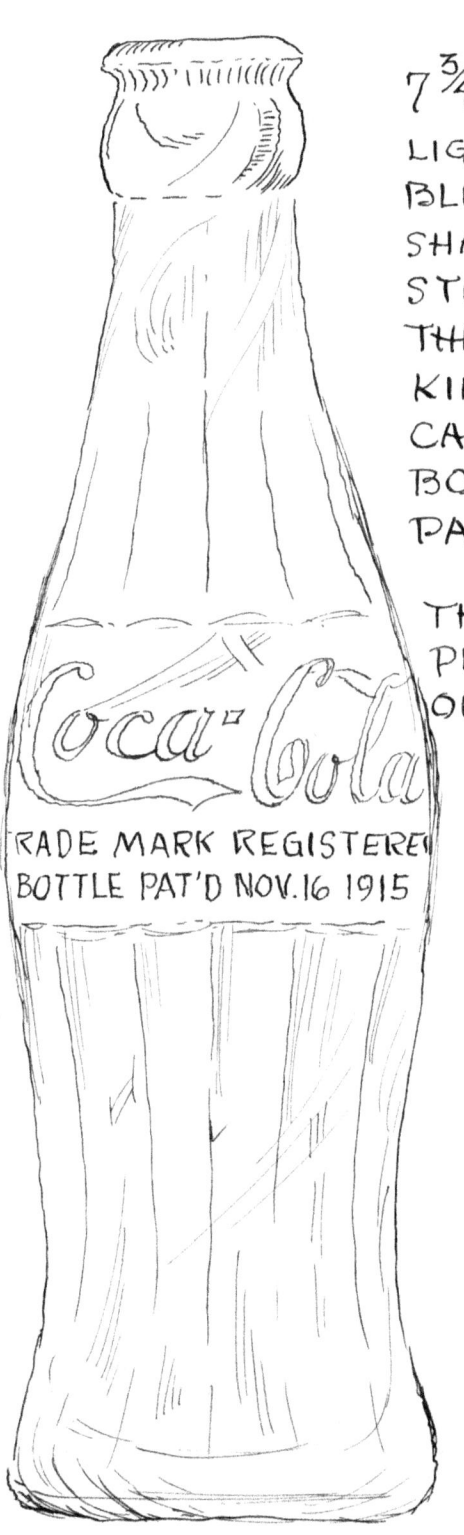

7 ¾ THESE COME IN CLEAR,
LIGHT GREEN , CORN FLOUR
BLUE , LIGHT BLUE & THIS
SHAPE THE COCA COLA CO.
STILL HAS. THEY RENEWED
THERE PAT'D ON THE SAME
KIND OF BOTTLE AND ITS
CALLED THE CHRISTMAS
BOTTLE BECAUSE THE
PAT'D DATE IS DEC. 25 1923.

THIS SHAPE THEY STARTED
PUTTING THE TOWNS NAMES
ON THE BOTTOMS...

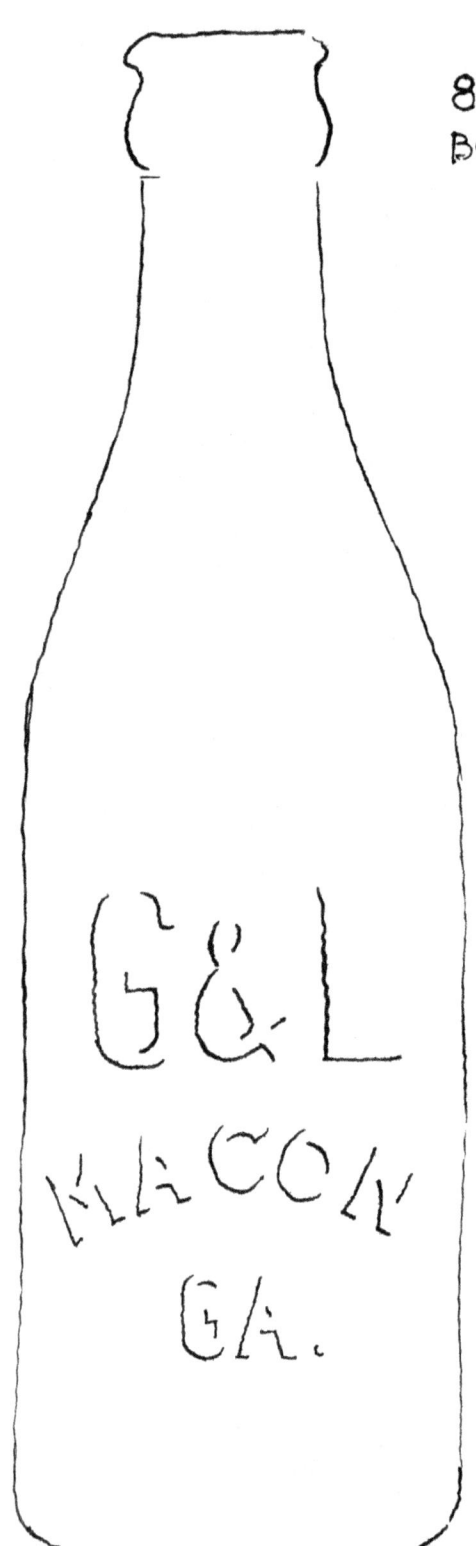

8 INCHES LIGHT, LIGHT GREEN
BOTTOM MARKING 123

G & L
MACON
GA.

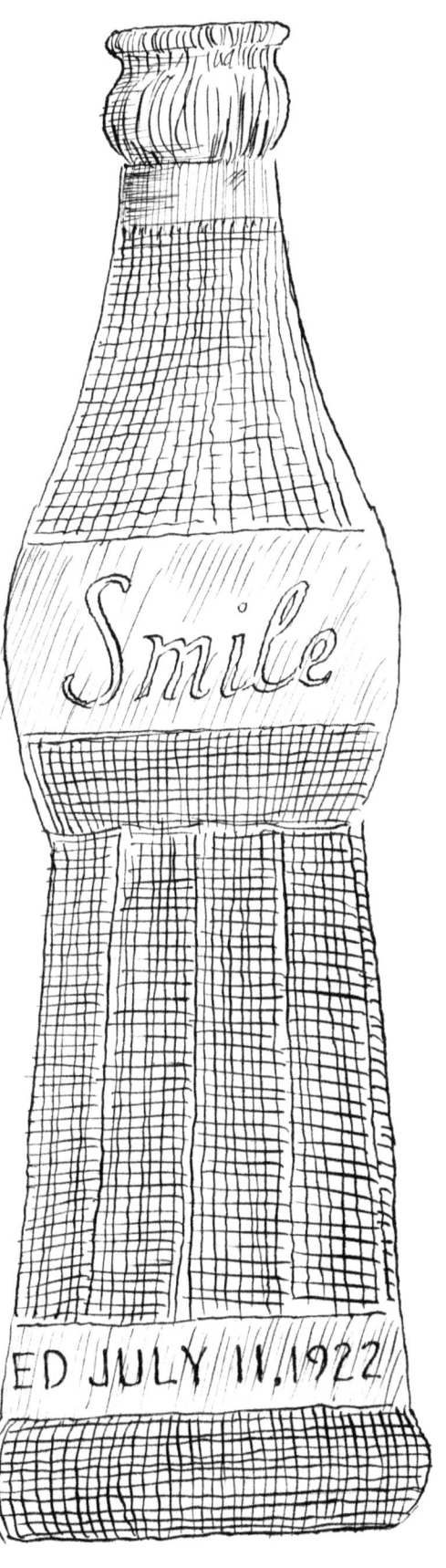

7 UP Green
CONTENTS 6½
FL. OZ PATENTED
JULY 11 1922
BOTTOM
MACON, GA.
MACHINE MADE

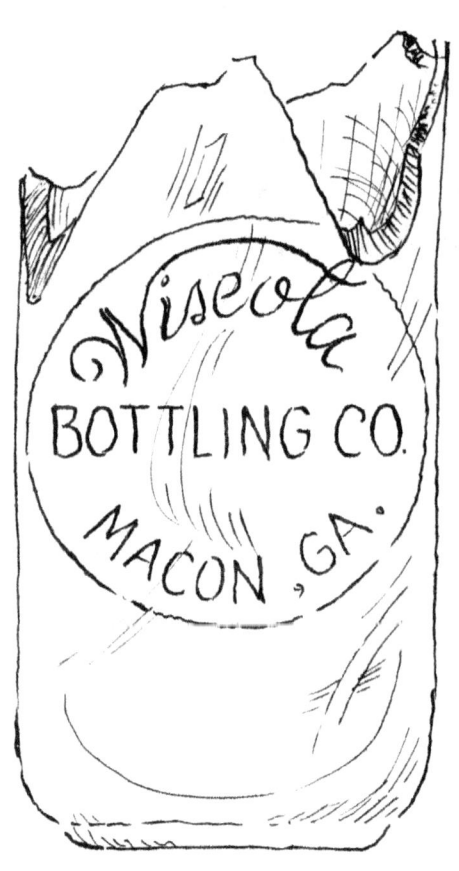

Wiscota
BOTTLING CO.
MACON, GA.

NO COMPLETE ONE
CLEAR
ON THE BOTTOM C

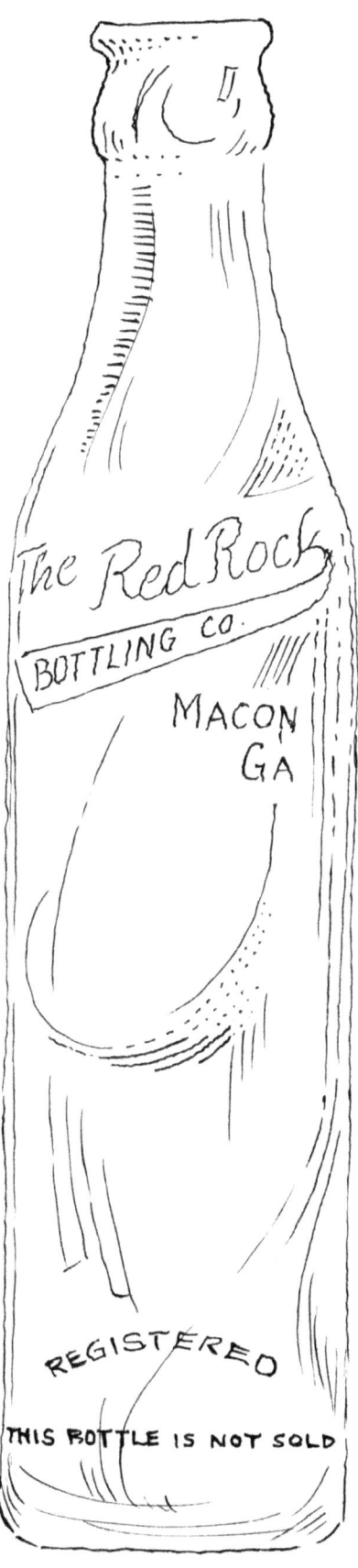

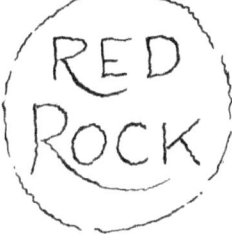

8¾ IN.
GREEN
BACK

MIN. CONT'S.
6½ FLU. OZS

BOTTOM

PURETY

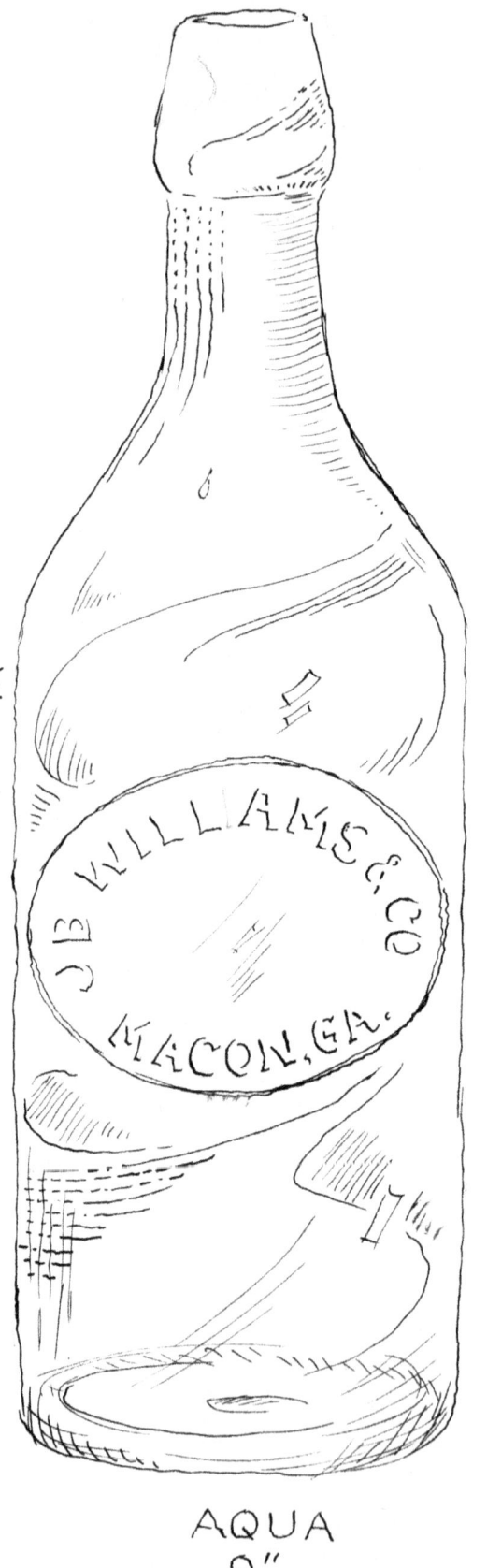

REVERSE

THIS BOTTLE

NOT TO

BE SOLD

JB WILLIAMS & CO

MACON, GA.

AQUA
9"

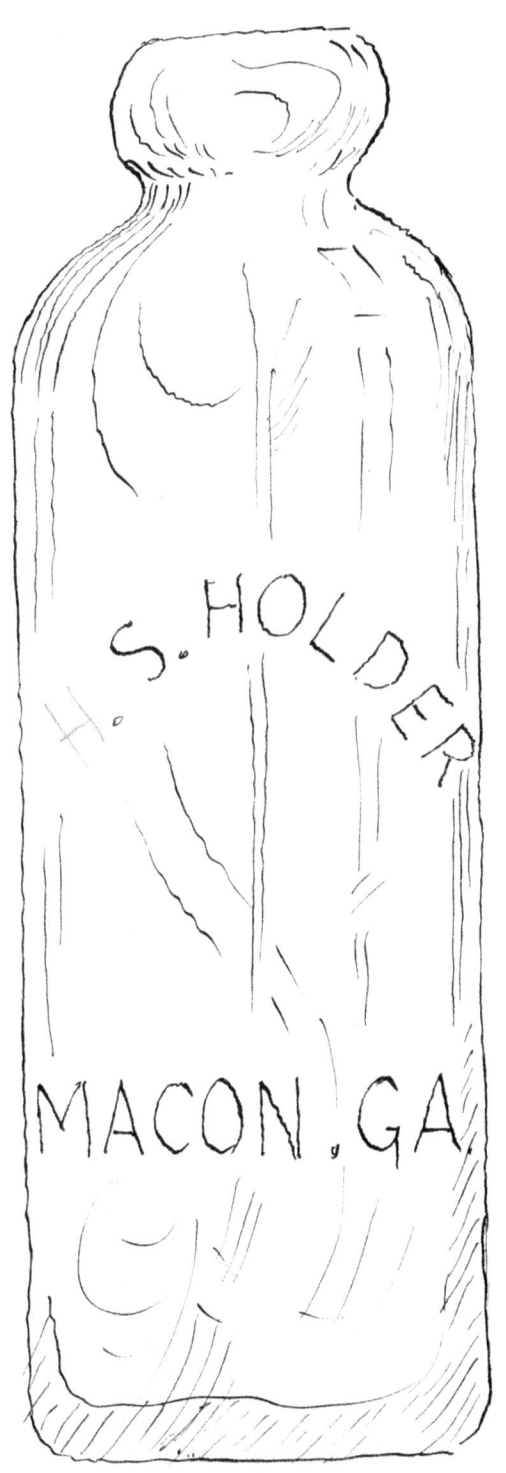

S. HOLDER

MACON, GA

THIS BOTTLE NEVER SOLD

E.J. BURKE

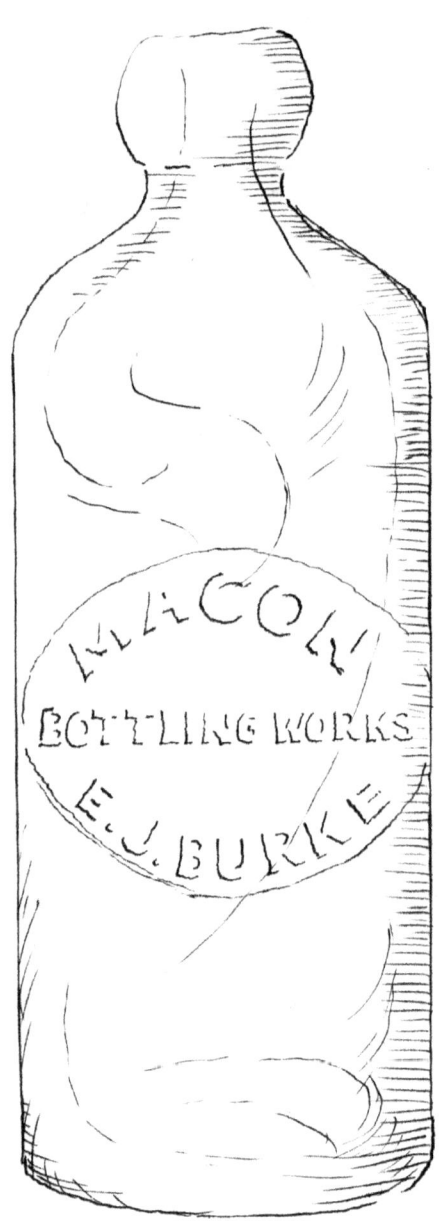

LIGHT GREEN
FOUND APR 70
6½ - 2⅜

55
BOTTOM

E.H.STUART

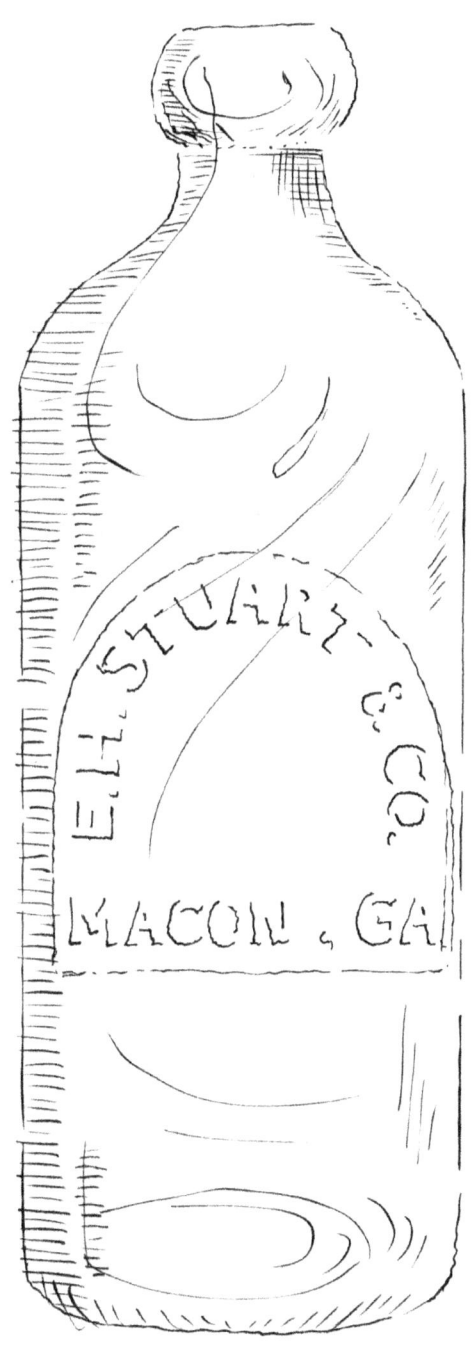

YELLOW GREEN   BOTTOM E.H.S
                         &
                         CO.

FOUND FEB 71

RALEY

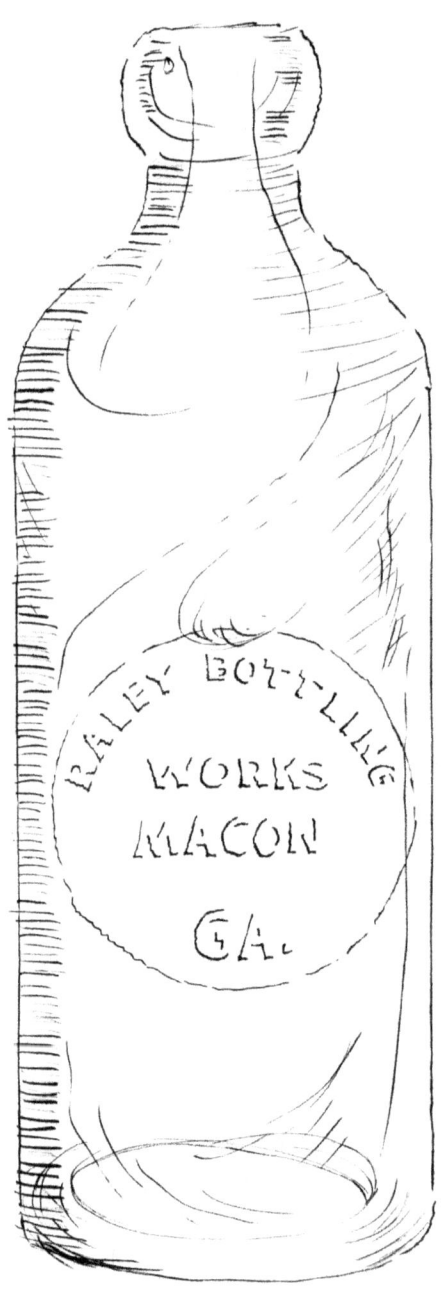

BLUE GREEN
6 3/4   2 3/8
FOUND JULY 70

MILLIRONS

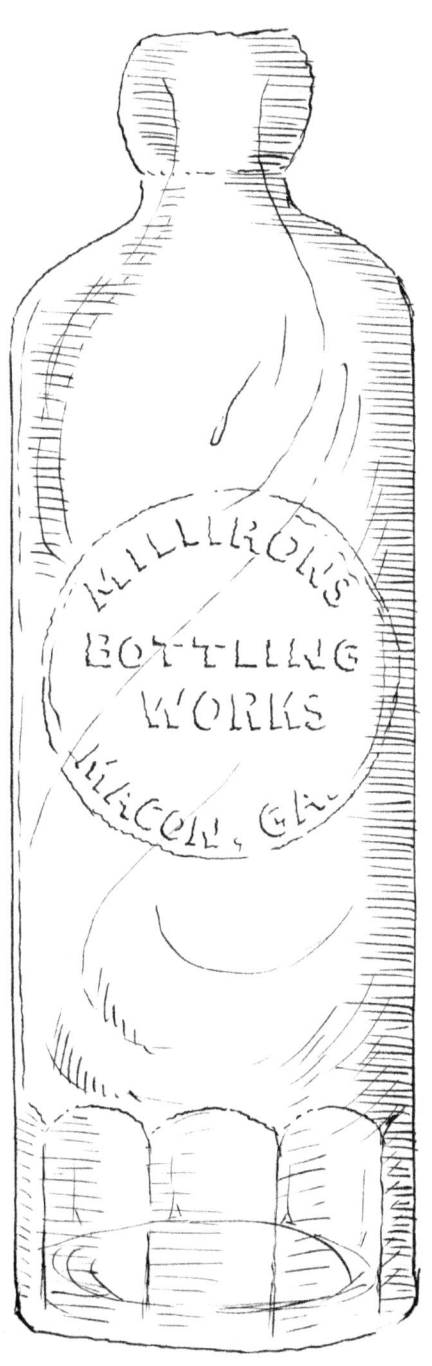

ALSO IN BLUE GREEN
WITH O.B. CO. ON
THE BOTTOM

CLEAR
7¼ - 2⅜
FOUND JUL 70

SAMPLE & LAKE

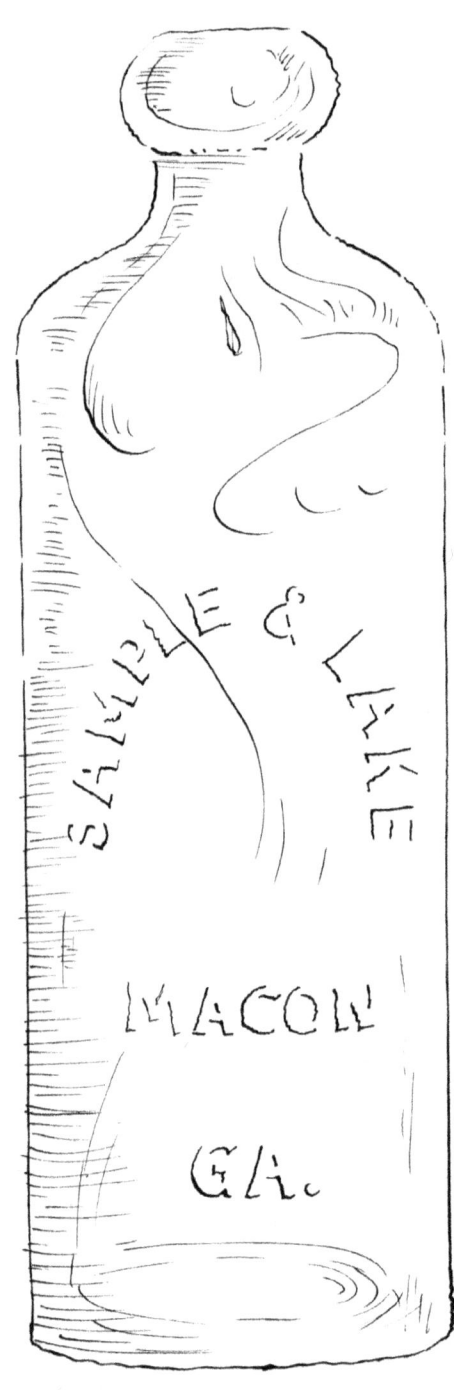

BLUE GREEN
7¼ - 2½
FOUND 1970

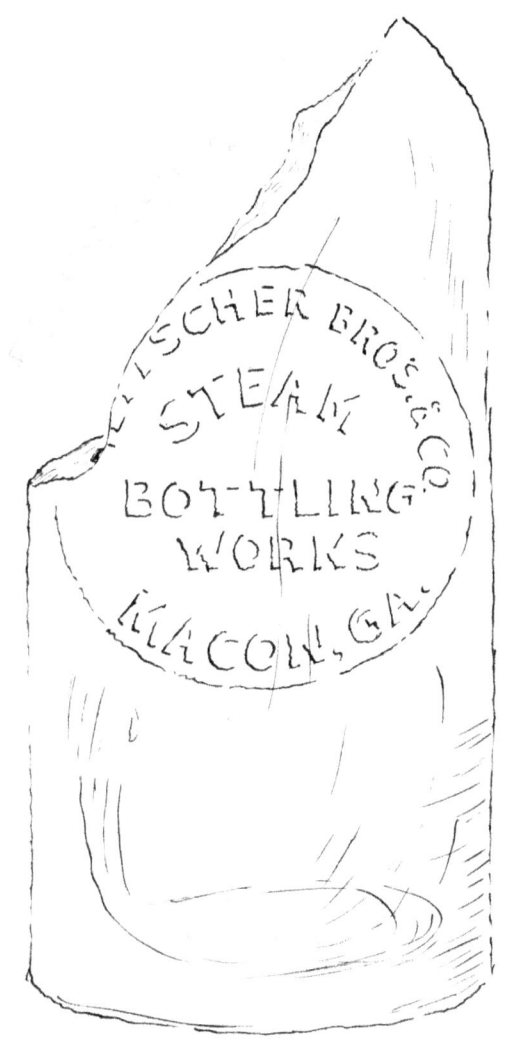

FISCHER BROS. & CO. STEAM BOTTLING WORKS MACON, GA.

BLUE
GREEN

FOUND JULY 1970

2 3/8 WIDE

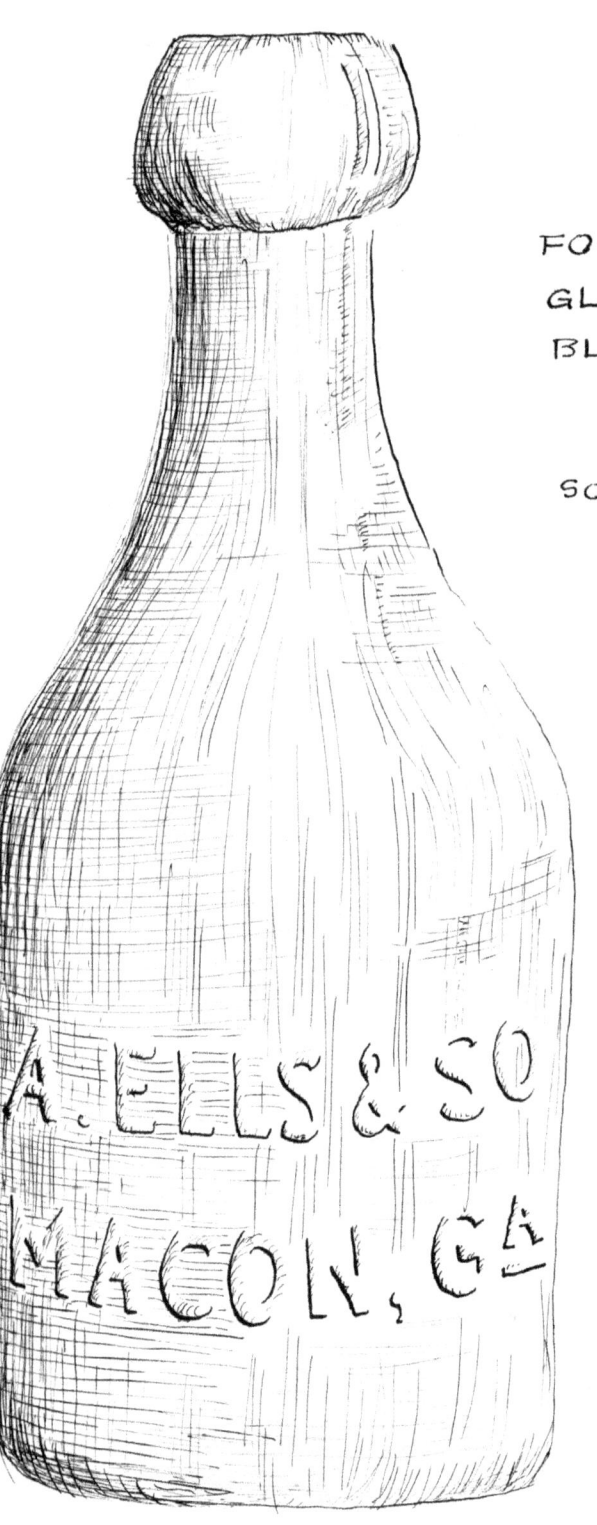

FOUND IN SAVA, GEO. 1972
GLOB TOP , COBALT
BLUE , IRON

SOLD FOR $150.00

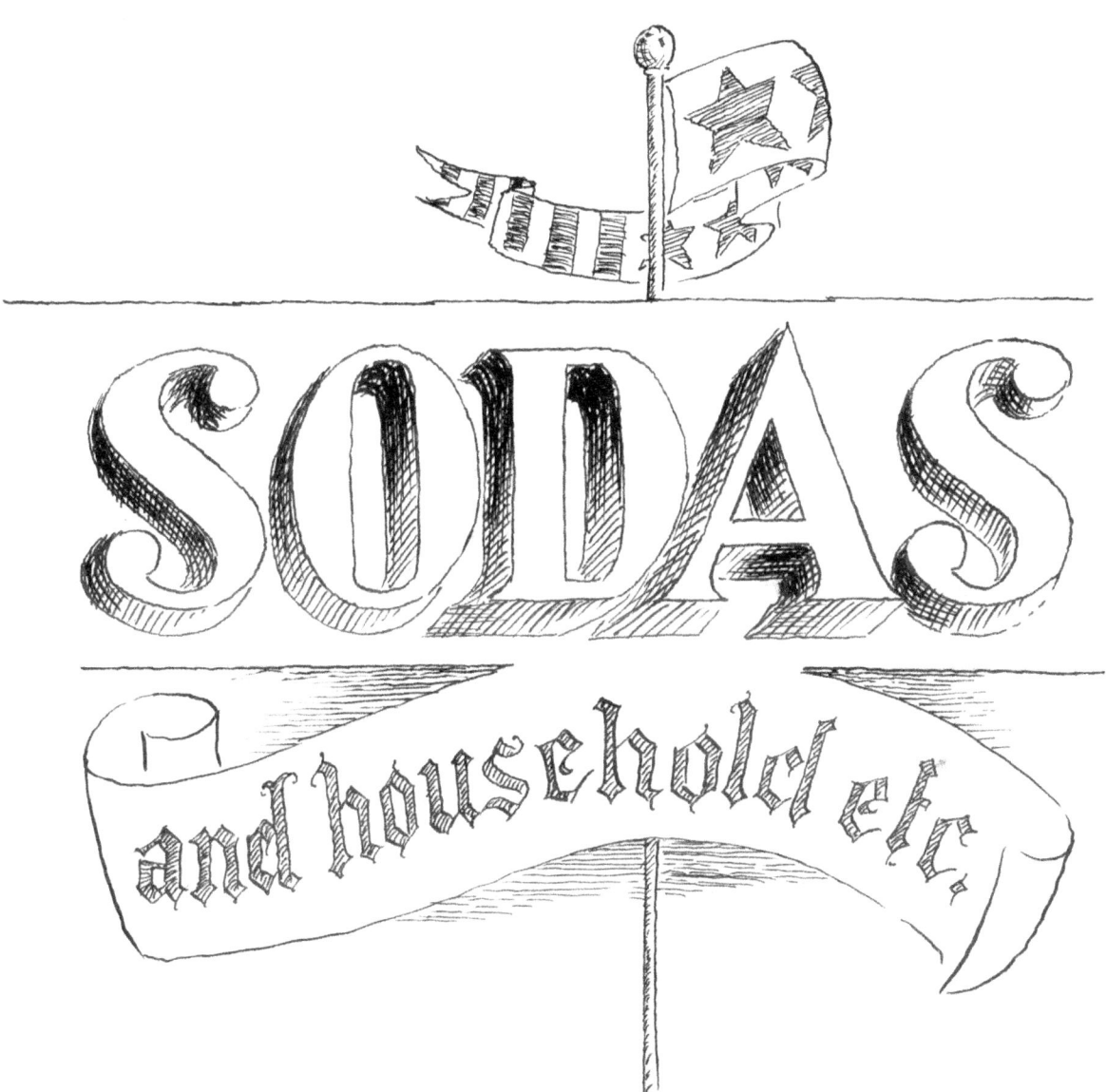

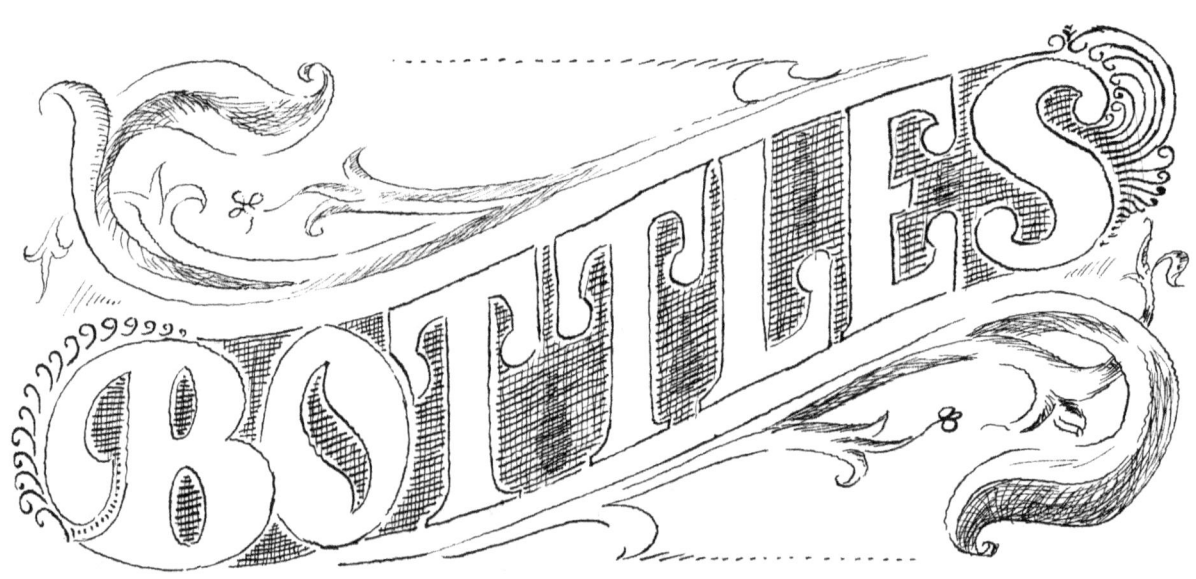

FROM MACON

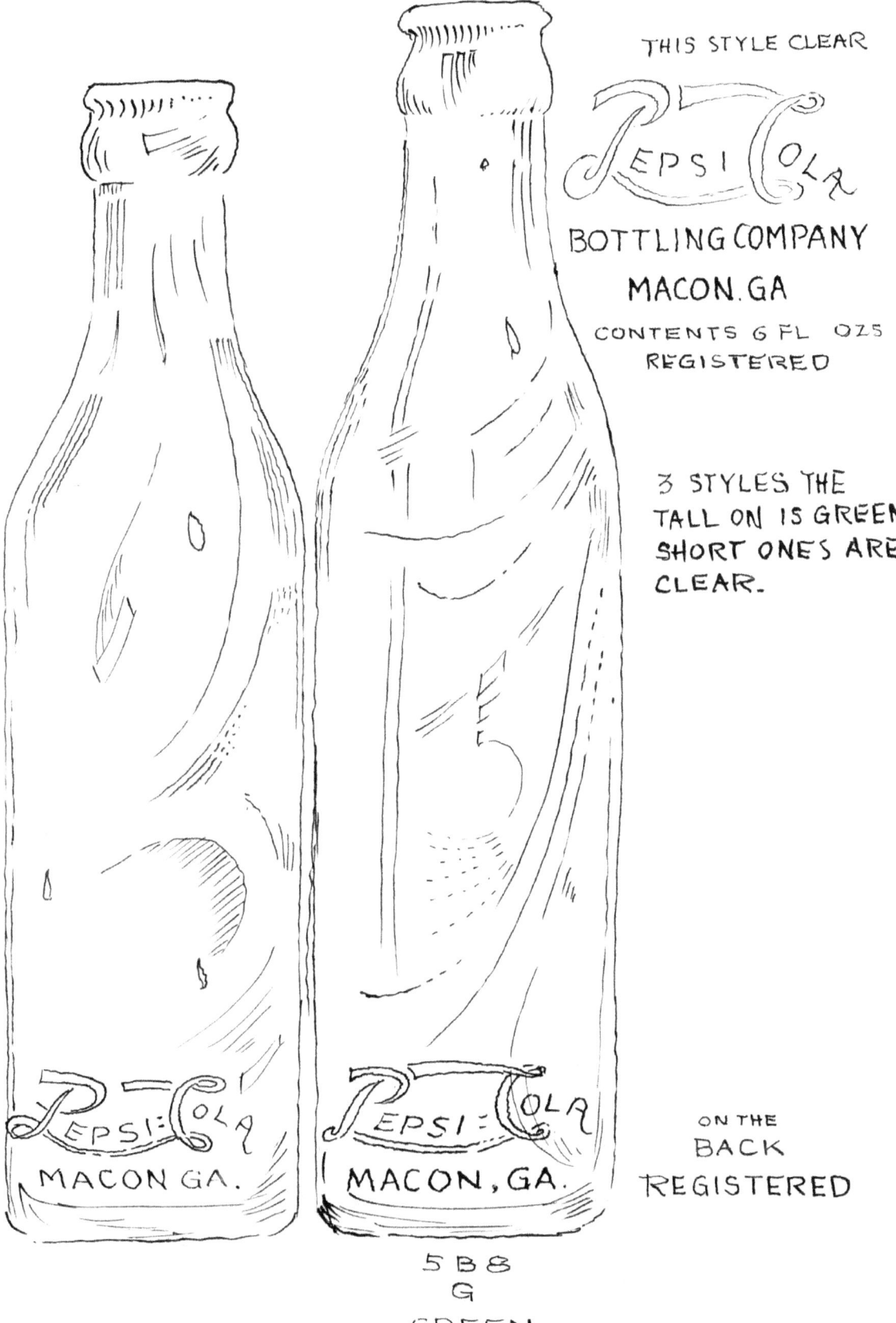

THIS STYLE CLEAR

PEPSI COLA

BOTTLING COMPANY

MACON. GA

CONTENTS 6 FL OZS
REGISTERED

3 STYLES THE
TALL ON IS GREEN
SHORT ONES ARE
CLEAR.

ON THE
BACK
REGISTERED

PEPSI COLA
MACON GA.

PEPSI COLA
MACON, GA.

5 B 8
G
GREEN

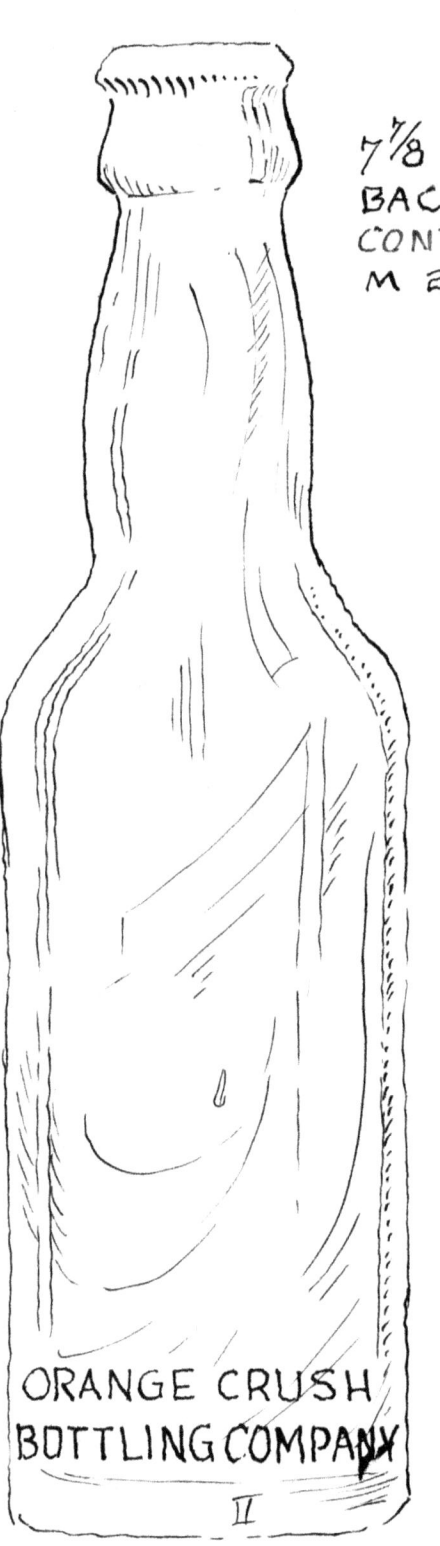

7⅞ LIGHT GREEN
BACK — MACON, GA
CONTENTS 6 FLU. OZS
M 28348 ROOT 20

ORANGE CRUSH
BOTTLING COMPANY

II

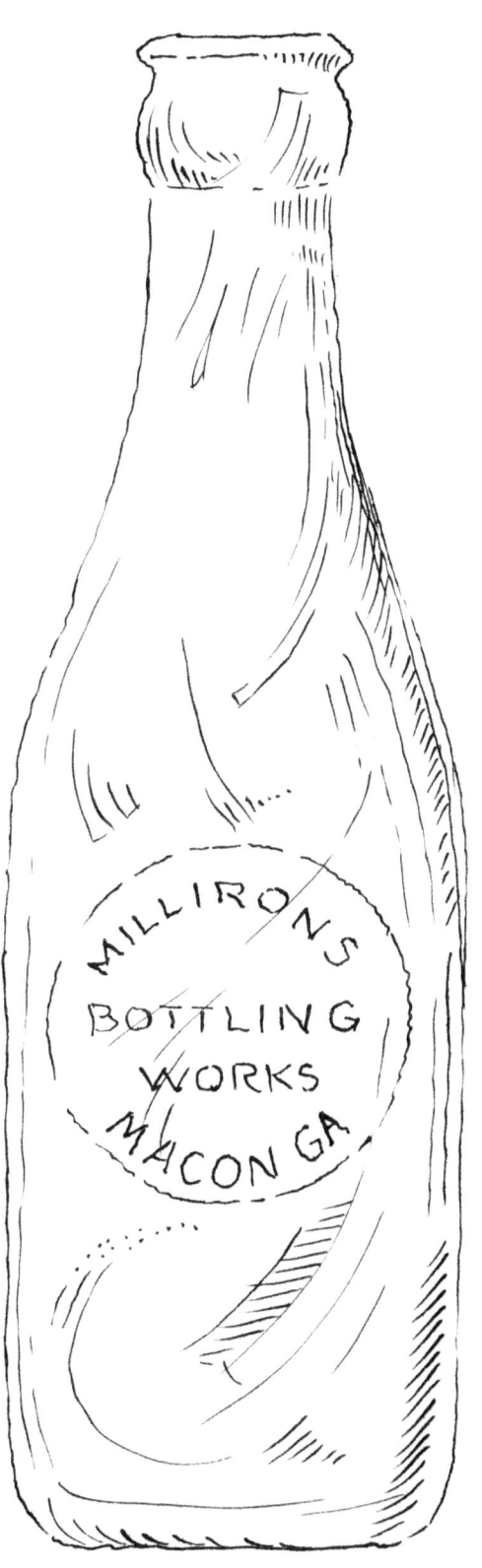

8 INCHES LIGHT GREEN
ON THE BOTTOM MILLIRONS

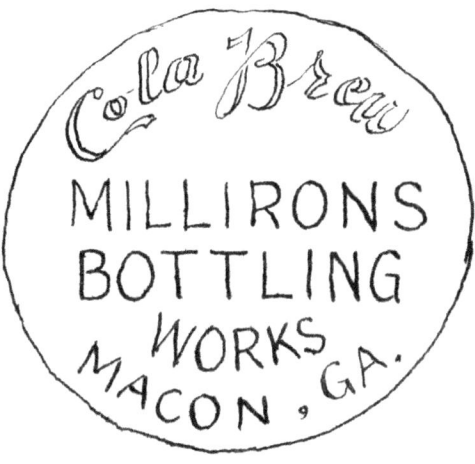

BOTTOM
MILLIRONS
CROWN TOP

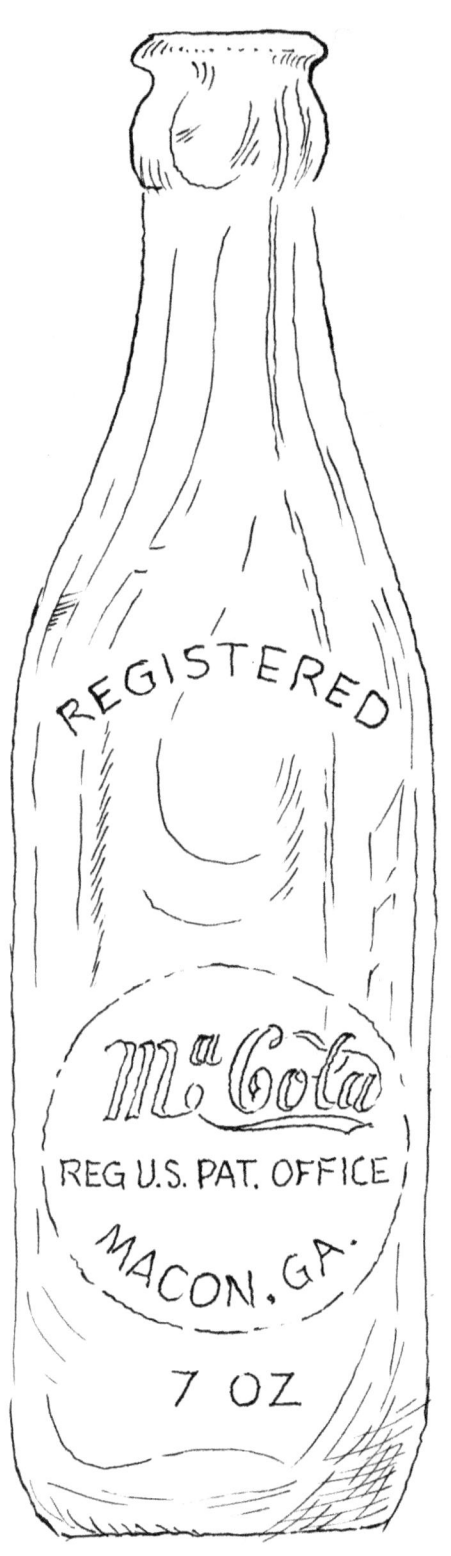

REGISTERED

Mª Cola

REG U.S. PAT. OFFICE

MACON, GA.

7 OZ

LIGHT, LIGHT GREEN
BACK- THIS BOTTLE
NOT TO BE SOLD
BOTTOM - Mª

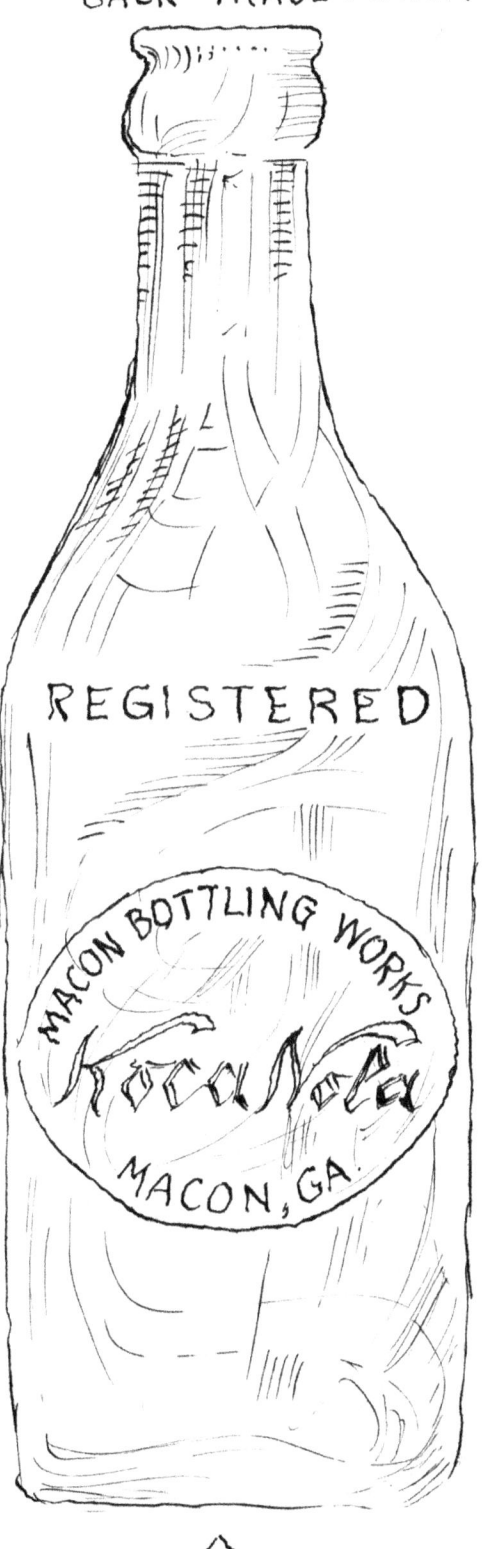

CLEAR
BACK-TRADE MARK

REGISTERED

MACON BOTTLING WORKS
KocaNola
MACON, GA.

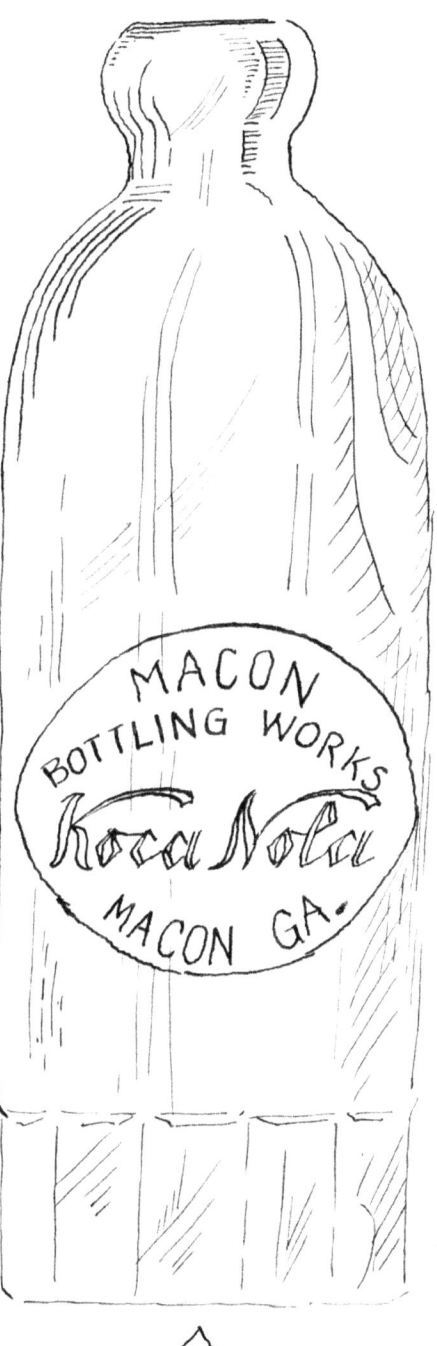

CLEAR

MACON
BOTTLING WORKS
KocaNola
MACON GA.

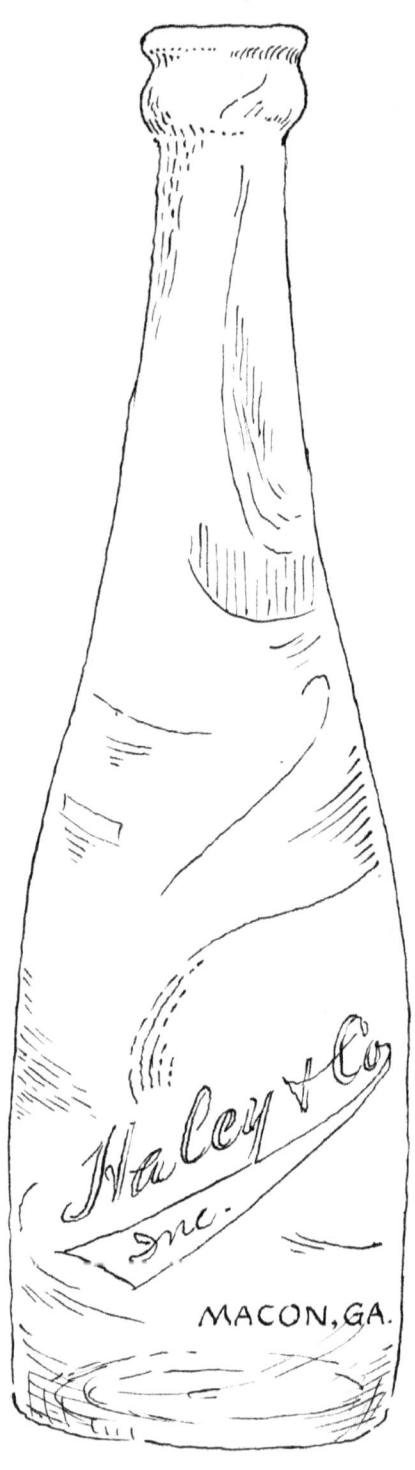

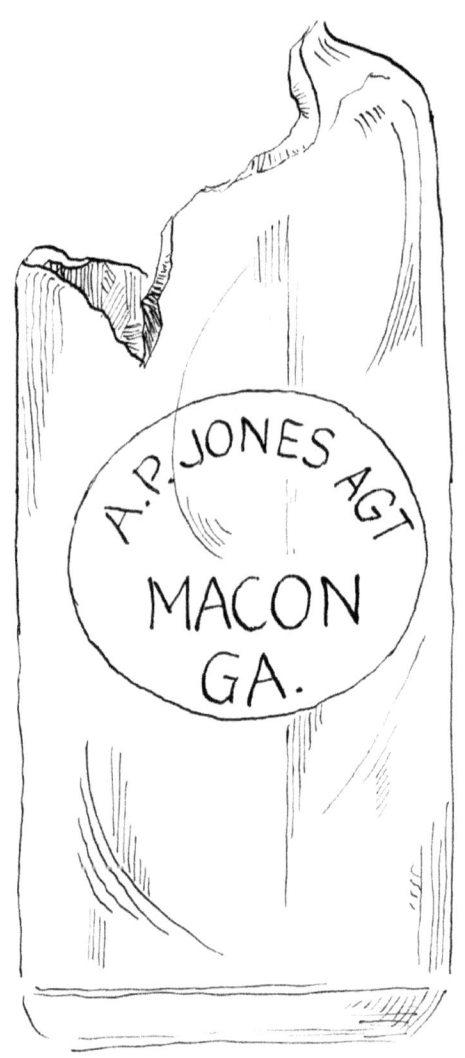

Haley & Co
Inc.

MACON, GA.

A.P. JONES AGT
MACON
GA.

AQUA
8 ¾

BOTTOM #
14G5
OWNER W H SUDDERTH
FOUND 7 TH ST.

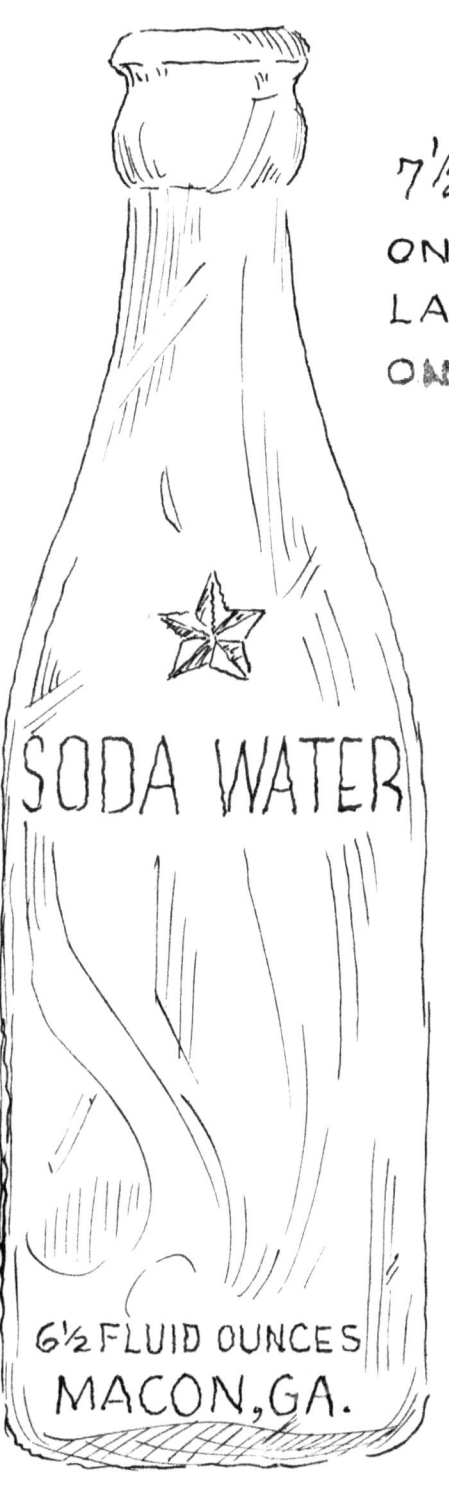

7½ LIGHT GREEN
ON THE BOTTOM A
LARGER STAR THAN
ON THE SHOULDER

SODA WATER

6½ FLUID OUNCES
MACON, GA.

REVERSE- SODA WATER
WITH A STAR ABOVE AND
PROPERTY OF COCA
COLA BOTTLING CO

Book 2

Medicines & Whiskies

E.J.BURKE

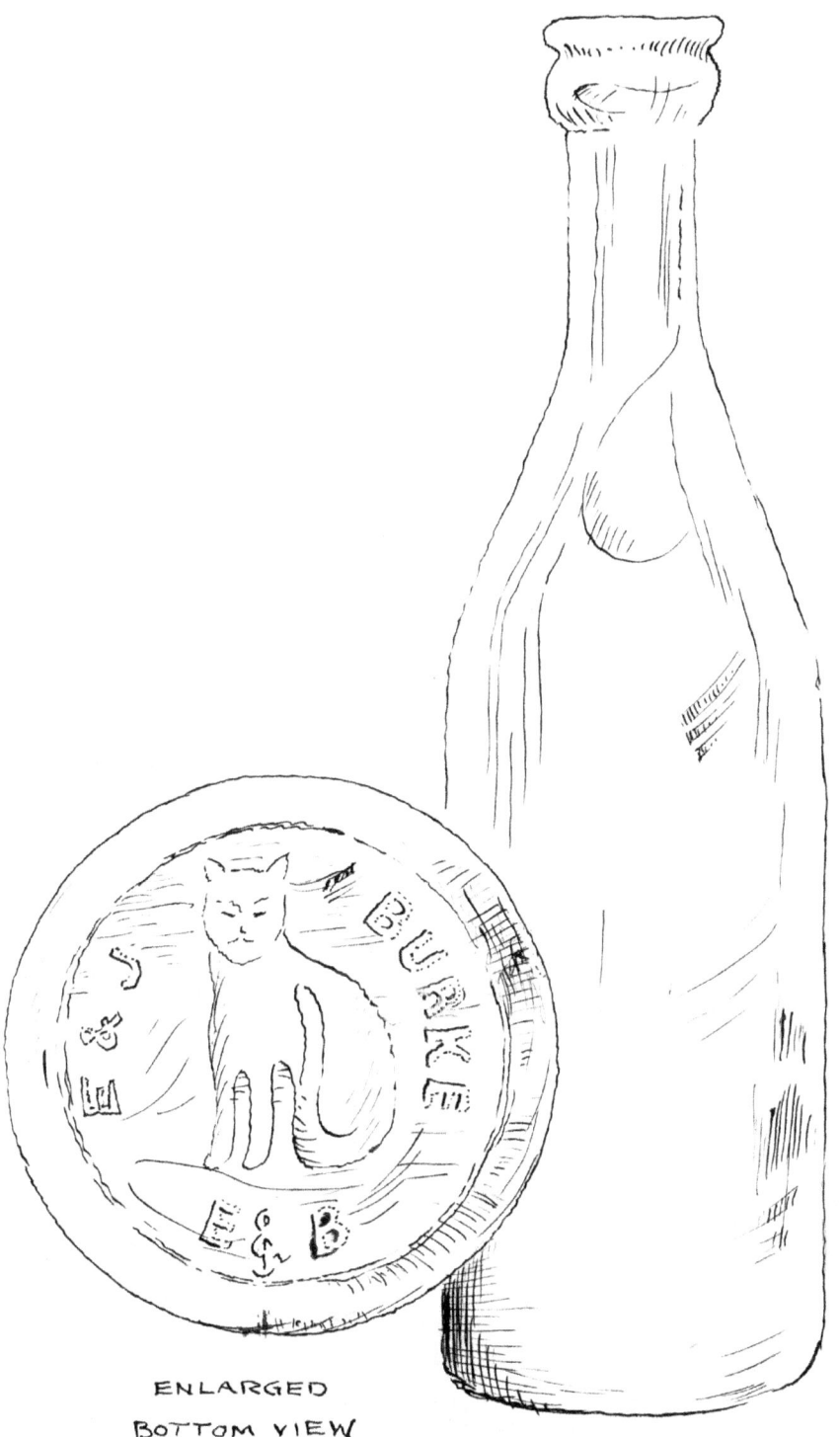

ENLARGED
BOTTOM VIEW

AMBER

FOUND 1971

3½" Tall
BLUE LETTERING
ON WHITE. TOP
BROWN

J.W. AMASON
NELSON CO WHISKEY
MACON. GA,

NOT COMPLETE
BLUE LETTERING
ON WHITE

Compliments of
☆ ⋇ ⋉ ☆
R.C.KEEN
212 COTTON AV

Compliments of
E.A.MIDDLEBROOKS
203 HARDEMAN AVE.

3½" Tall
Gray glaze
blue lettering

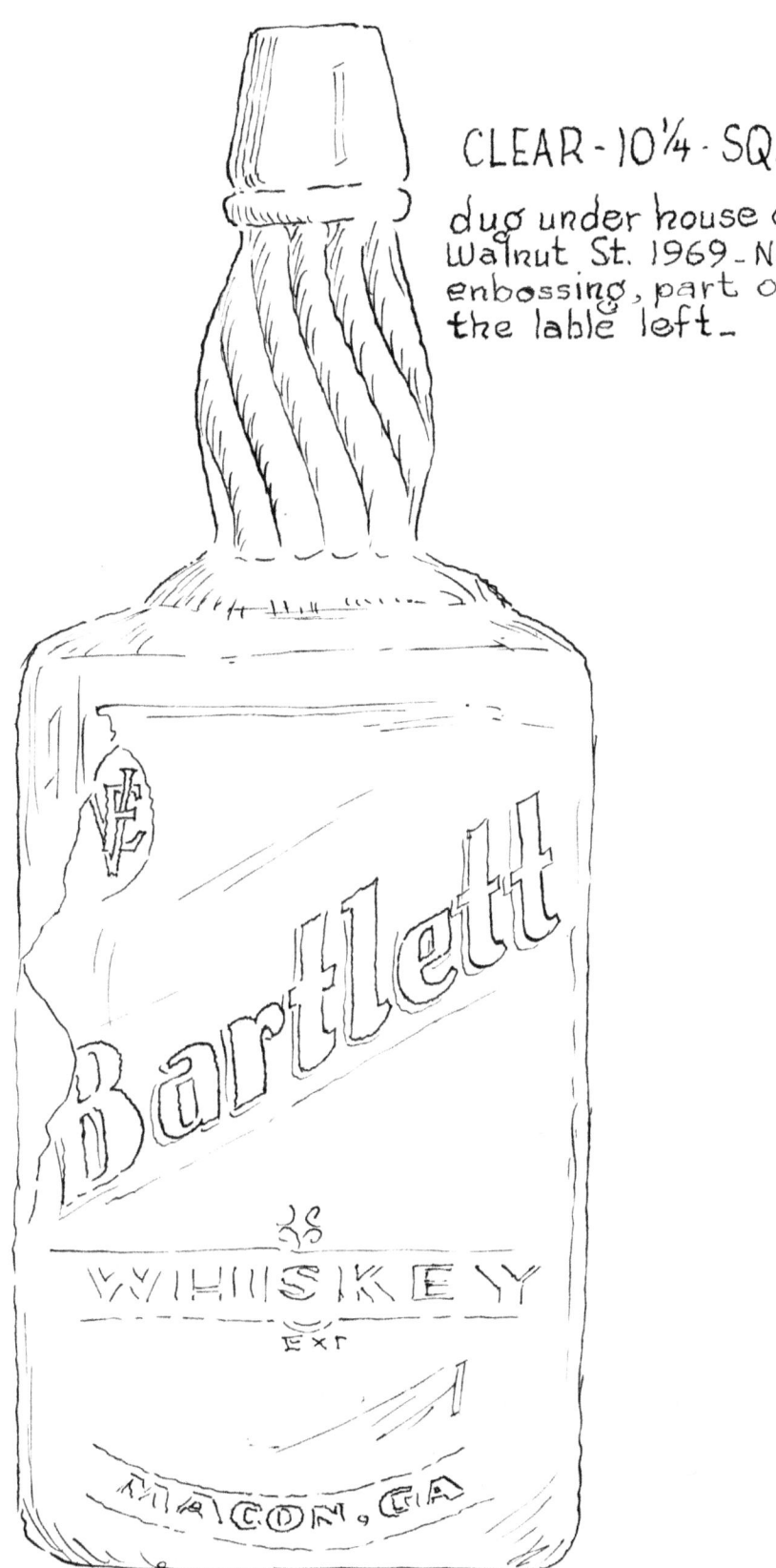

CLEAR - 10¼ - SQ.

dug under house on
Walnut St. 1969 - No
enbossing, part of
the lable left _

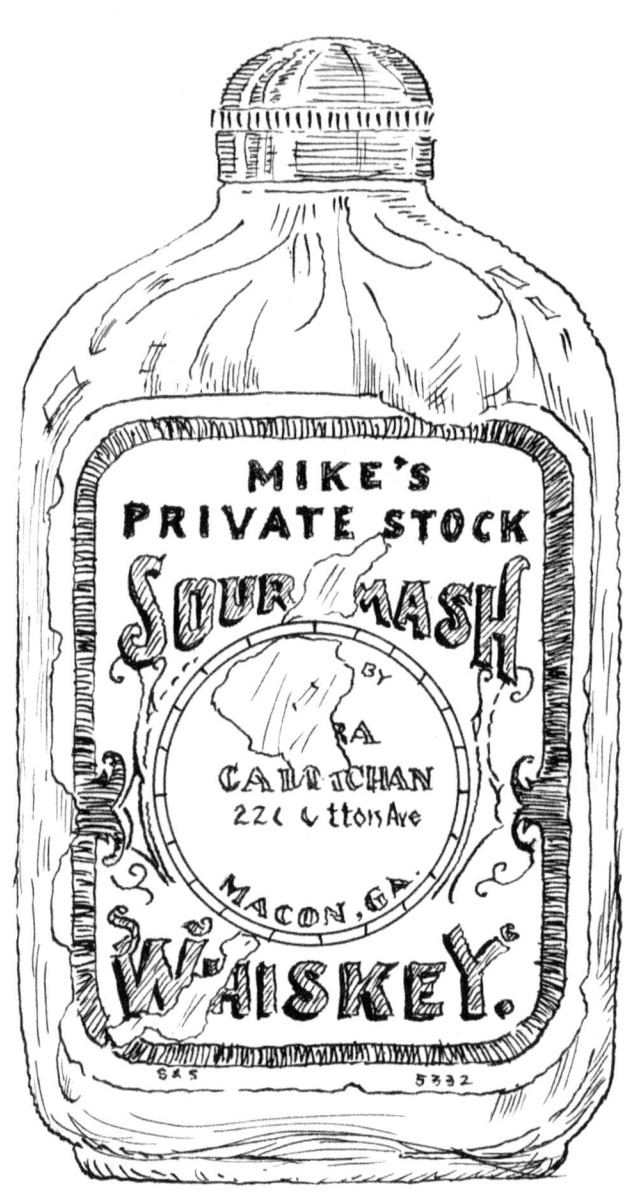

6"

CLEAR

LABEL GOLD LETTERS
& TRIM , BLACK OUT LINE
on white paper
silver metal top

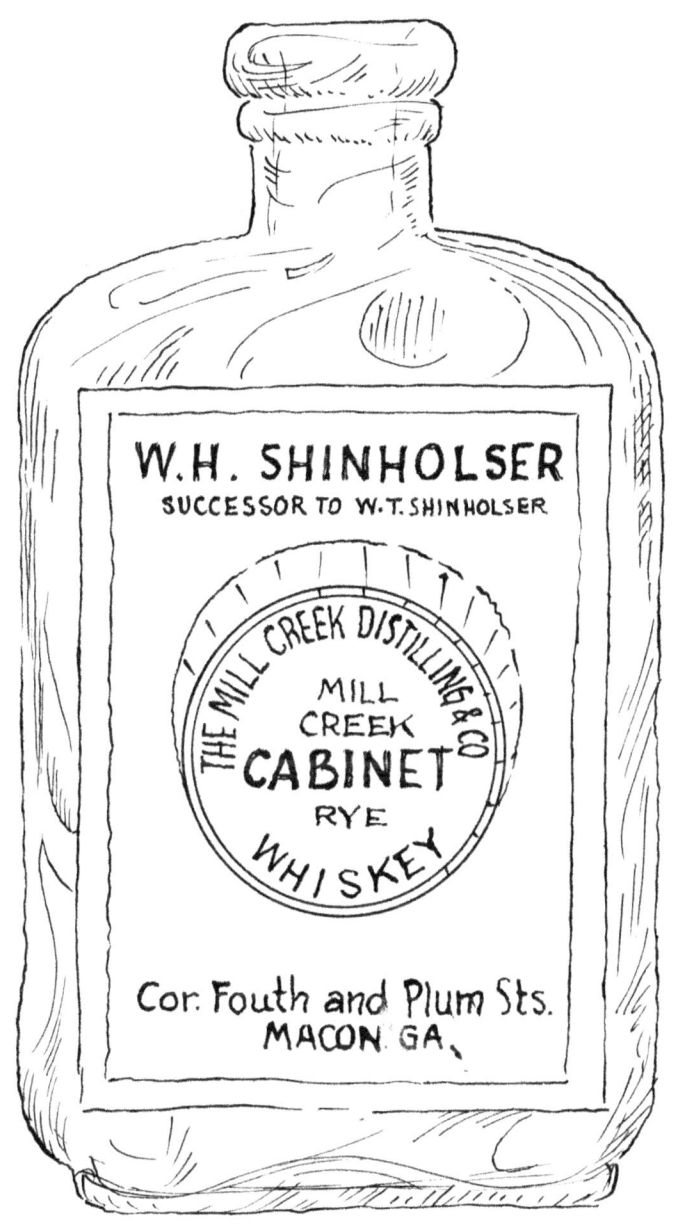

W.H. SHINHOLSER
SUCCESSOR TO W.T. SHINHOLSER

THE MILL CREEK DISTILLING & CO
MILL CREEK CABINET RYE
WHISKEY

Cor. Fouth and Plum Sts.
MACON GA.

CLEAR 6⅛"

BLACK LETTERS - YELLOW
BARREL HEAD & OUT LINE

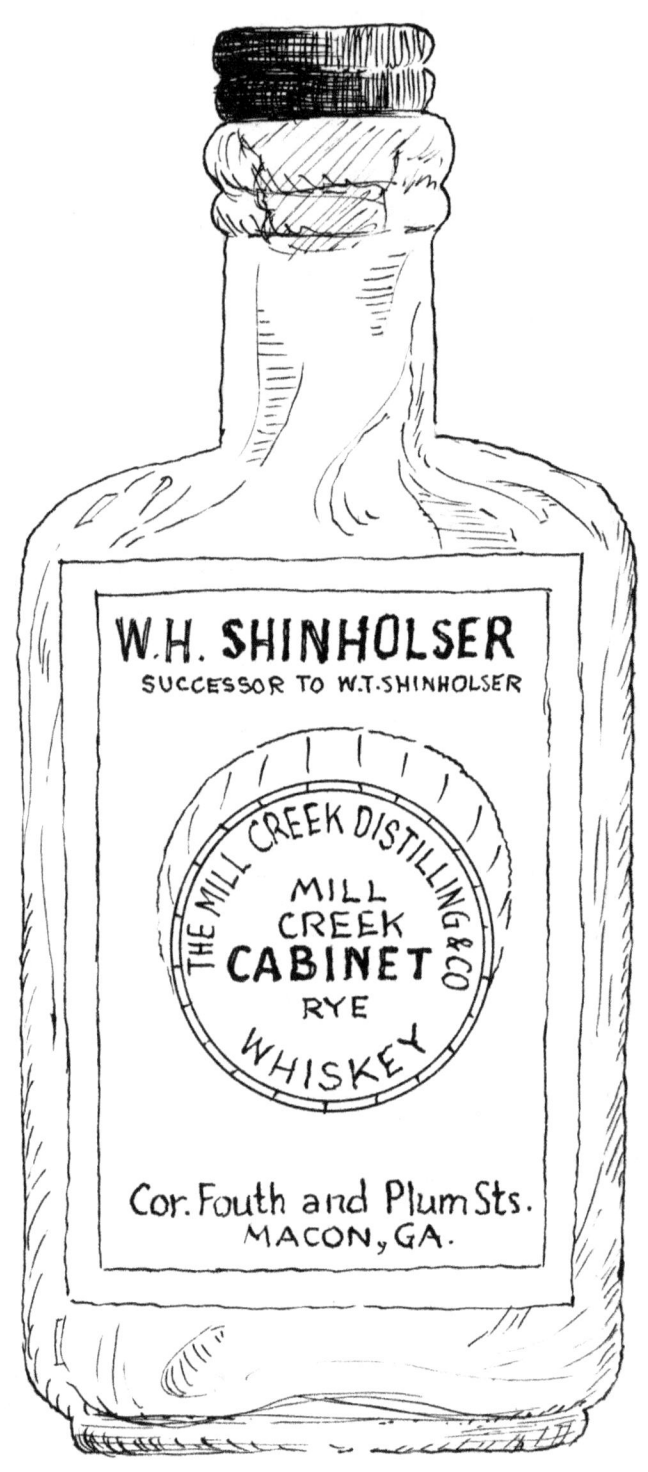

W.H. SHINHOLSER
SUCCESSOR TO W.T. SHINHOLSER

THE MILL CREEK DISTILLING & CO

MILL
CREEK
CABINET
RYE

WHISKEY

Cor. Fouth and Plum Sts.
MACON, GA.

CLEAR 7¼

WITH CAP

INSIDE THREAD

CAP MADE OF WOOD PAINTED

BLACK.

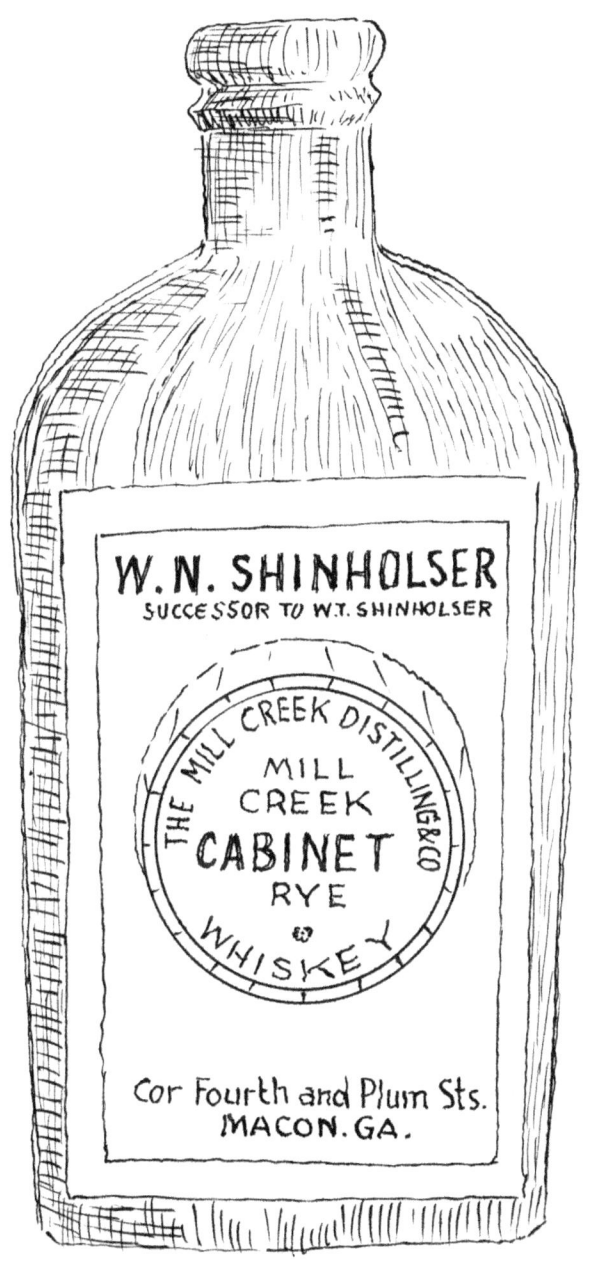

AMBER. 6³/₈
SIDE STRAPS

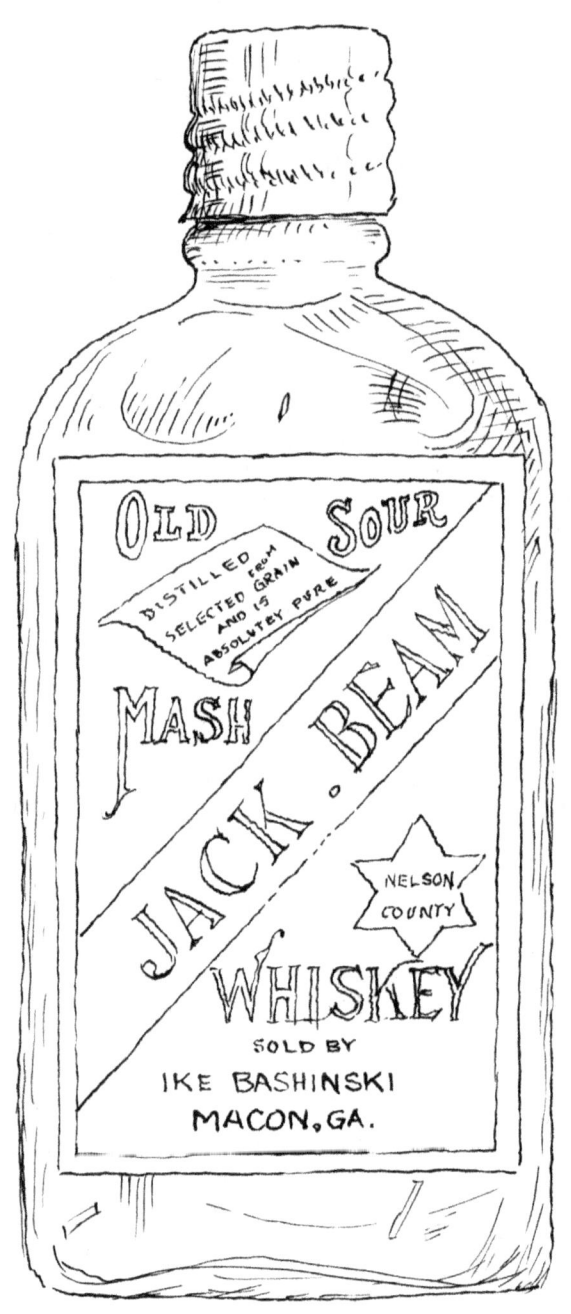

CLEAR 6½ WITH CAP

LABEL YELLOW, RED

SILVER AND BLACK

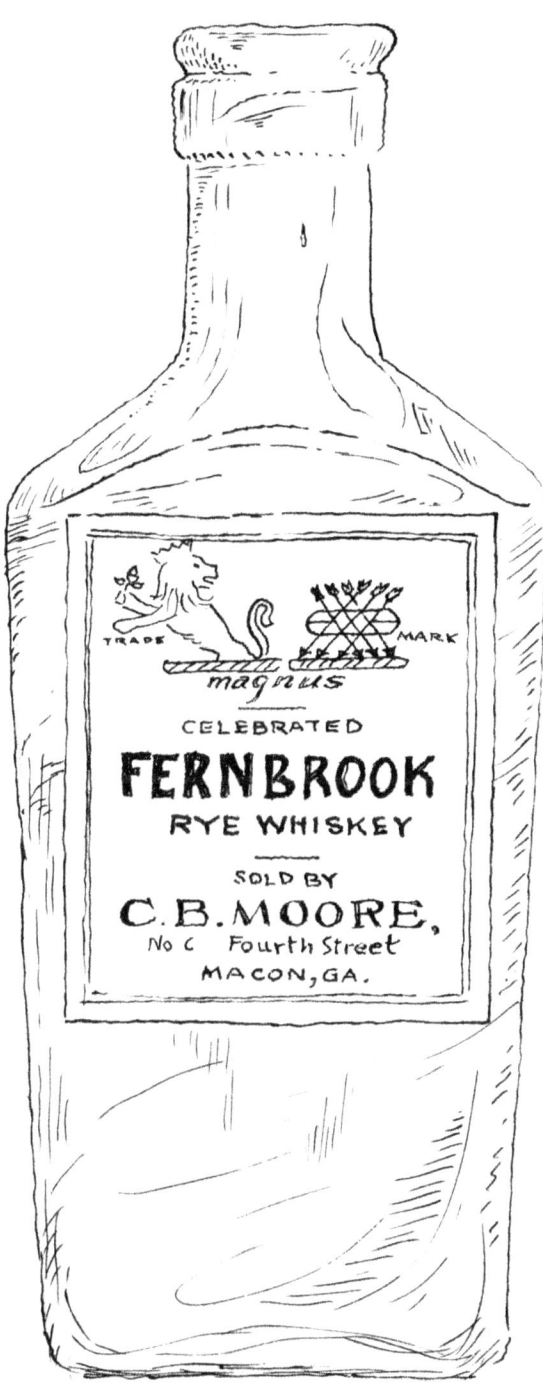

TRADE MARK

magnus

CELEBRATED

FERNBROOK

RYE WHISKEY

SOLD BY

C.B.MOORE,

No 6 Fourth Street

MACON, GA.

7" CLEAR

LABEL - BLACK, GOLD,
BLUE ON WHITE

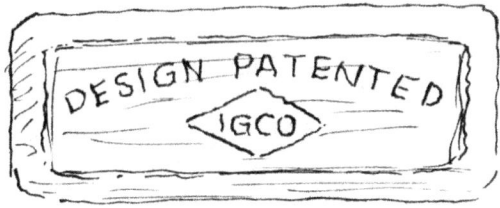

DESIGN PATENTED

IGCO

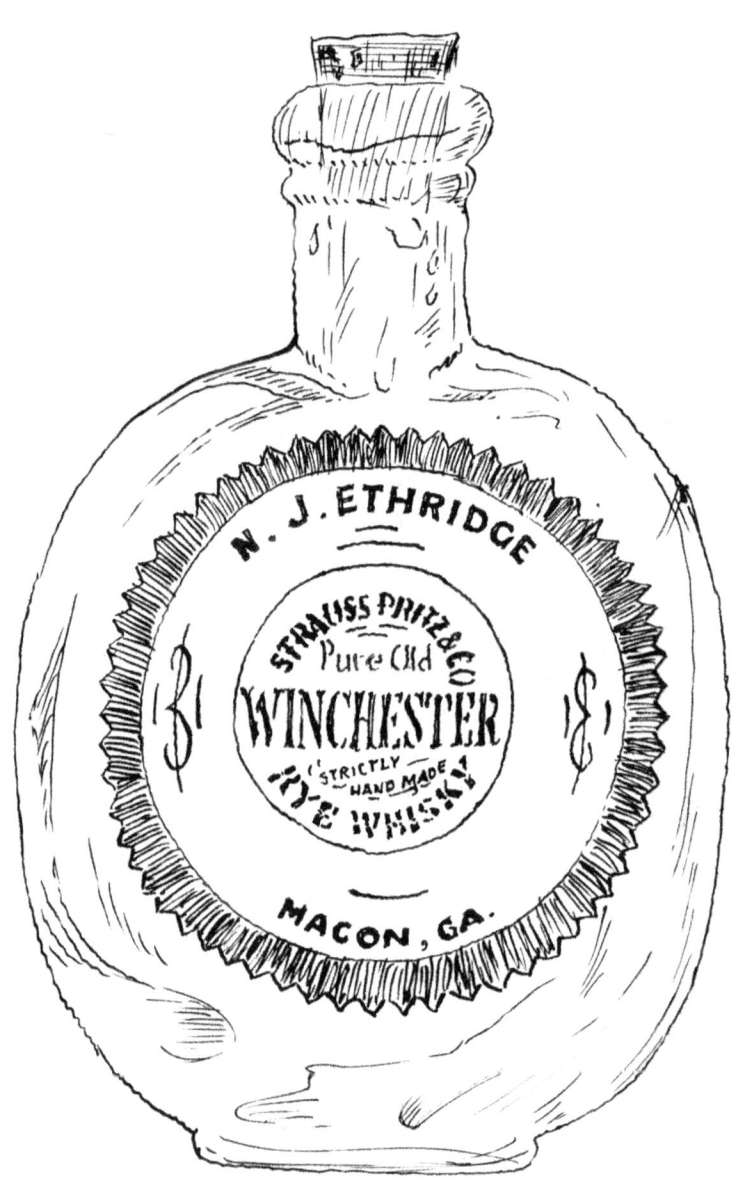

N. J. ETHRIDGE

STRAUSS PRITZ & CO
Pure Old
WINCHESTER
STRICTLY
HAND MADE
RYE WHISKY

MACON, GA.

CLEAR
5½
LABEL DARK BLUE
& WHITE

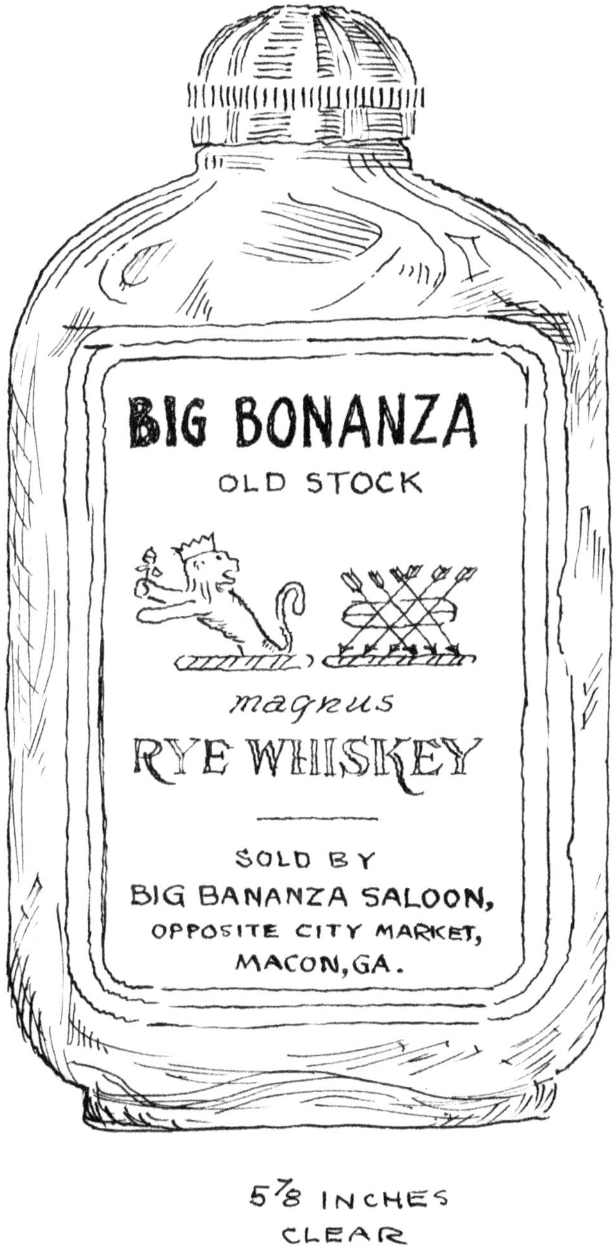

BIG BONANZA
OLD STOCK

magnus
RYE WHISKEY

SOLD BY
BIG BANANZA SALOON,
OPPOSITE CITY MARKET,
MACON, GA.

5⅞ INCHES
CLEAR
METAL CAP

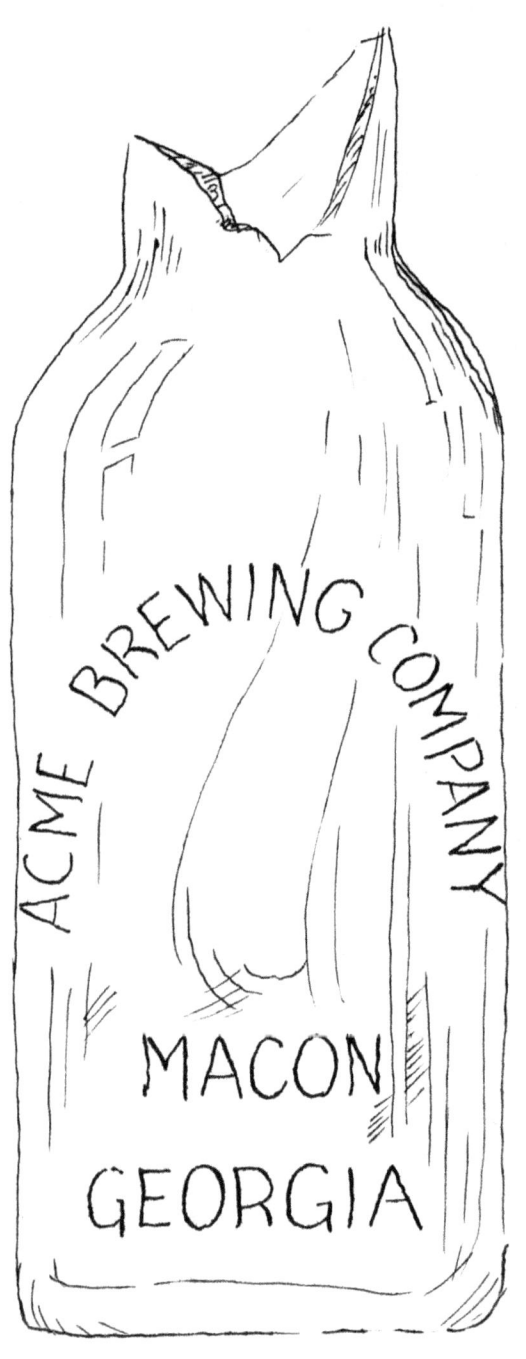

ACME BREWING COMPANY

MACON

GEORGIA

NO COMPLETE ONE
LIGHT GREEN
ON THE SIDE AT THE
BOTTOM D.O.C. 234

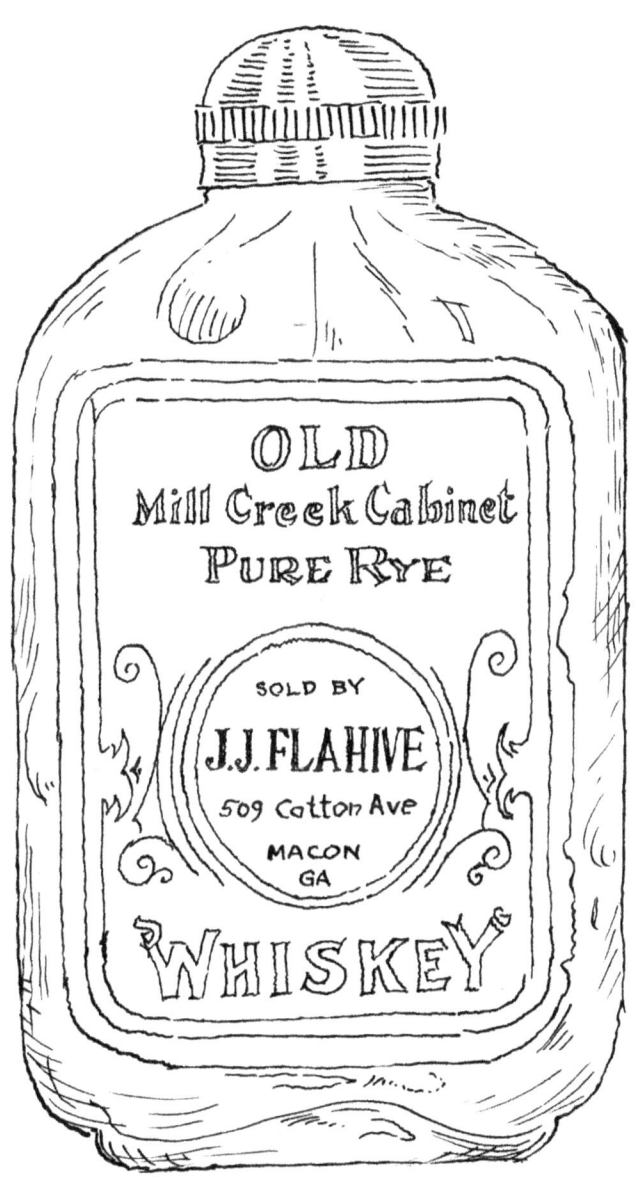

5 7/8 INCHES
CLEAR
METAL CAP

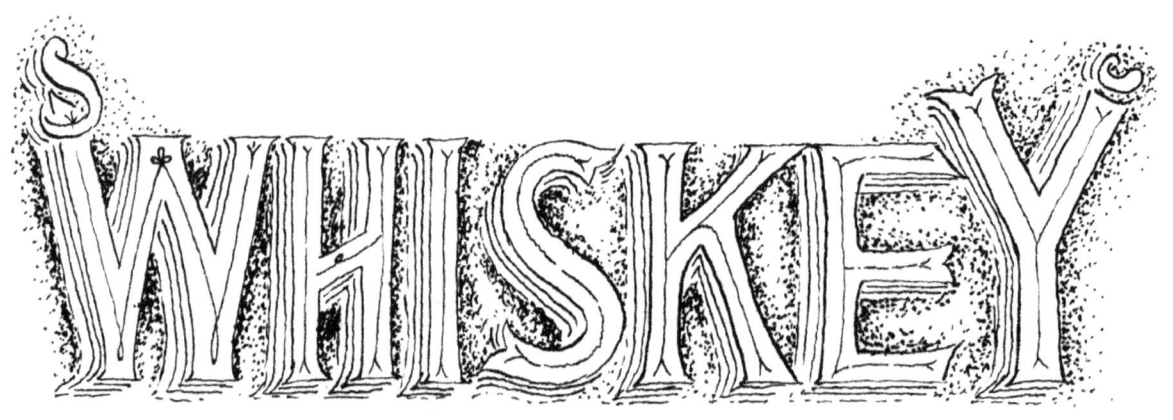

CLEAR 5"

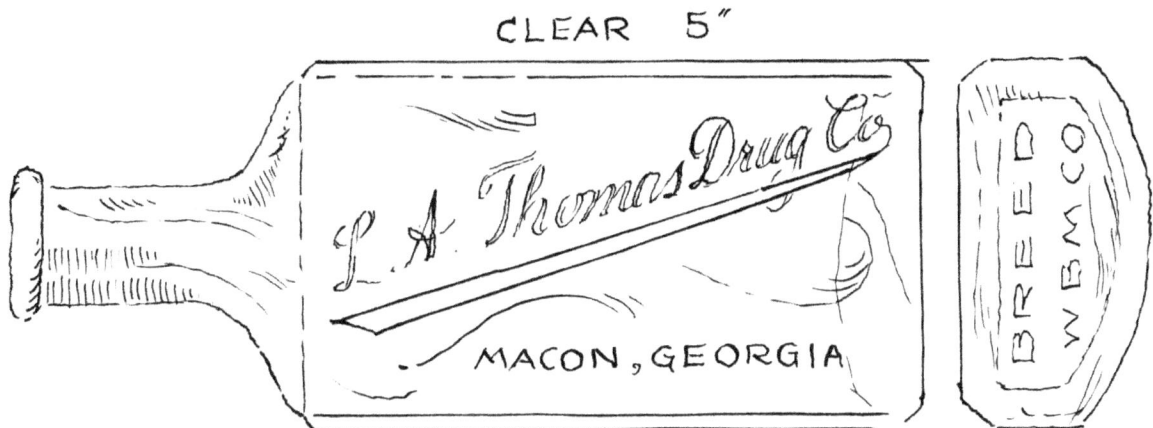

L. A. Thomas Drug Co.

MACON, GEORGIA

BREED
W.B.M.CO

CLEAR 3¾ ALSO 4¾ 5 11 & 6¾

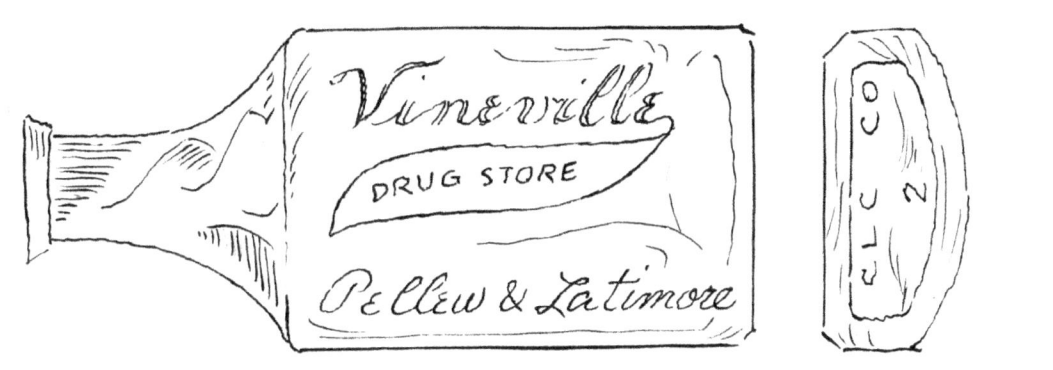

Vineville
DRUG STORE
Pellew & Latimore

CLC CO
2

CLEAR 5⅜ dug on 7th St. JUN-71

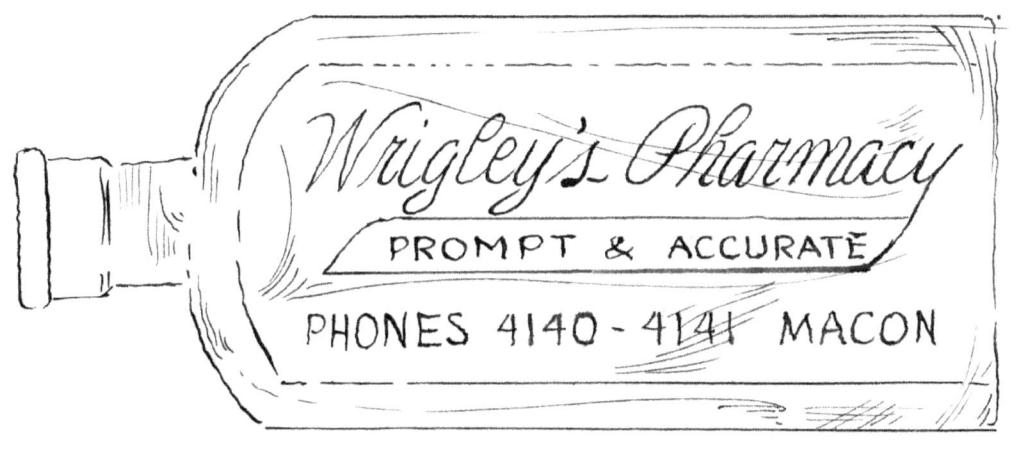

Wrigley's Pharmacy
PROMPT & ACCURATE
PHONES 4140 - 4141 MACON

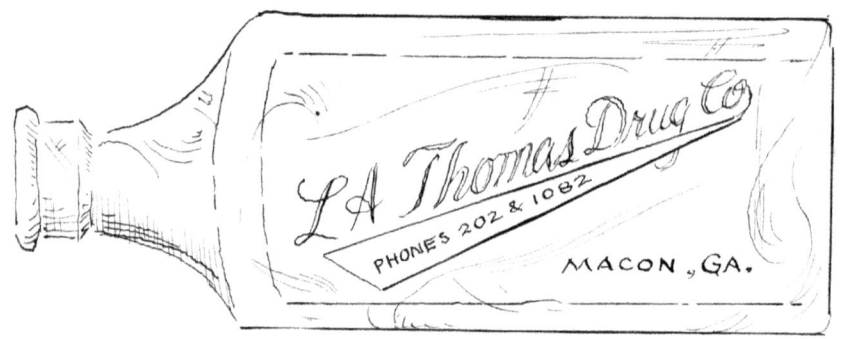

L A Thomas Drug Co

PHONES 202 & 1082

MACON, GA.

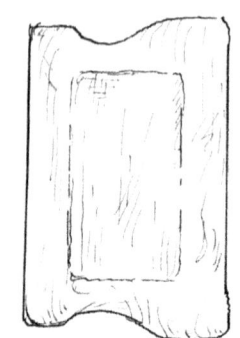

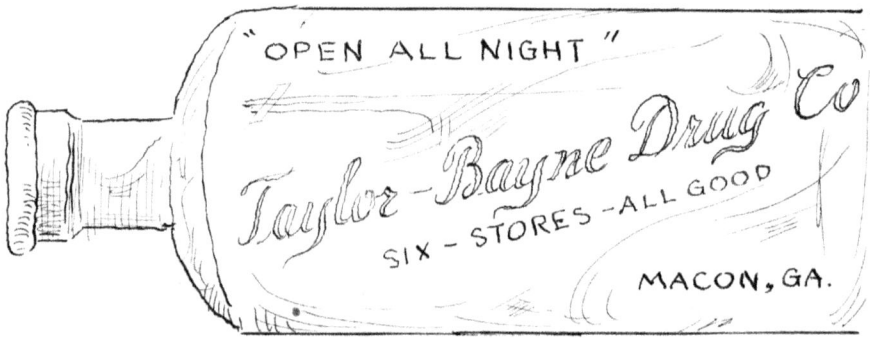

"OPEN ALL NIGHT"

Taylor - Bayne Drug Co

SIX - STORES - ALL GOOD

MACON, GA.

REVERSE SIDE → | TAYLOR - BAYNE |

MOST TAYLOR BAYNE WAS MADE BY WT CO

SOME HAS NO MARKING

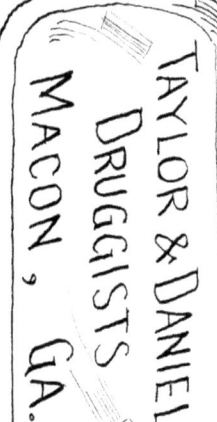

TAYLOR & DANIEL DRUGGISTS MACON, GA.

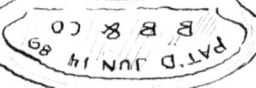

PAT'D JUN 14 89   B B & CO

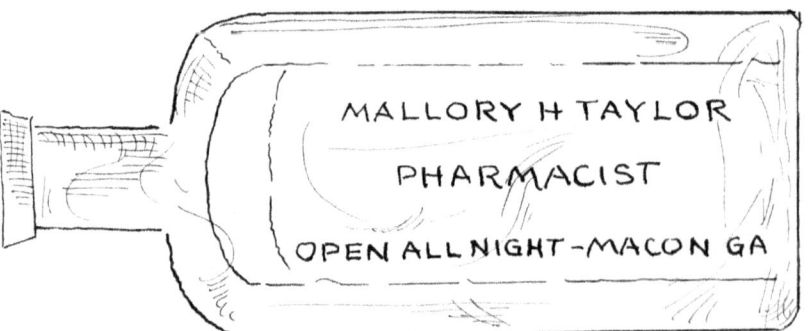

MALLORY H TAYLOR

PHARMACIST

OPEN ALL NIGHT - MACON GA

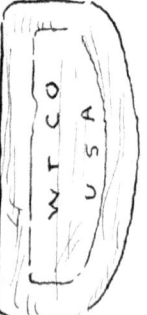

W T CO   U S A

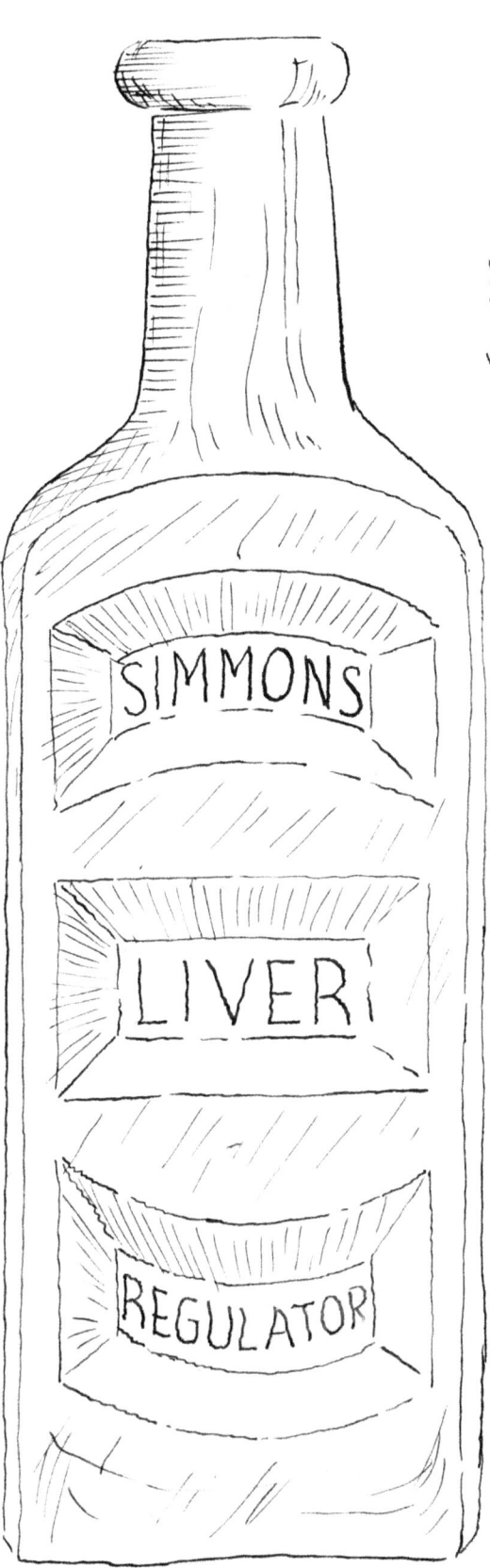

Back –
J.H. ZEILIN & Co
DEEP COCAVES ON
4 SIDES   Large size
2 SIZES –

MACON, GA

PHILADELPHIA

SIMMONS

LIVER

REGULATOR

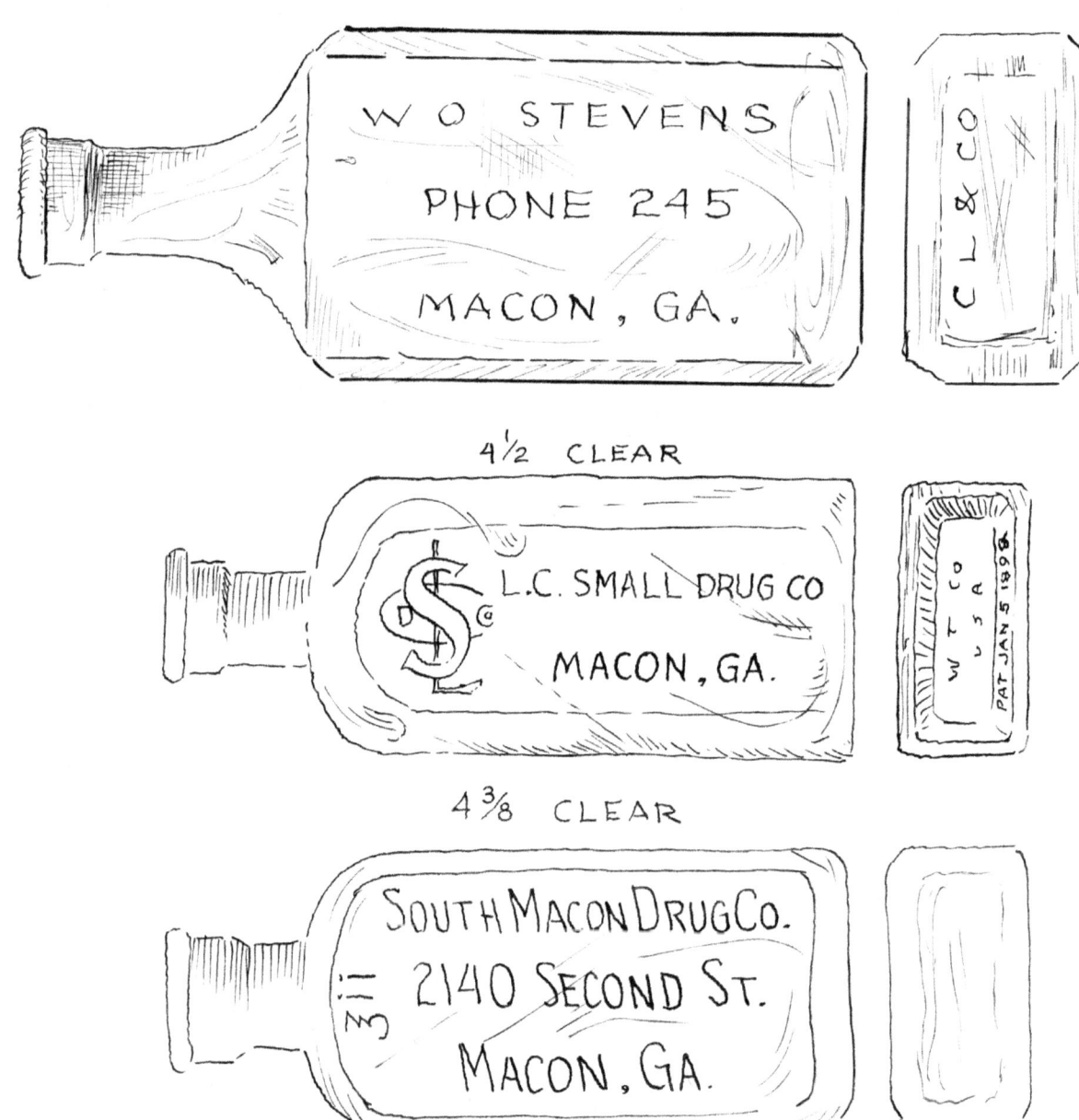

CLEAR 6½

W O STEVENS

PHONE 245

MACON, GA.

C L & CO

4½ CLEAR

L.C. SMALL DRUG CO

MACON, GA.

W T CO
U S A
PAT JAN 5 1898

4⅜ CLEAR

SOUTH MACON DRUG CO.

2140 SECOND ST.

MACON, GA.

Ʒii

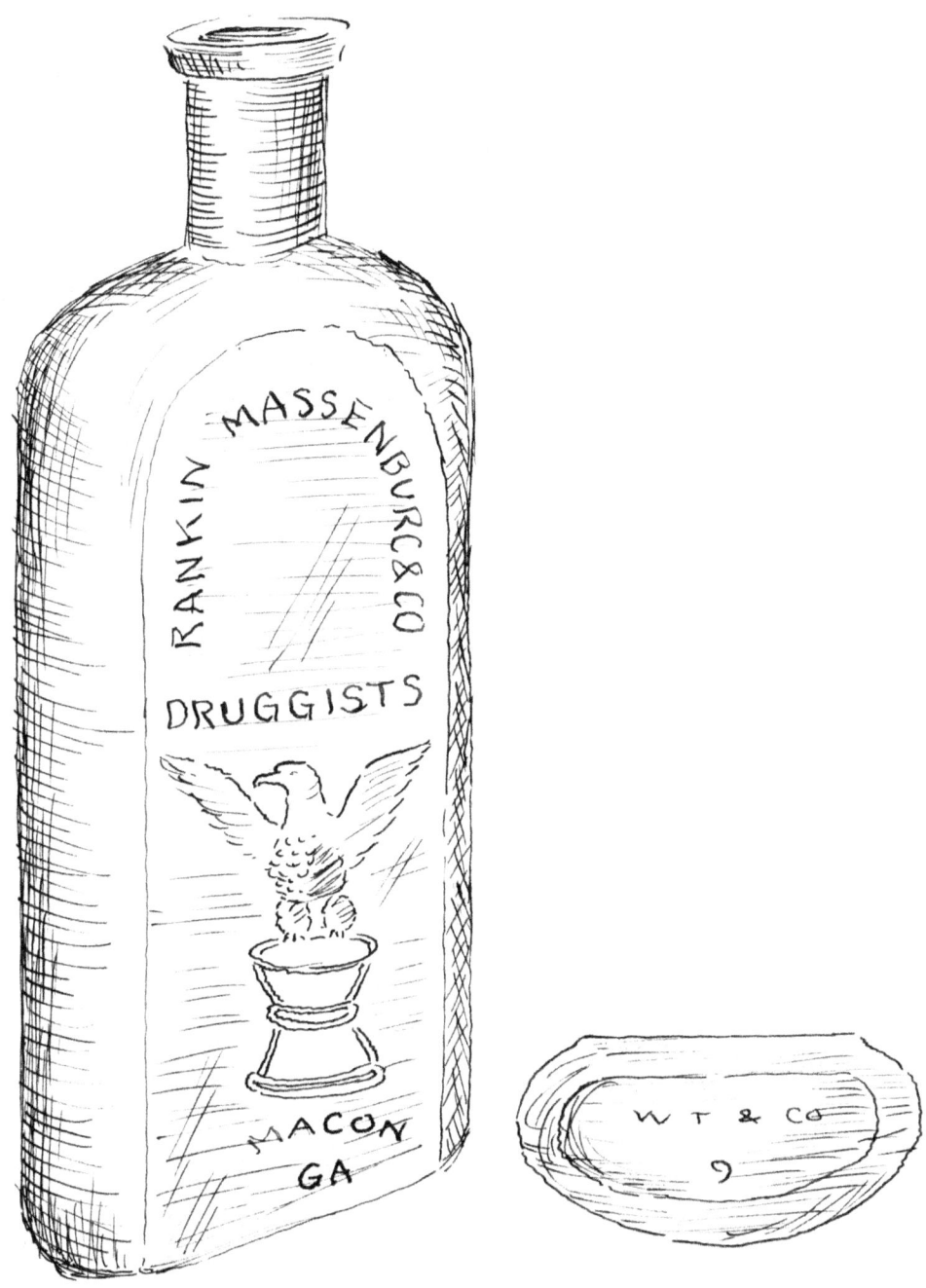

RANKIN MASSENBURG&CO

DRUGGISTS

MACON GA

WT & CO

9

EMERALD GREEN

CLEAR 4"

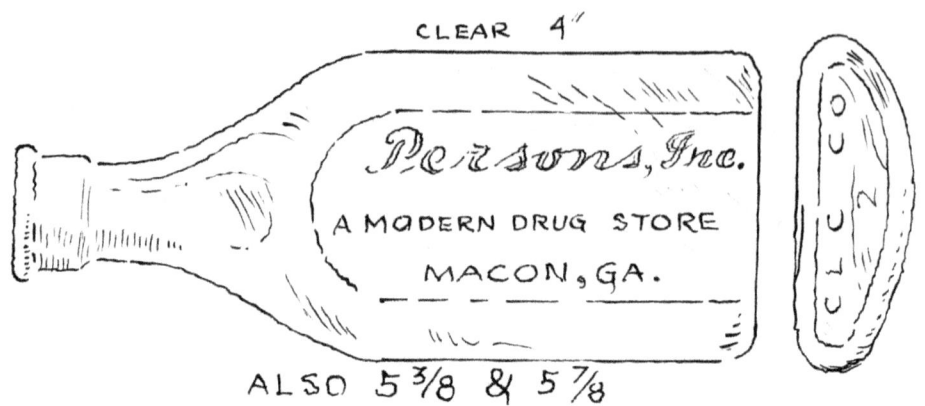

Persons, Inc.

A MODERN DRUG STORE

MACON, GA.

ALSO 5 3/8 & 5 7/8

CLEAR 3 5/8

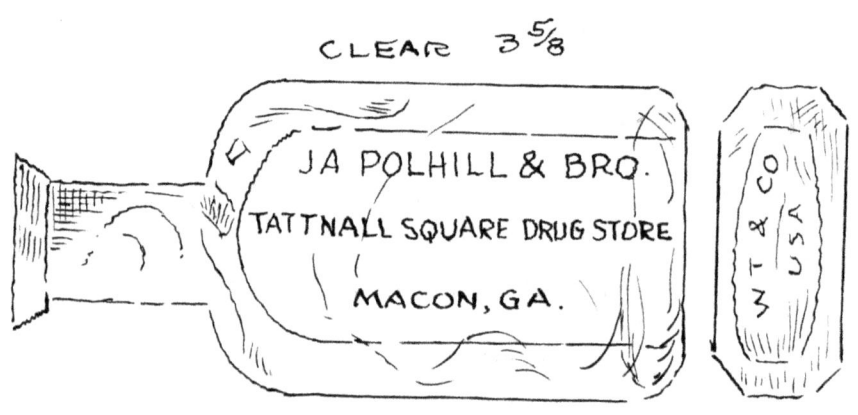

JA POLHILL & BRO.

TATTNALL SQUARE DRUG STORE

MACON, GA.

CLEAR 5 3/8

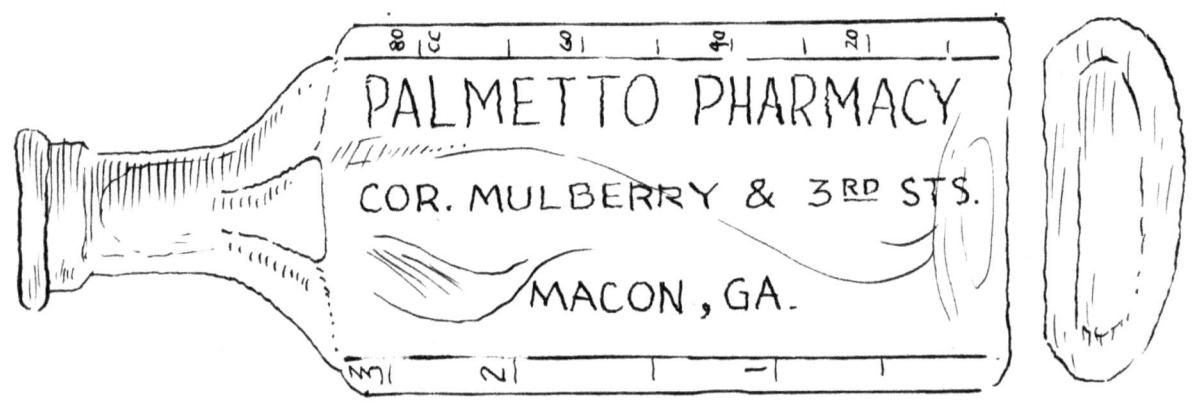

PALMETTO PHARMACY

COR. MULBERRY & 3RD STS.

MACON, GA.

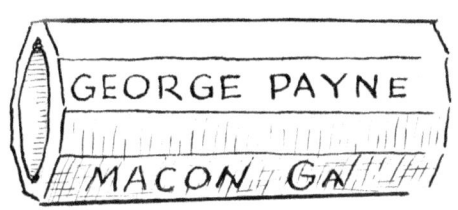

CLEAR – 2 1/16 IN. TALL TAPPERS OFF
1/8" FROM TOP TO BOTTOM. 10 SIDED
GEORGE PAYNE
FEVER & AGUE
PILLS
MACON, GA.

CLEAR 6"

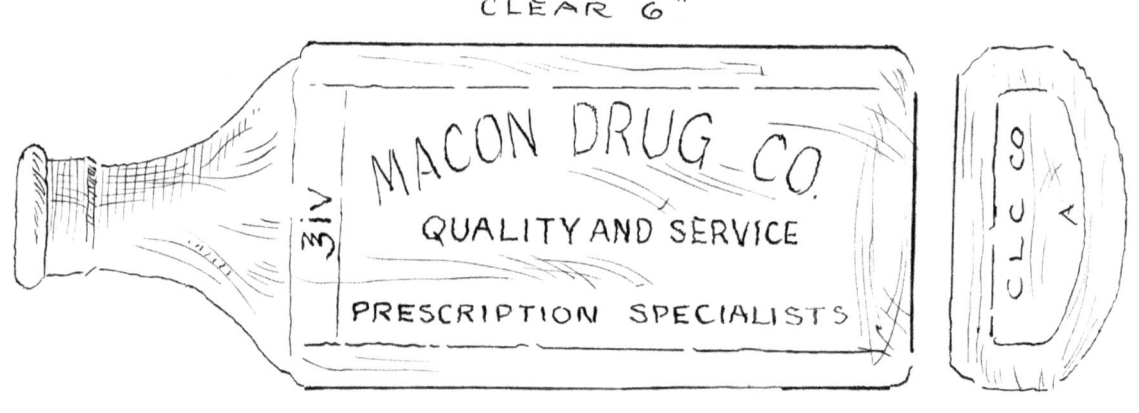

ℨiv MACON DRUG CO.
QUALITY AND SERVICE
PRESCRIPTION SPECIALISTS

CLC CO A

CLEAR 6⅜ SQ

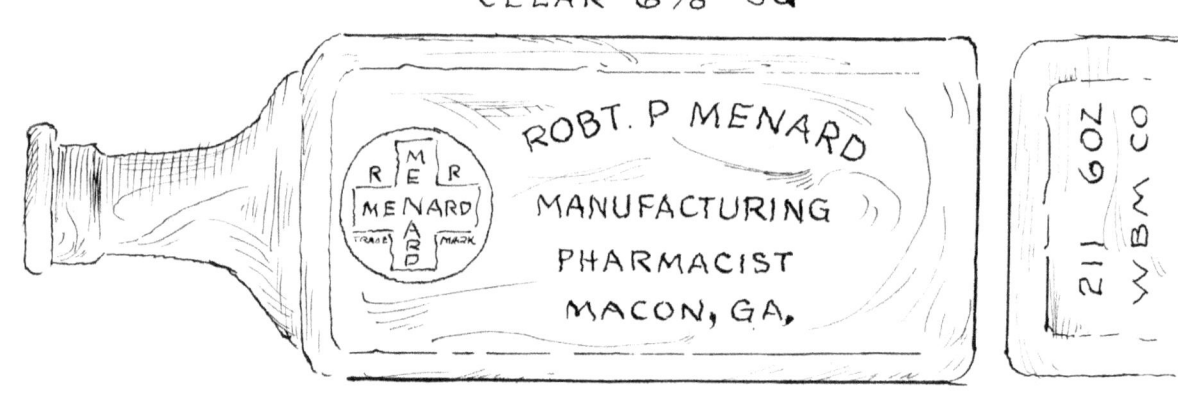

ROBT. P MENARD
MANUFACTURING
PHARMACIST
MACON, GA.

R E MENARD A D
TRADE MARK

211 6OZ WBM CO

CLEAR 5¼ CONCAVE FRONT & SIDES

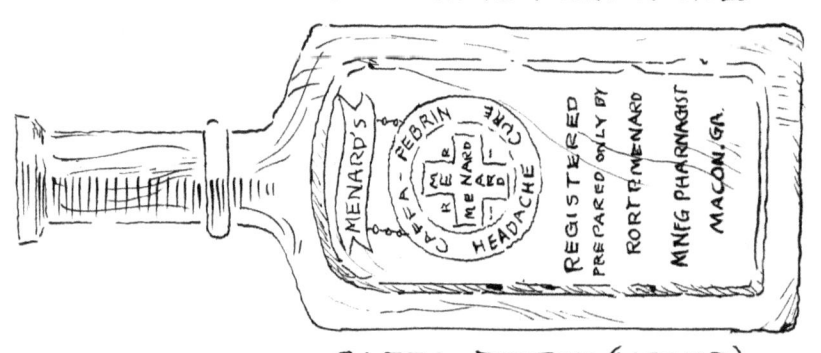

MENARD'S GAFFA FEBRIN CURE HEADACHE

R E MENARD A D

REGISTERED
PREPARED ONLY BY
ROBT. P. MENARD
MNFG PHARMACIST
MACON. GA.

OWNER
W H SUDDERTH
FOUND ON 7ᵗʰ St.

GAFFA - FEBRIN (LIQUID)
ON EACH SIDE

CLEAR 4$\frac{1}{2}$ dug on 7Th St. Jun. 71

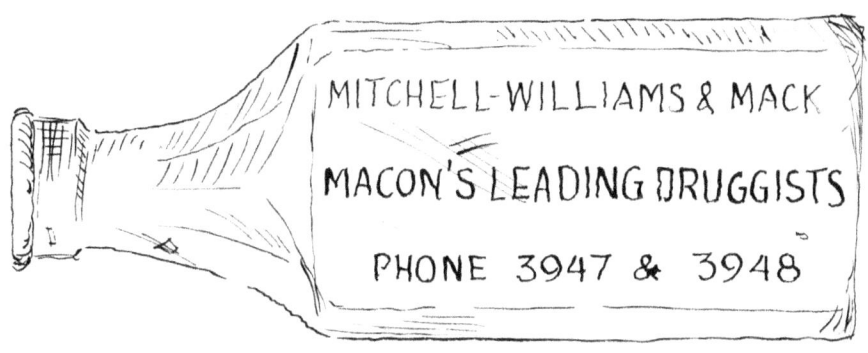

MITCHELL-WILLIAMS & MACK

MACON'S LEADING DRUGGISTS

PHONE 3947 & 3948

CLEAR 5$\frac{3}{4}$ dug on 7th St.

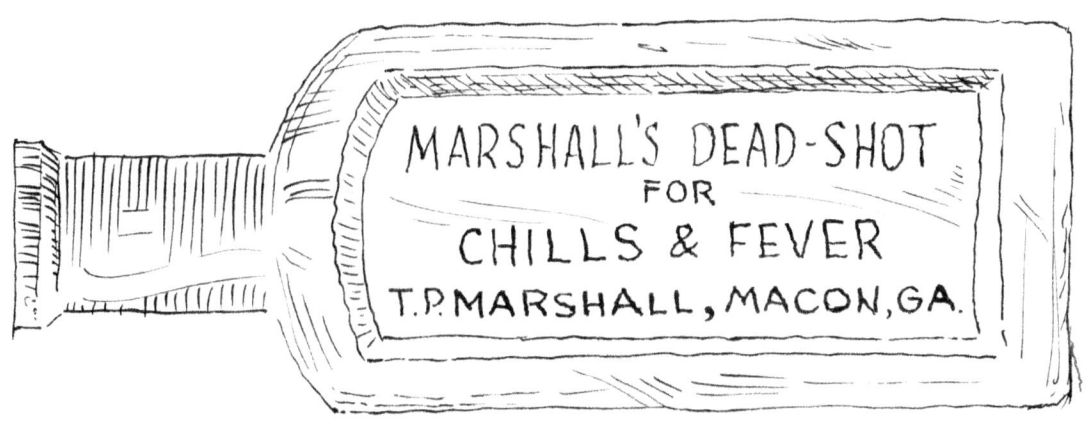

MARSHALL'S DEAD-SHOT
FOR
CHILLS & FEVER
T.P. MARSHALL, MACON, GA.

2 1/8 AMBER

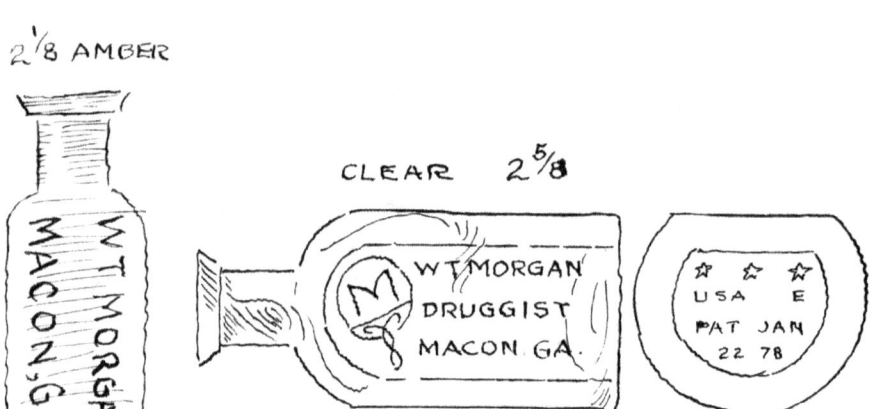

CLEAR 2 5/8

WT MORGAN
MACON, GA.

WT MORGAN
DRUGGIST
MACON. GA.

☆ ☆ ☆
U S A   E
PAT JAN
22 78

LIGHT BLUE GREEN 5" & 5 1/2

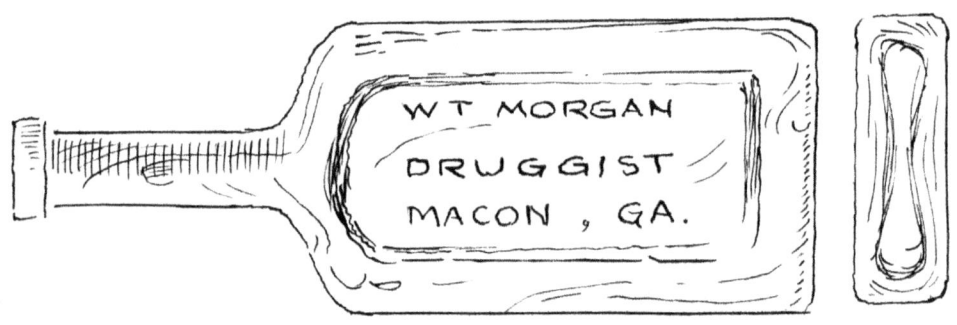

WT MORGAN
DRUGGIST
MACON , GA.

SHAPED LIKE EXTRACT BOTTLE
CONCAVE 4 SIDES

CLEAR 6 1/4 ALSO 3 3/4

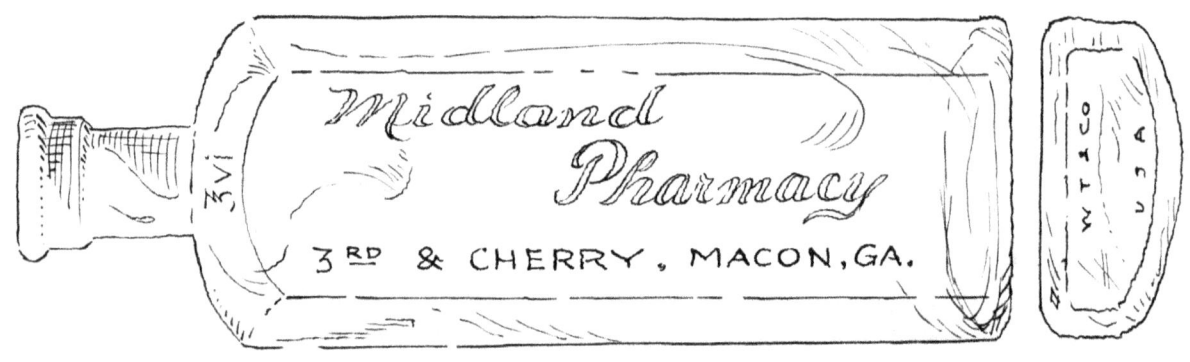

Midland
Pharmacy

3RD & CHERRY, MACON, GA.

CLEAR 4³⁄₈

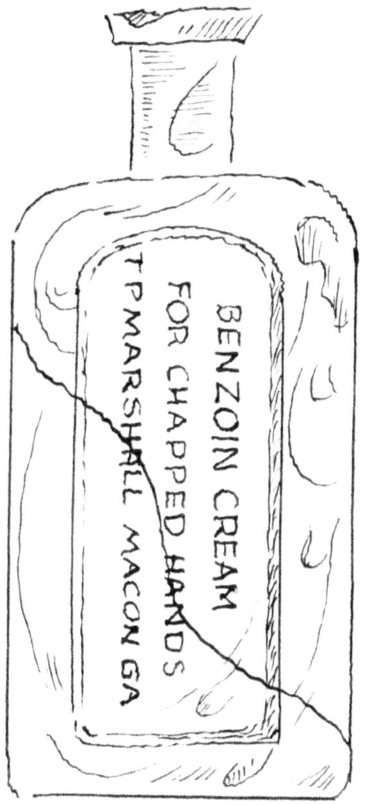

CLEAR 4³⁄₈

2³⁄₄
SIZE
ALSO

BENZOIN CREAM
FOR CHAPPED HANDS
T P MARSHALL MACON GA

Marshalls
DRUG
STORES
MACON

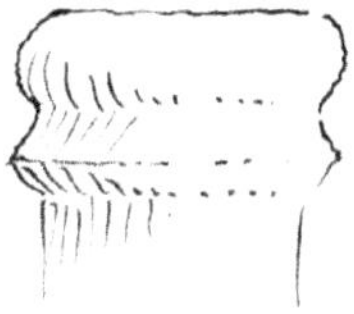

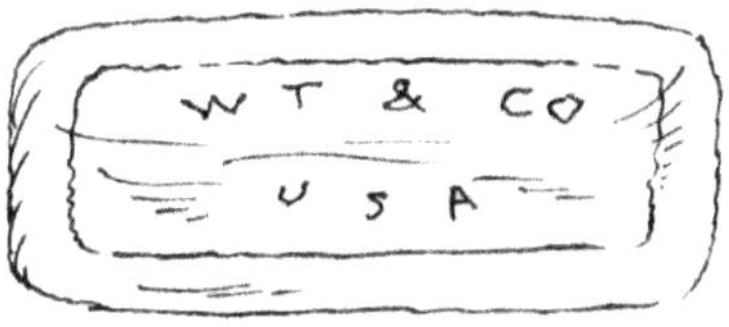

CLEAR

5½ INCHES FLAT
TYPE, CONCAVE
FRONT & SIDES
T. P. MARSHALL
MACON
GA.

CONCAVE FRONT

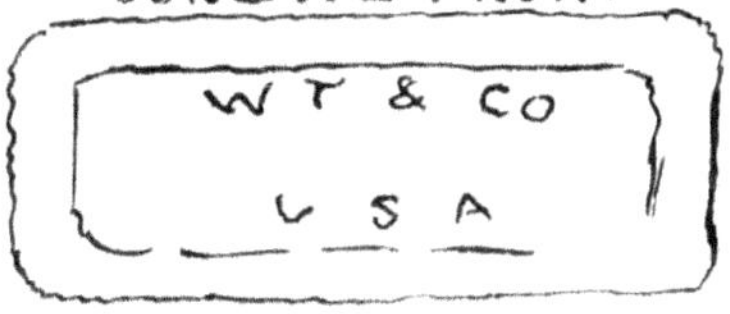

WT & CO

USA

CRACKED
CHIPPED

WT & CO

USA

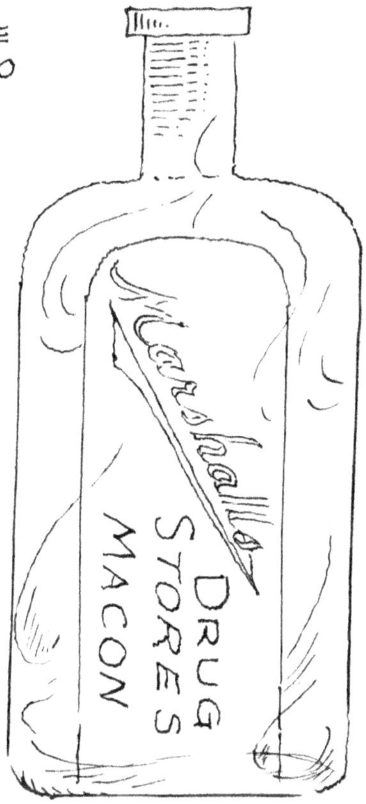

CLEAR 3⁵⁄₈

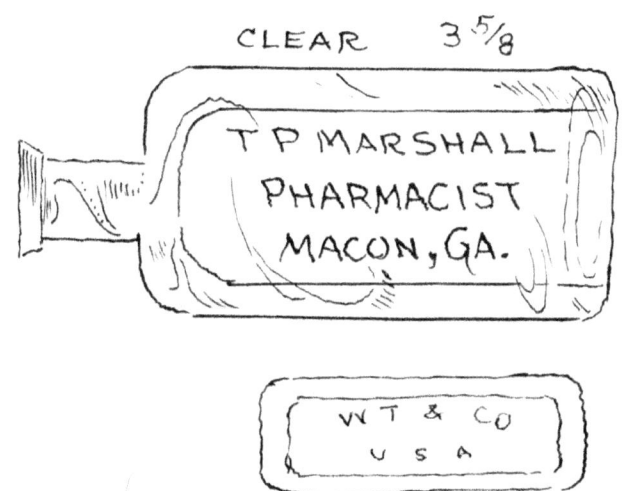

T P MARSHALL
PHARMACIST
MACON, GA.

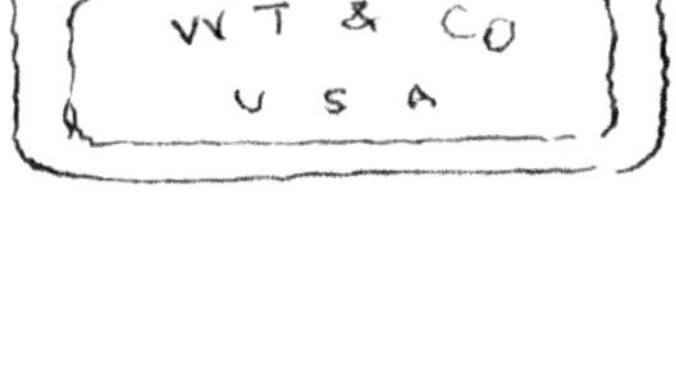

WT & CO

USA

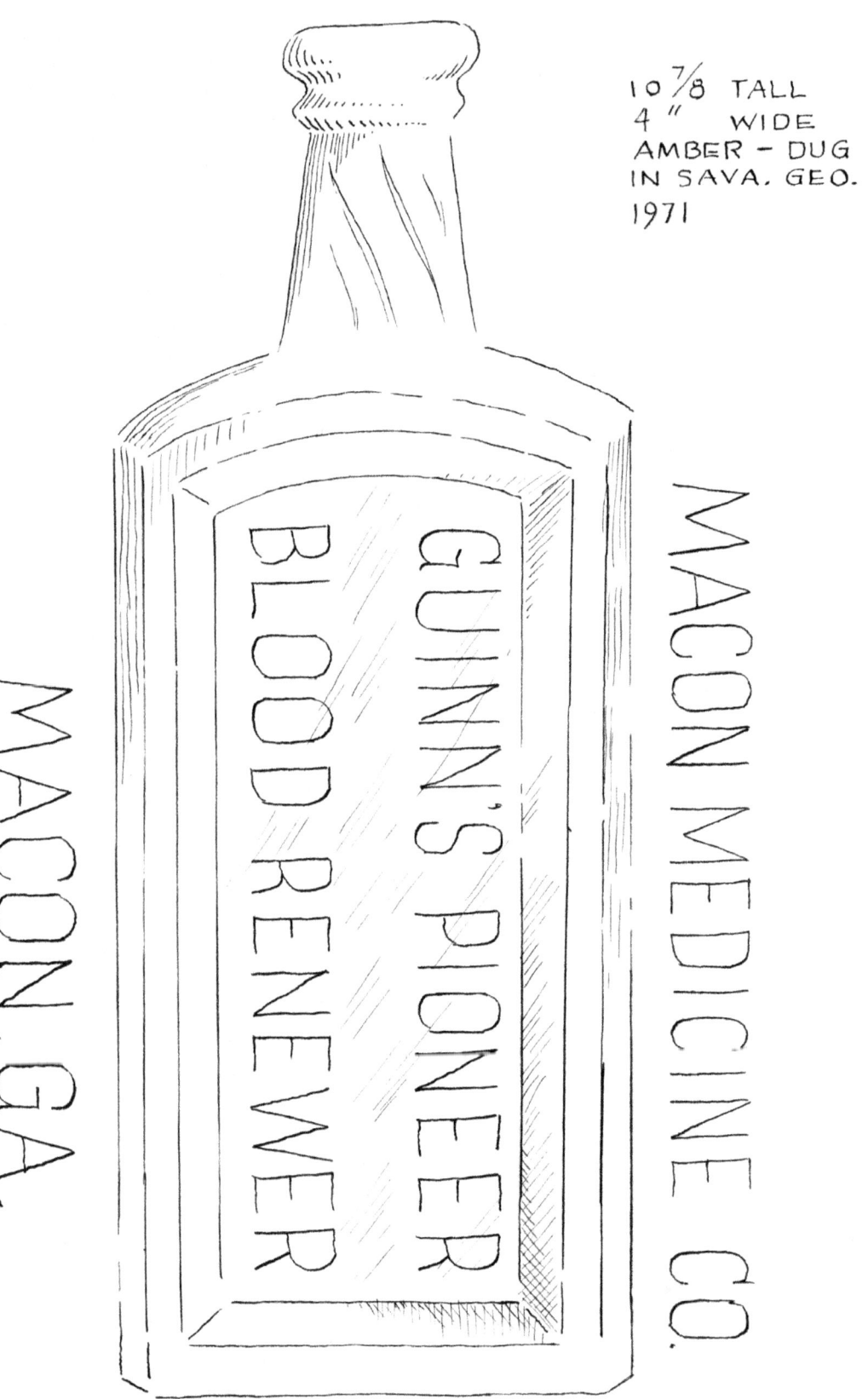

10 7/8 TALL
4" WIDE
AMBER – DUG
IN SAVA, GEO.
1971

GUINN'S PIONEER
BLOOD RENEWER

MACON MEDICINE CO.

MACON, GA.

CLEAR 3½ SQ.

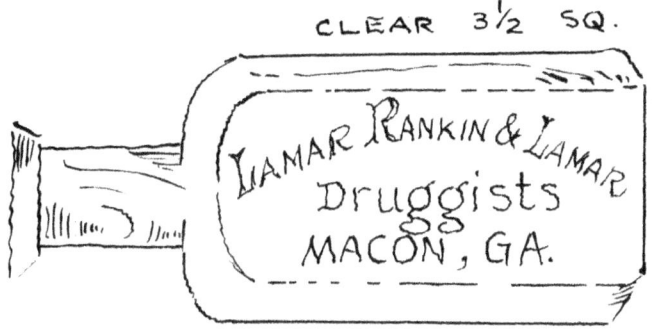 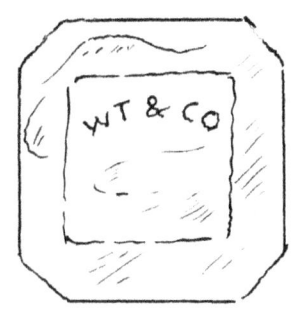

CLEAR 4¼

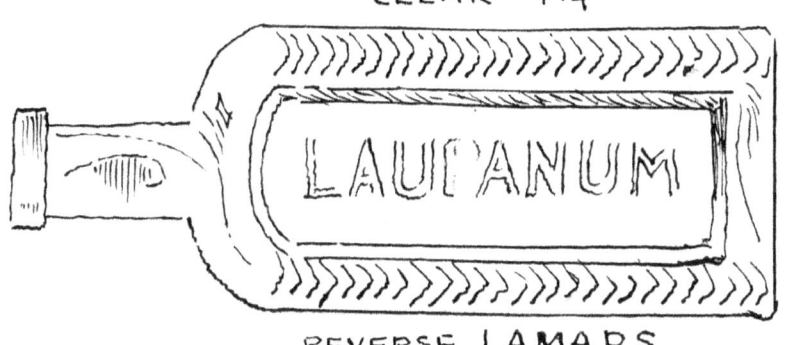 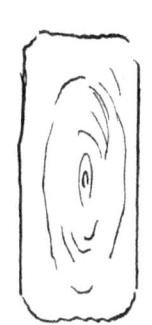

REVERSE LAMARS
CONCAVE 4 SIDES

ALSO 4⅜ IN LIGHT BLUE

CLEAR 3¾

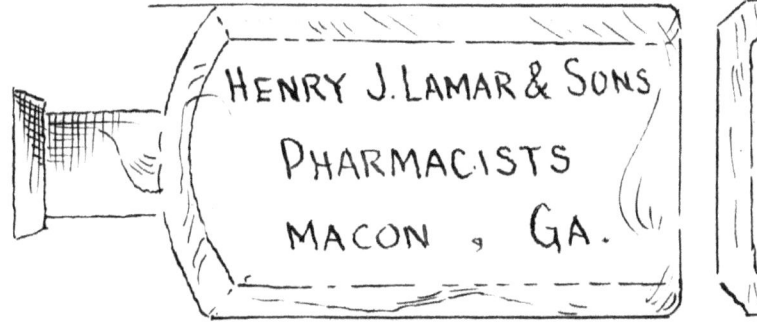 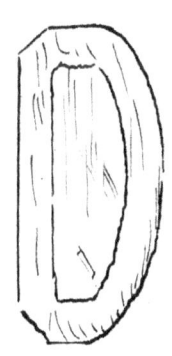

CLEAR 3

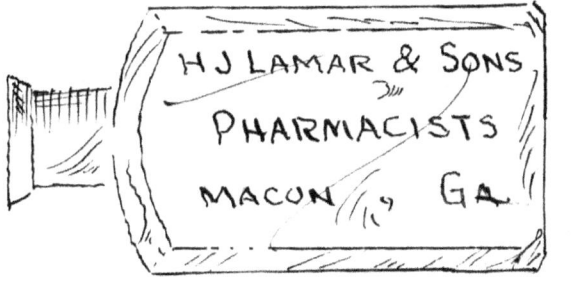 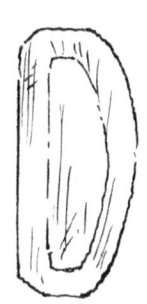

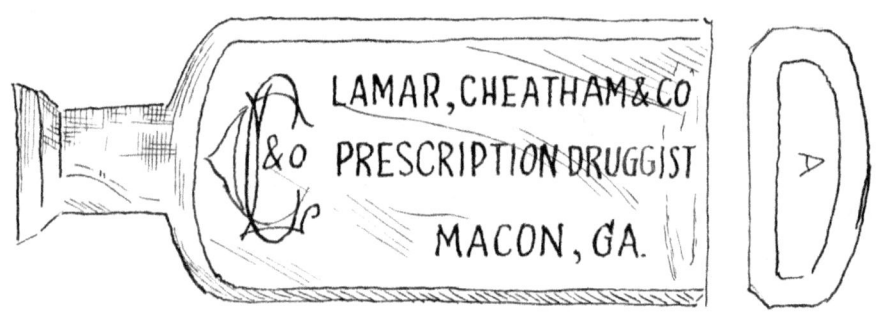

LAMAR, CHEATHAM & CO

PRESCRIPTION DRUGGIST

MACON, GA.

CLEAR 3½ IN. TALL

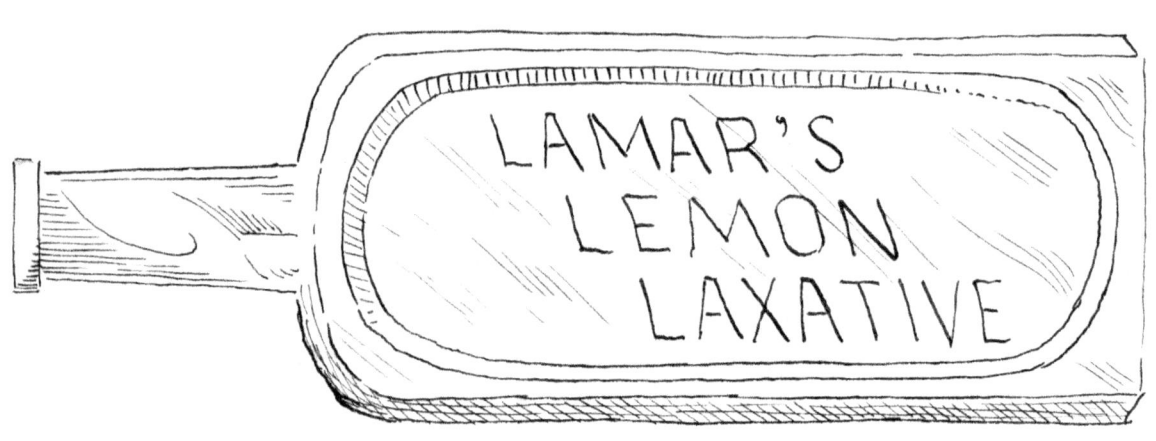

LAMAR'S
LEMON
LAXATIVE

CLEAR ~ 7 ¾ by 2½

AQUA 9"

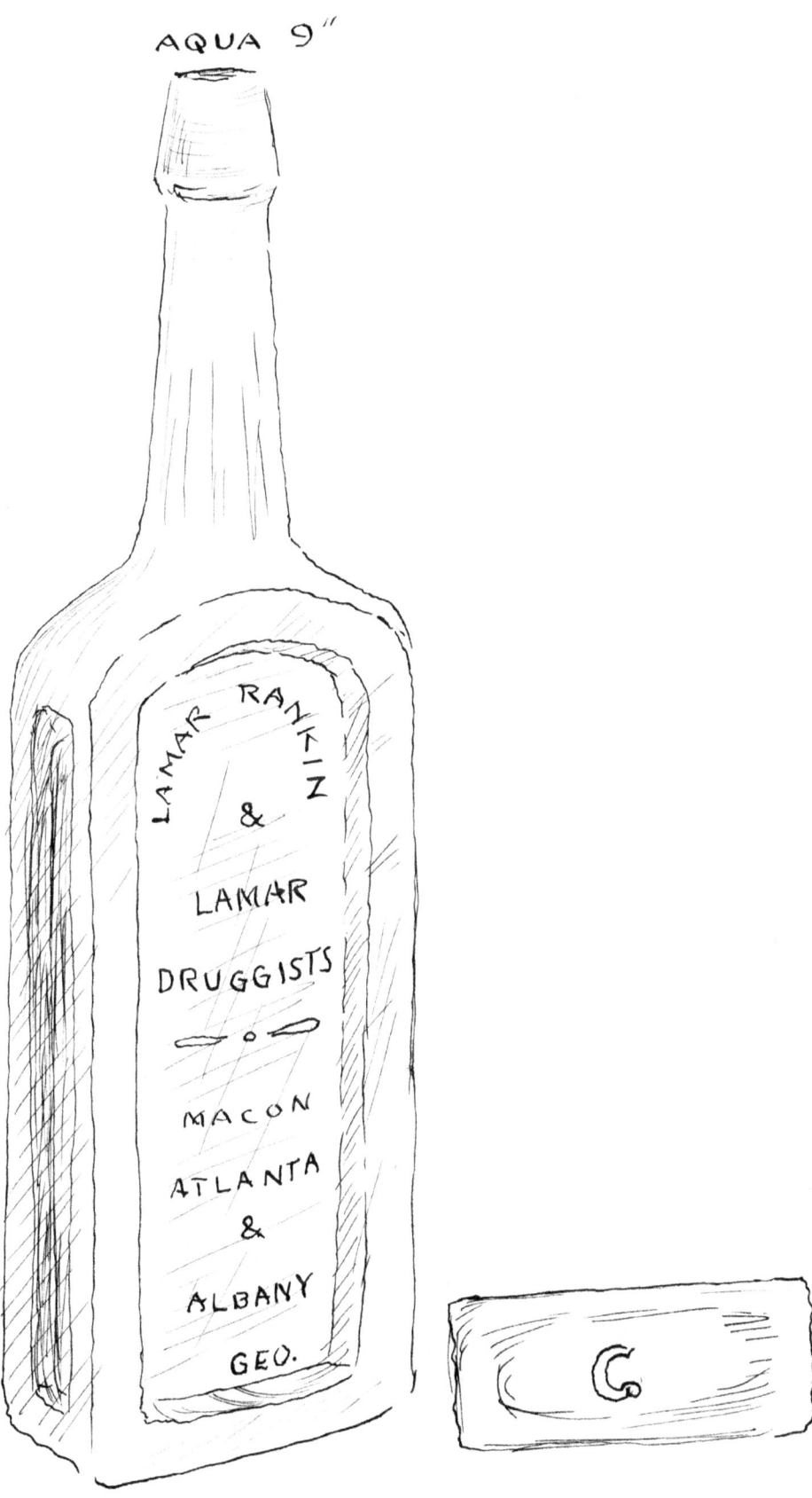

LAMAR RANKIN
&
LAMAR
DRUGGISTS
MACON
ATLANTA
&
ALBANY
GEO.

G

CLEAR 4½ & 2⅞

CLEAR 3½

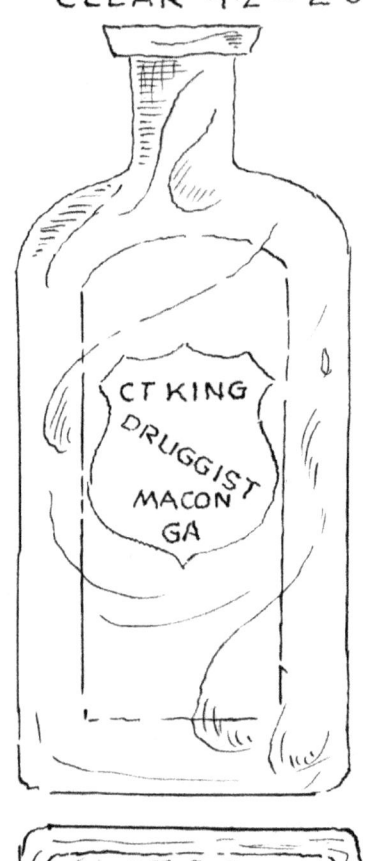

CT KING
DRUGGIST
MACON
GA

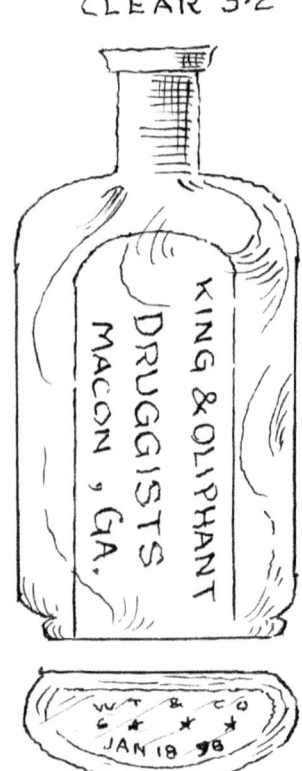

KING & OLIPHANT
DRUGGISTS
MACON , GA.

WT & CO
JAN 18 98

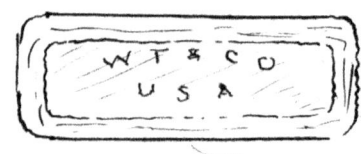

WT & CO
USA

CLEAR 4⅜

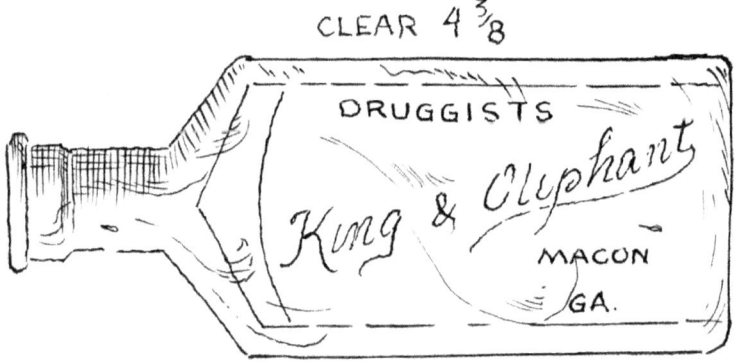

DRUGGISTS
King & Oliphant
MACON
GA.

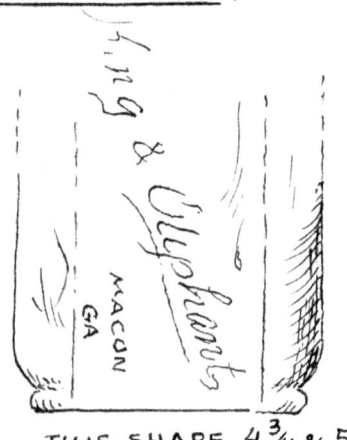

King & Oliphant
MACON
GA

THIS SHAPE 4¾ & 5⅛
BOTTOM
JAN 8 1898
WT CO
C
U S A

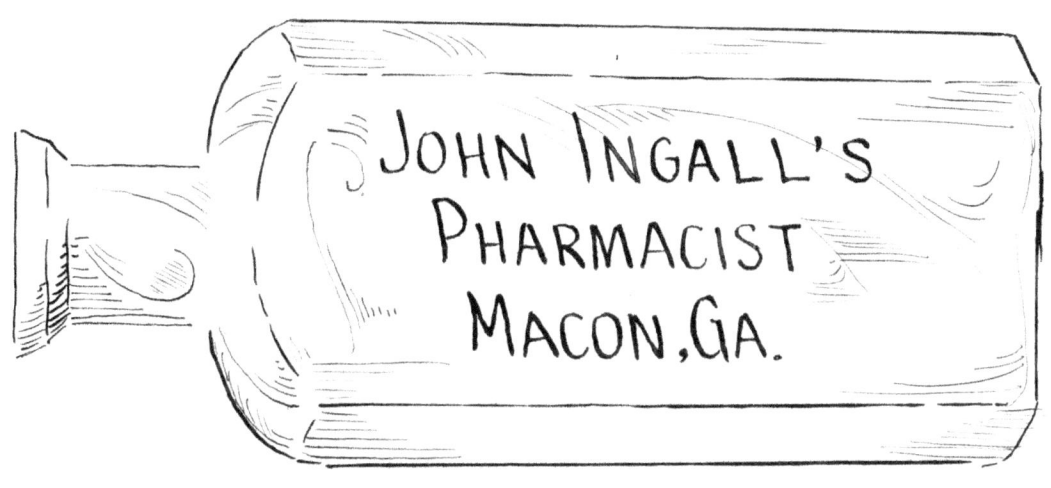

CLEAR 5½

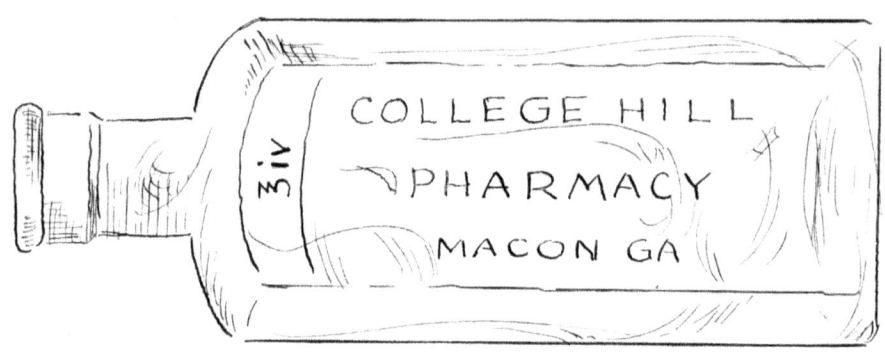

COLLEGE HILL
PHARMACY
MACON GA

℥iv

CLEAR 6¼

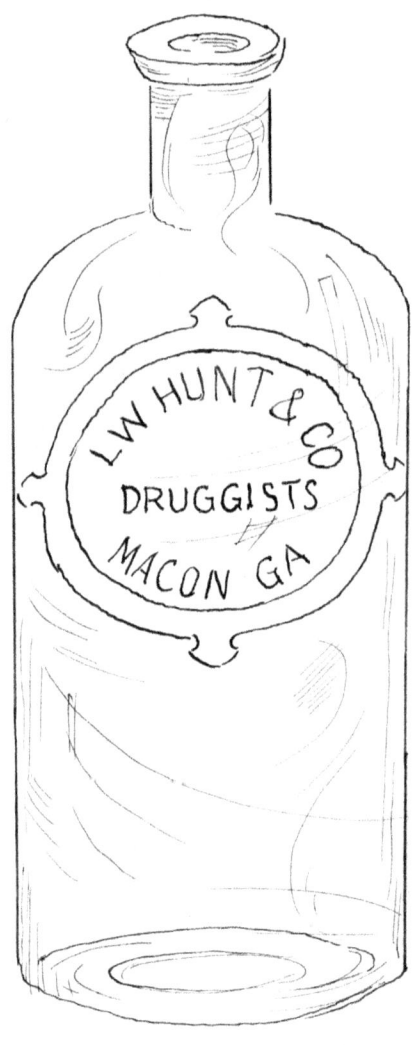

L.W HUNT & CO
DRUGGISTS
MACON GA

ALSO A COPPER TRADE
TOKEN
"GOOD FOR ONE GLASS"

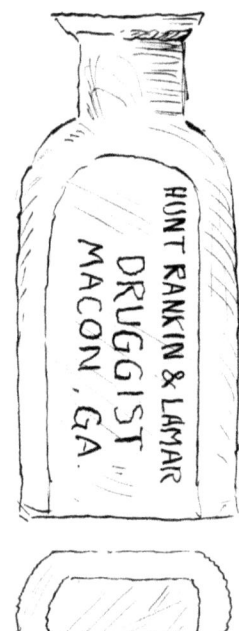

HUNT RANKIN & LAMAR
DRUGGIST
MACON, GA.

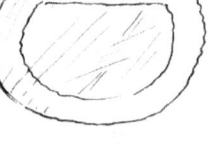

CLEAR

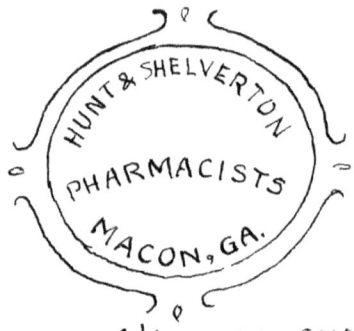

HUNT & SHELVERTON
PHARMACISTS
MACON, GA.

CLEAR 4⅛ OVAL SHAPE

CLEAR 3⅝ SQ.

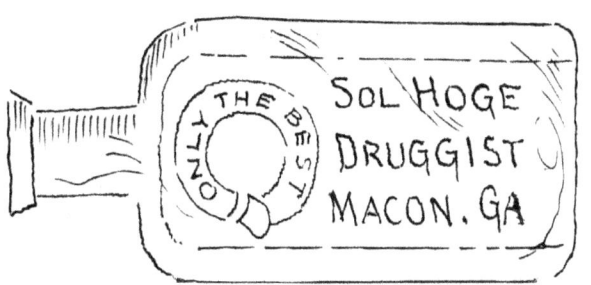

ONLY THE BEST

SOL HOGE
DRUGGIST
MACON. GA

CLEAR 6¼

CLEAR 5⅔

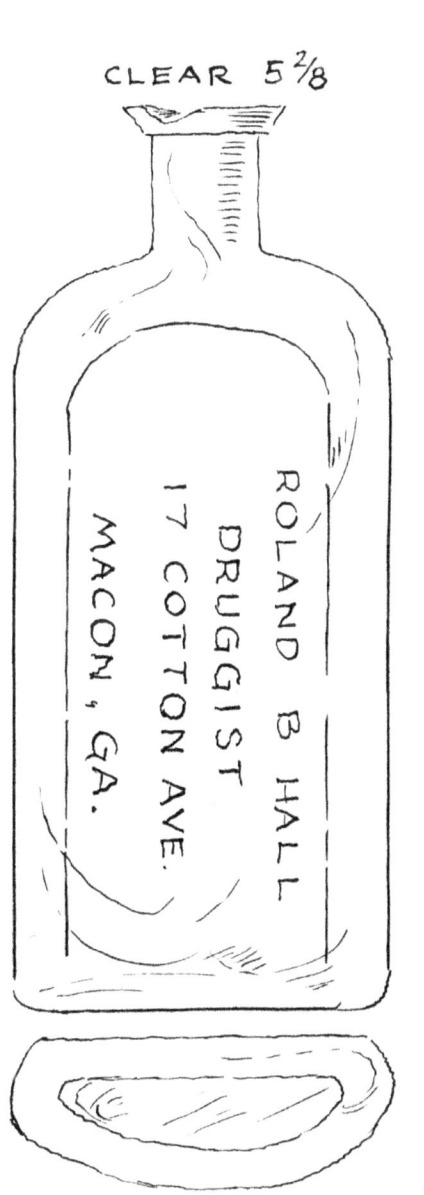

ROLAND B HALL
DRUGGIST
17 COTTON AVE.
MACON, GA.

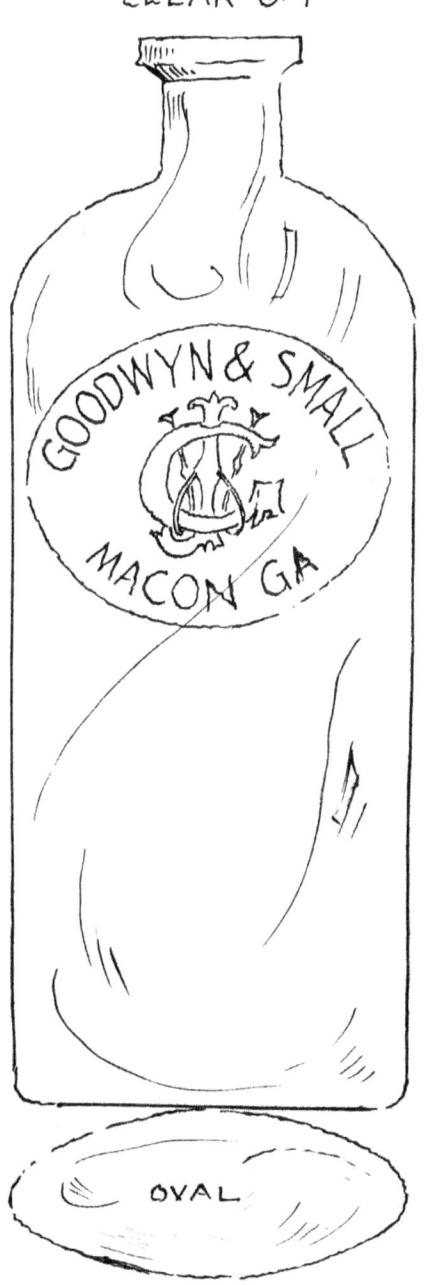

GOODWYN & SMALL
MACON GA

OVAL

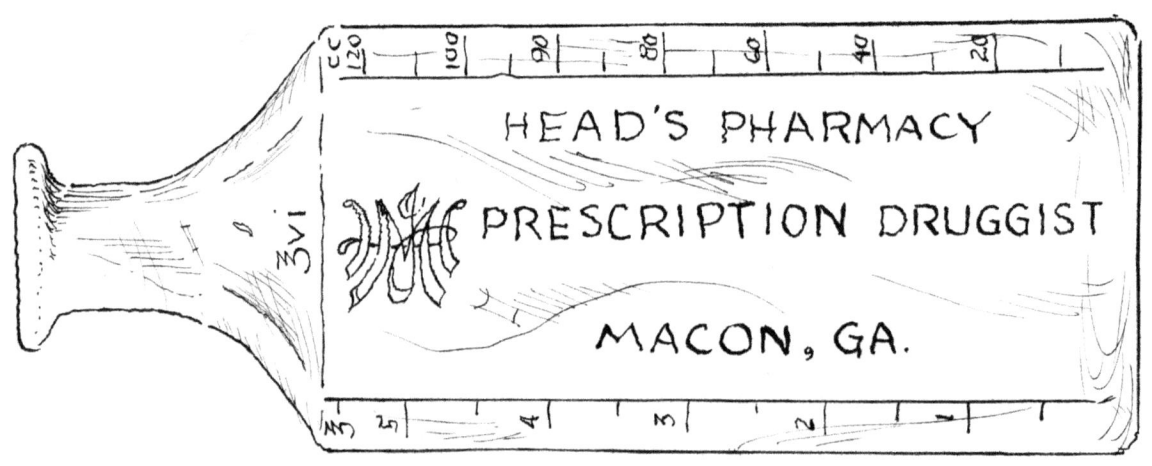

GOODWYN'S DRUG

CLEAR – BOTTOM ★ ★ ★
D
U S A

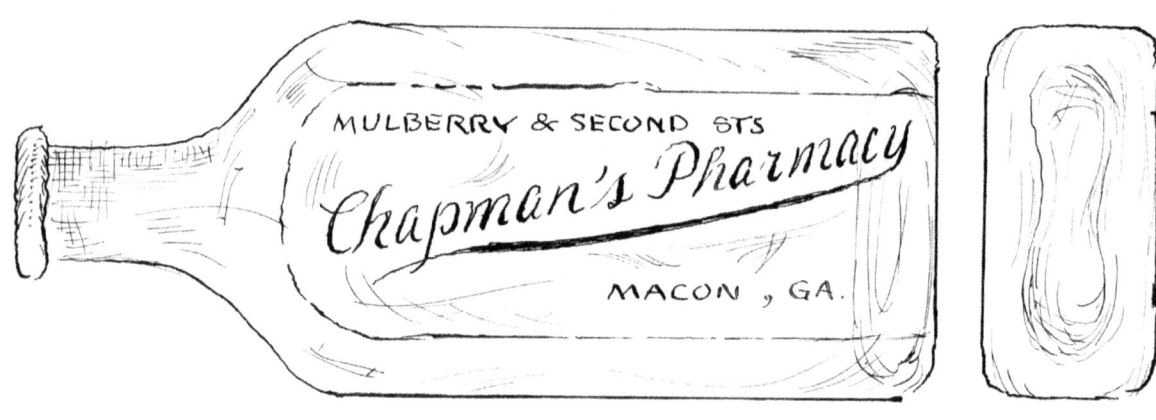

MULBERRY & SECOND STS

Chapman's Pharmacy

MACON , GA.

AQUA   6 7/8 dug by G.W. Pierce

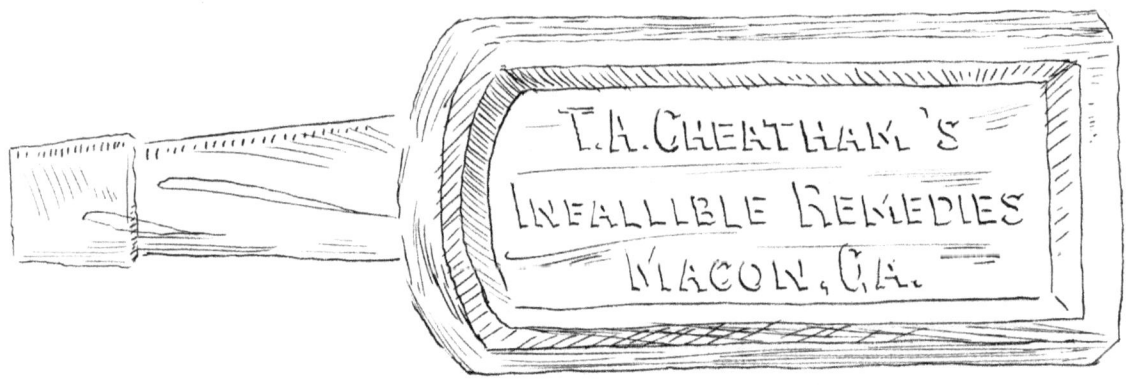

T.A.CHEATHAM'S
INFALLIBLE REMEDIES
MACON, GA.

BRUNNERS $6\frac{3}{8}$-$\overline{3}$vi

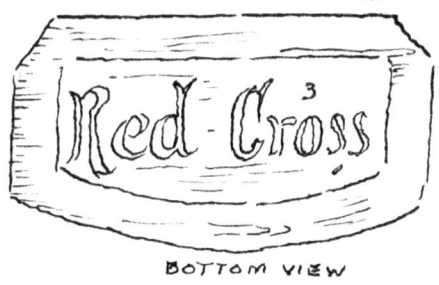

Red·Cross

BOTTOM VIEW

CLEAR 3"

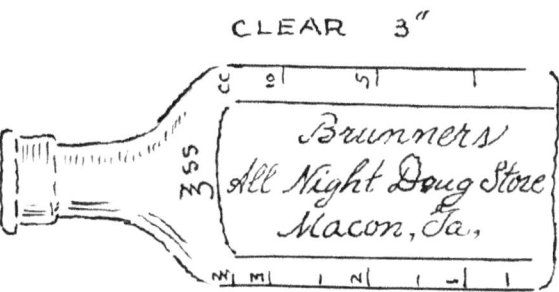

Brunners
All Night Drug Store
Macon, Ga.,

CLEAR 4"

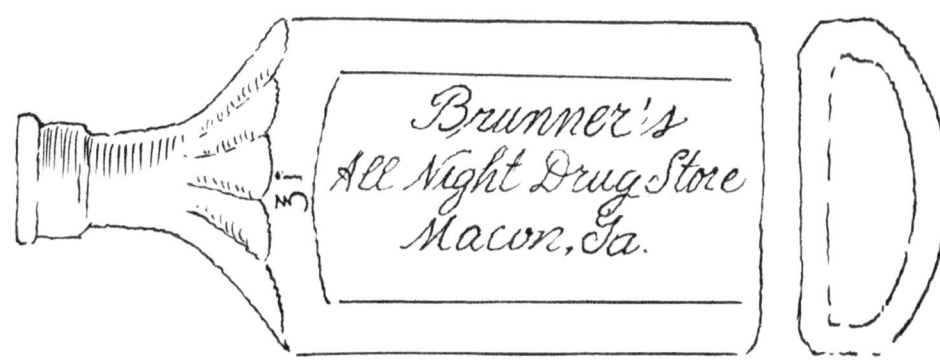

Brunner's
All Night Drug Store
Macon, Ga.

CLEAR 5" OVAL

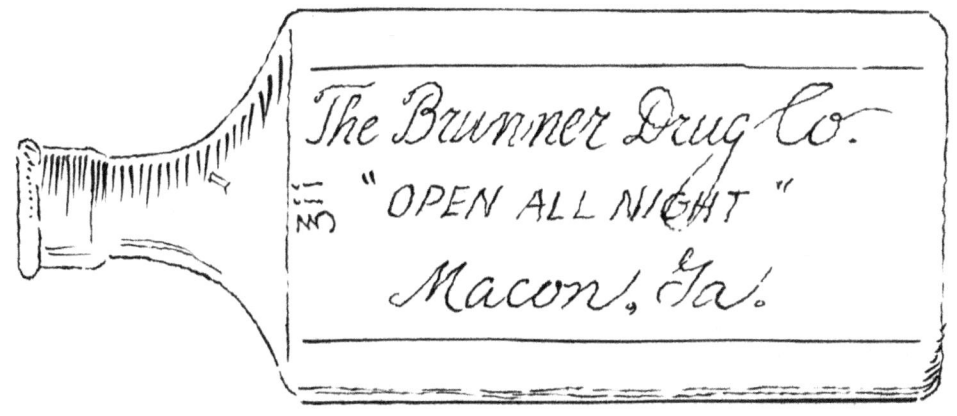

The Brunner Drug Co.
"OPEN ALL NIGHT"
Macon, Ga.

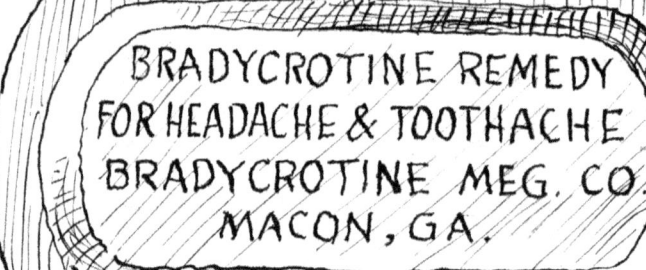

BRADYCROTINE REMEDY
FOR HEADACHE & TOOTHACHE
BRADYCROTINE MEG. CO.
MACON, GA.

AMBER HICKS
SHAPE
dug on 7th st.

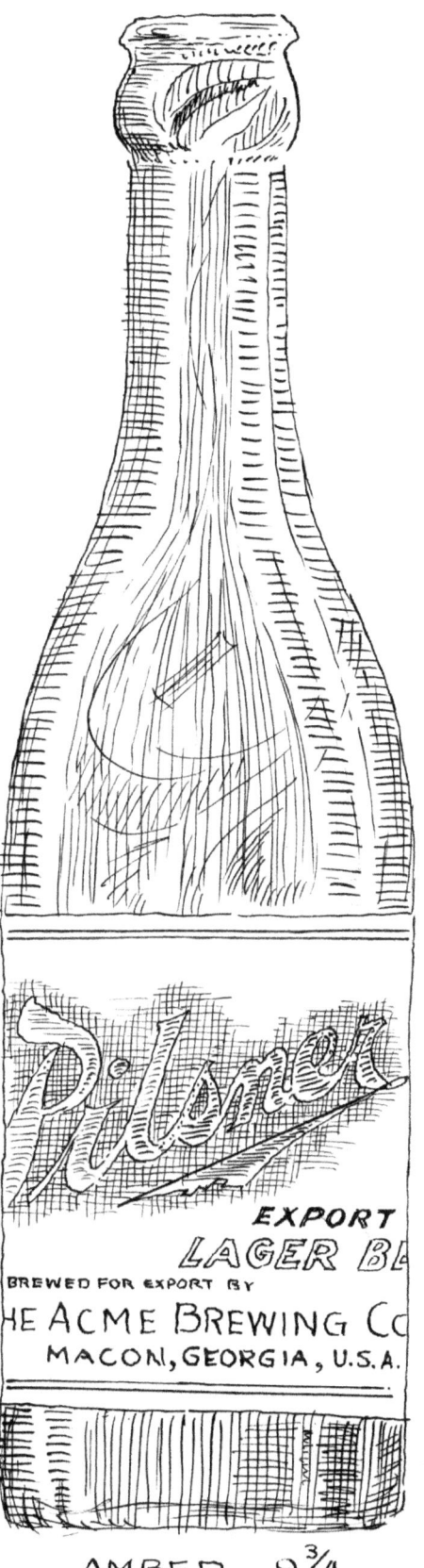

ACME BREWING CO.
BEER

WHITE LABLE WITH
BLUE PRINTING

Pilsner

EXPORT
LAGER BE

BREWED FOR EXPORT BY

HE ACME BREWING CO

MACON, GEORGIA, U.S.A.

AMBER   9¾

S B & G Co.
3
BOTTOM

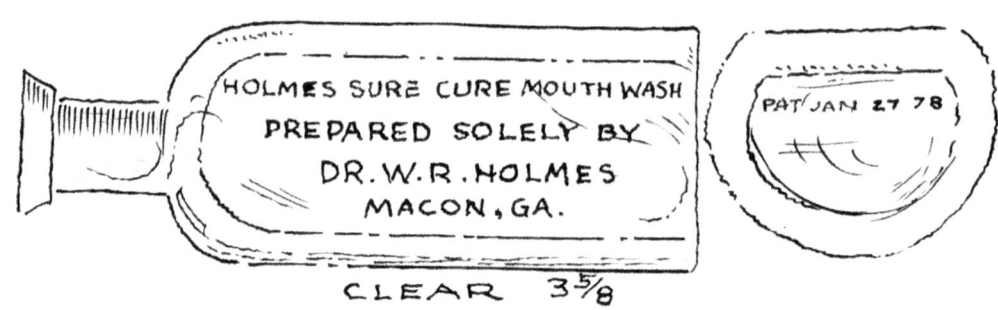

HOLMES SURE CURE MOUTH WASH
PREPARED SOLELY BY
DR. W. R. HOLMES
MACON, GA.

CLEAR 3⅝

ALSO BY DRS. J. P & WR HOLMES

PREPAIRED

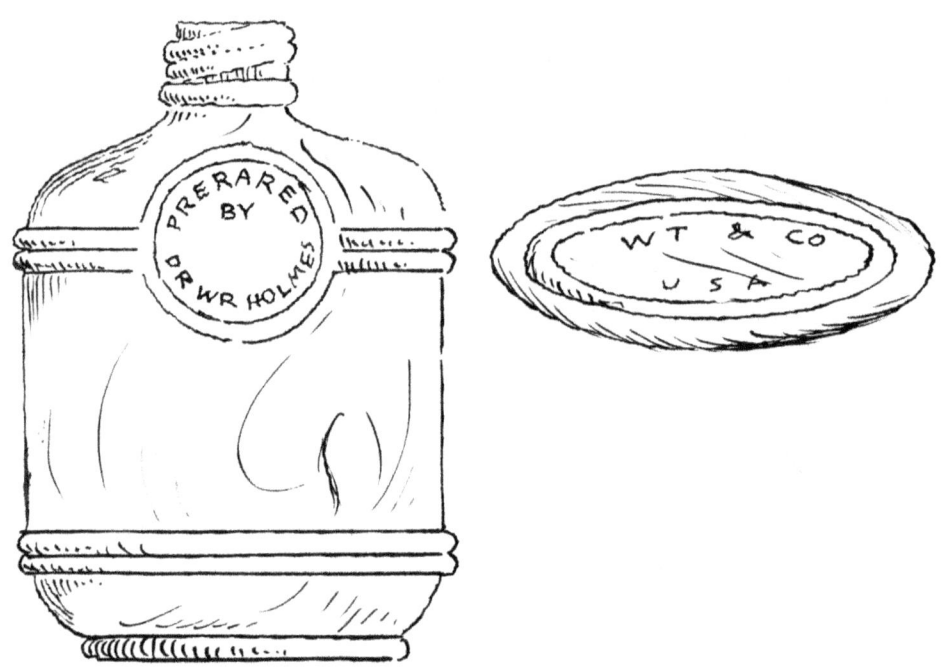

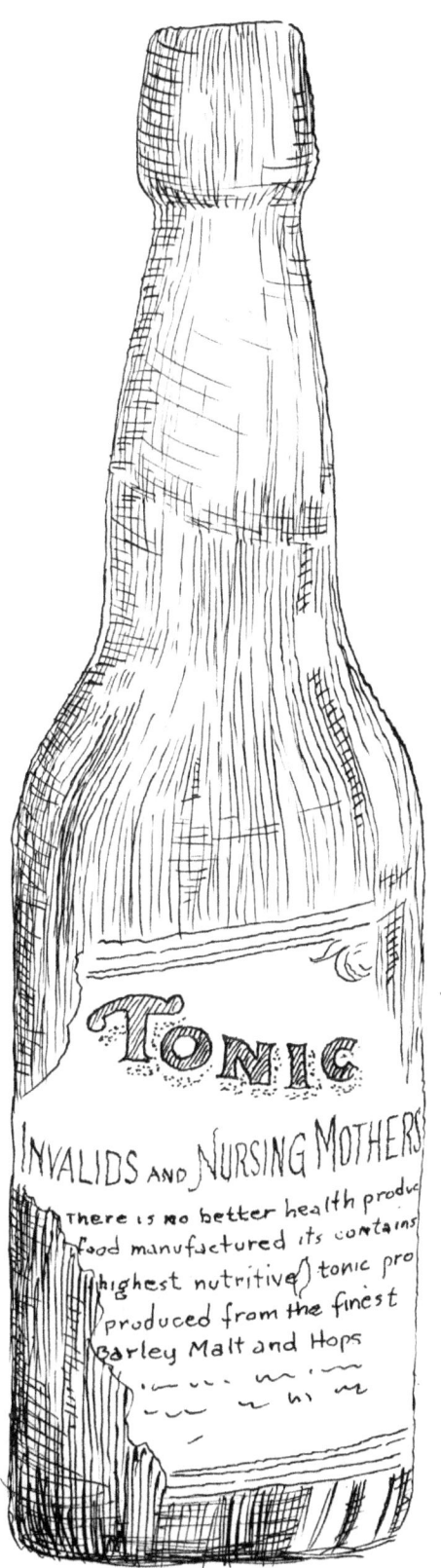

TONIC

INVALIDS AND NURSING MOTHERS

There is no better health produ
food manufactured its contains
highest nutritive tonic pro
produced from the finest
barley Malt and Hops

ACME TONIC from
ACME BREWING CO.
A Tonic from Malt
and hops brewed
for Invalids and
Nursing Mothers, a
body builder.

AMBER 9½" (WF&S 16 MIL)
BOTTOM

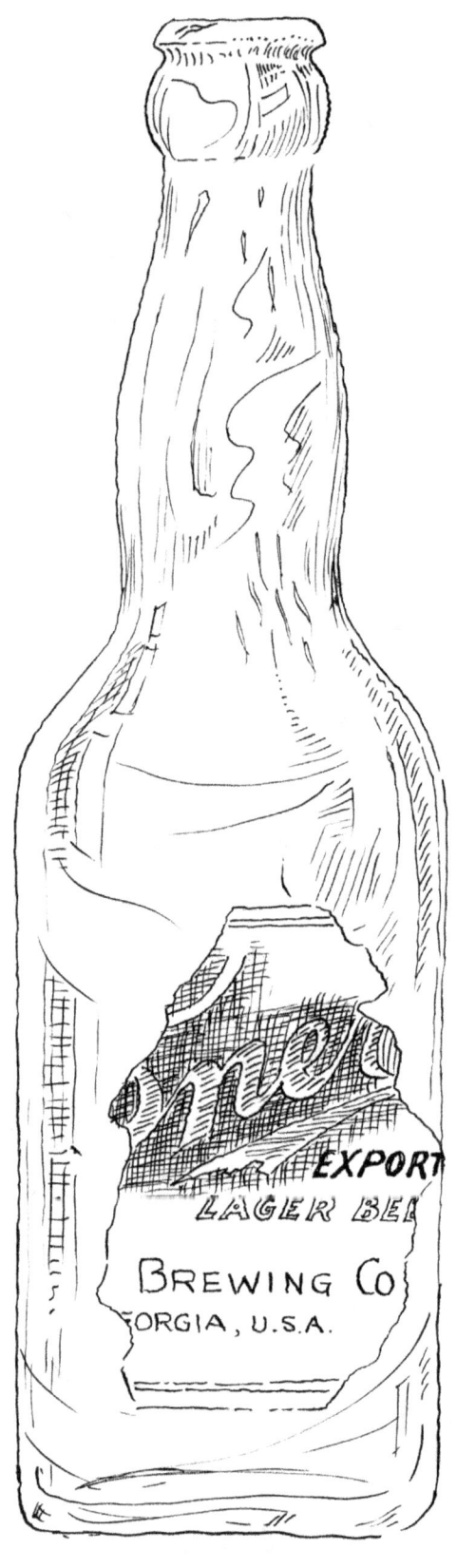

EXPORT

LAGER BE[

BREWING Co

[G]ORGIA, U.S.A.

ACME BREWING Co.
BEER

WHITE LABLE WITH
BLACK PRINTING.

LIGHT BLUE 9½

BOTTOM
S B & Co
7

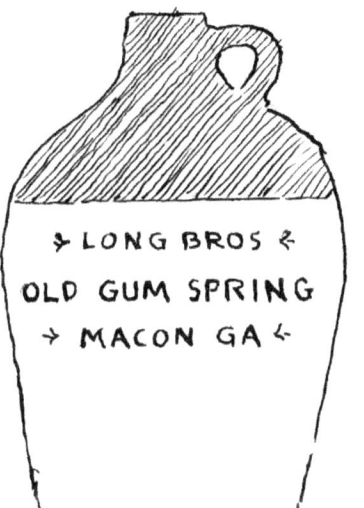

* LONG BROS *
OLD GUM SPRING
+ MACON GA +

3" TALL
BLUE LETTERING ON
WHITE, TOP BROWN.

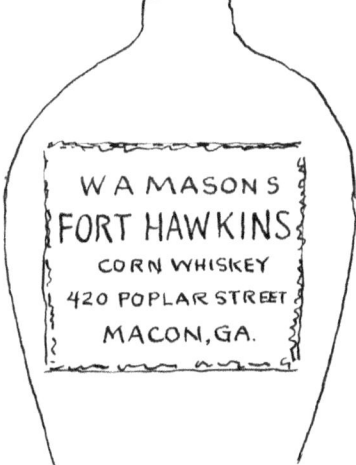

WA MASONS
FORT HAWKINS
CORN WHISKEY
420 POPLAR STREET
MACON, GA.

3" TALL
OFF WHITE
LETTERING BLUE

FINE LIQUORS
FROM
THE FLATMAYER &
FLATAU
LIQUOR CO.
MACON , GA.

3 GAL.
WHITE JUG
BLUE LETTERS

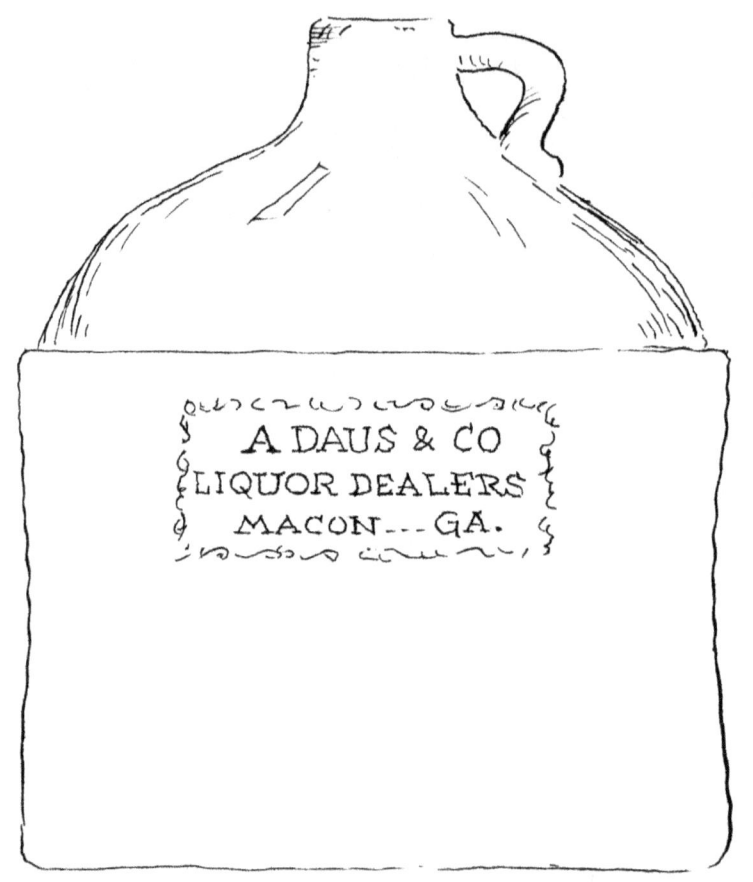

GRAY, BLUE
LETTERS
14¼ TALL

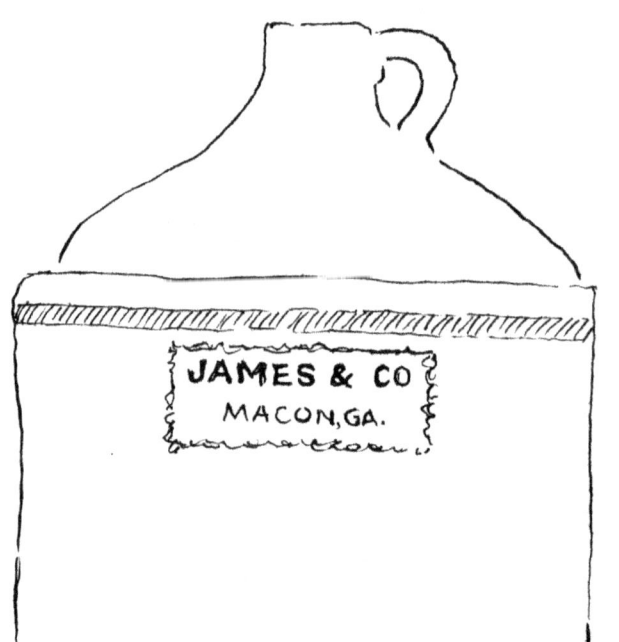

GRAY TOP
WHITE BOTTOM
& BLUE STRIP
AND LETTERS
7¾ TALL

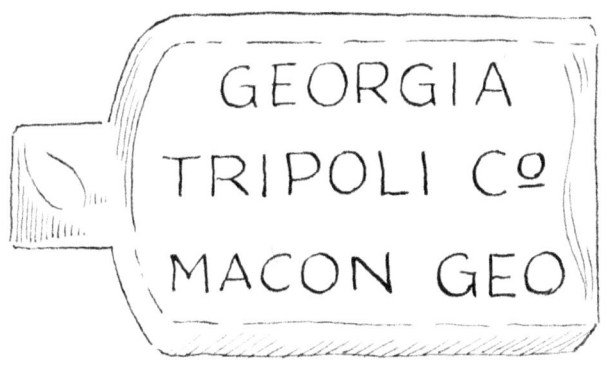
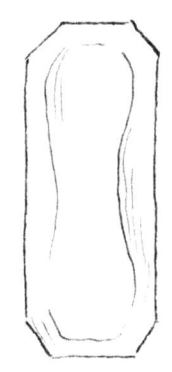

GEORGIA
TRIPOLI C<u>O</u>
MACON GEO

CLEAR - GROUNDED TOP

CLEAR 5⅛ dug on 7th St. Jun. 71

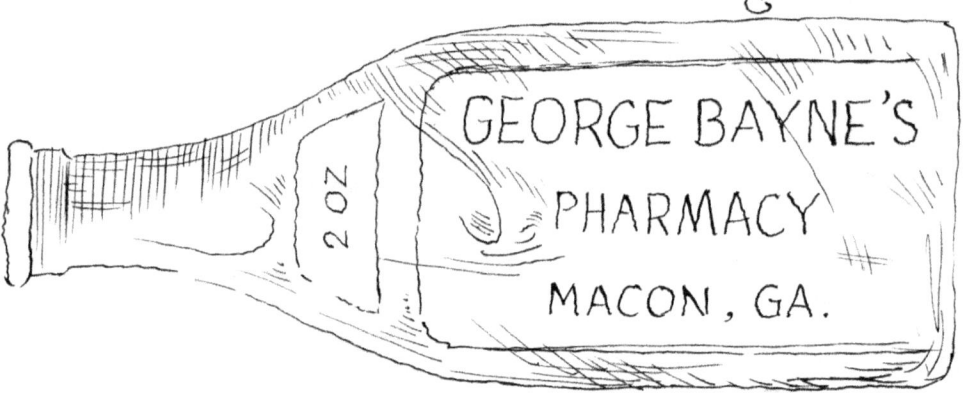

GEORGE BAYNE'S PHARMACY MACON, GA.

2 OZ

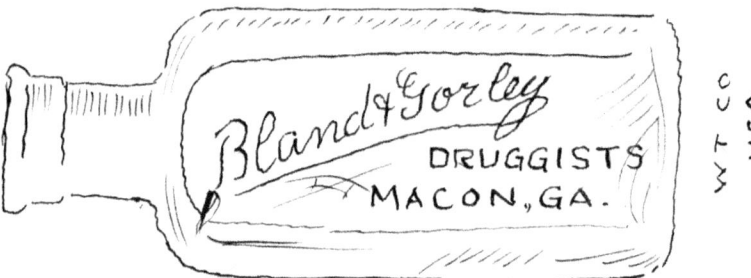

Bland & Gorley DRUGGISTS MACON, GA.

W T CO USA

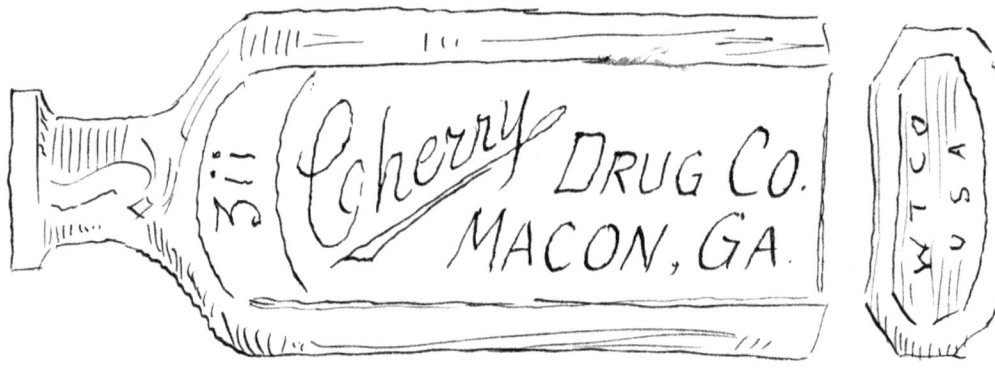

Cherry DRUG CO. MACON, GA.

℥ii

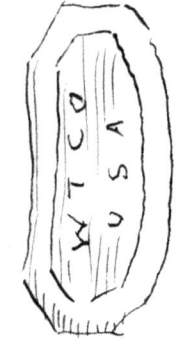

W T CO USA

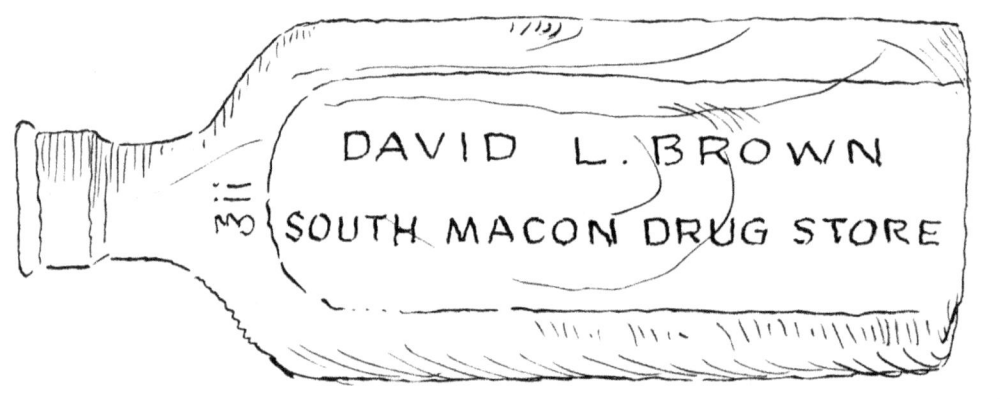

DAVID L. BROWN SOUTH MACON DRUG STORE

℥ii

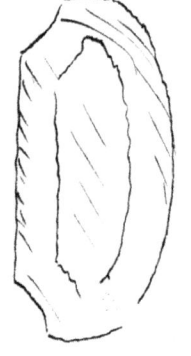

Book 3

Various

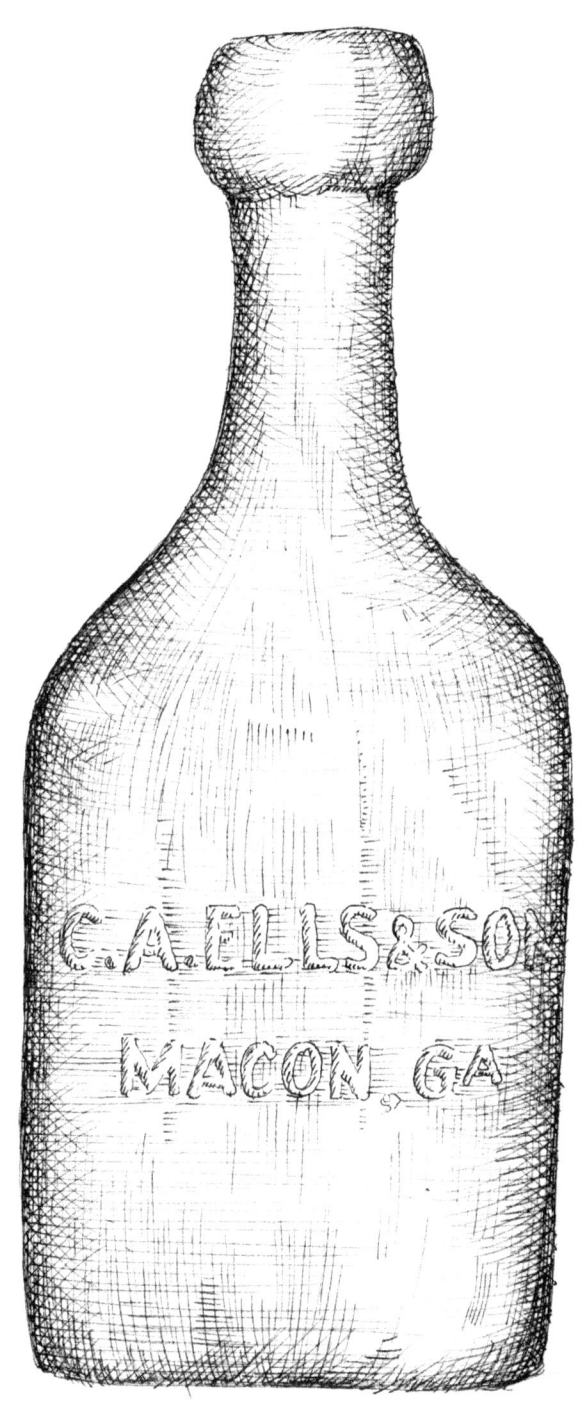

COLBALT BLUE - GROUND PONTIAL   7 x 2 5/8

BACK --- MINERALWATER

UNION GLASS WORKS

PHIL^A

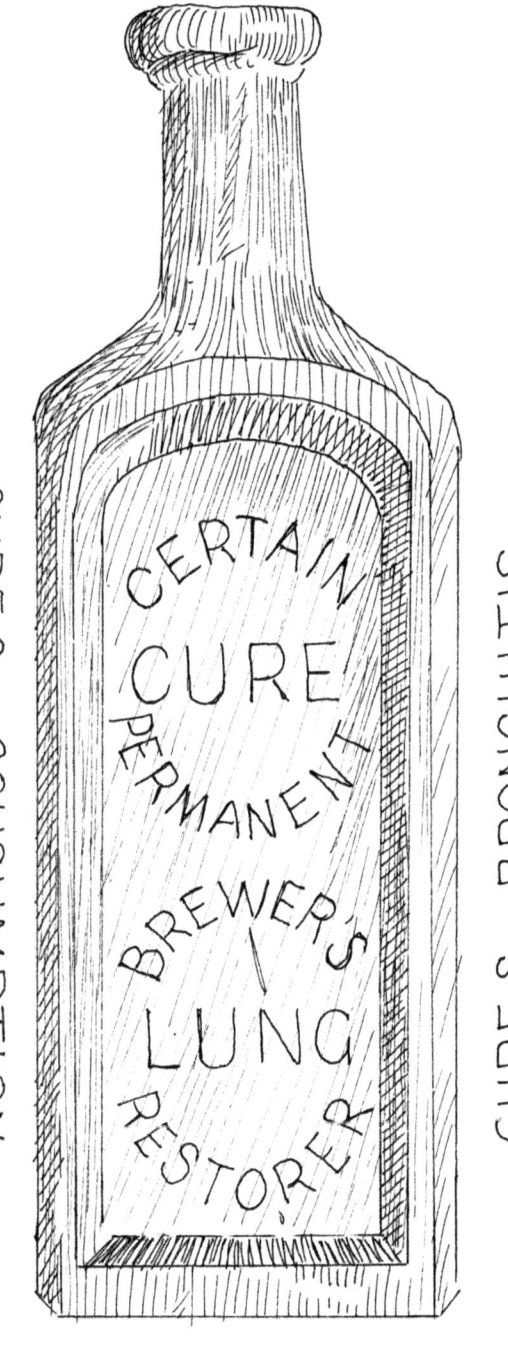

CURES CONSUMPTION

CURES BRONCHITIS

CERTAIN CURE PERMANENT BREWER'S LUNG RESTORER

THE LARGE SIZE 9½ × 3

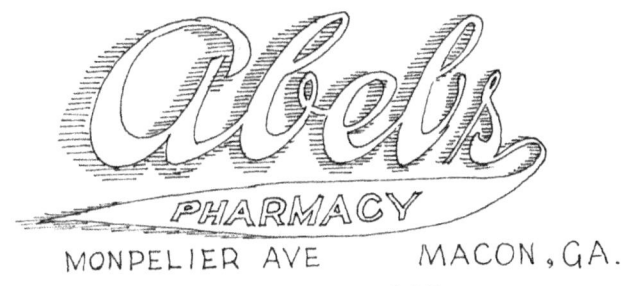

Abels

PHARMACY

MONPELIER AVE   MACON, GA.

PHONE 646 - 647

ARCHER'S

Compound Syrup of Tar with Cod Liver Oil Extract and
Menthol, Alcohol 2%, Chloroform 3 mins, Morphine 200g
Cannabis Ind 1-4 Gr. For coughs, hoarseness & loss of
voice, resulting from colds, simple laryngitis & bronchitis
Mild bronchial asthma and catarrhal croup
Distributed by ARCHER'S PHARMACY Quick Service Store
Cor Giles & Second Sts Macon, Ga. **35** ¢ This store
later became Middlebrook's Drugs, sometime in
the middle 1930's

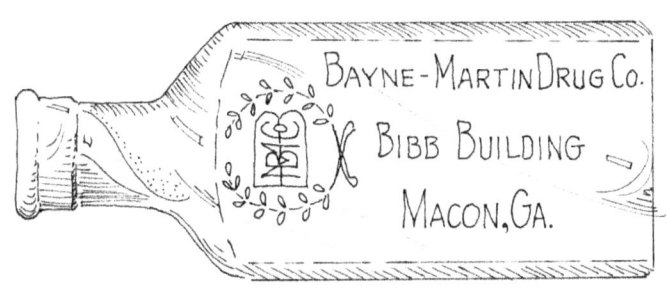

BAYNE-MARTIN DRUG CO.

BIBB BUILDING

MACON, GA.

labled crown type bottle from **BAYNE'S** PHARMACY
CHERRY ST & COTTON AVE MACON GA

contained Housekeepers
         AMMONIA
Also same lable on a round amber, medical top
bottle

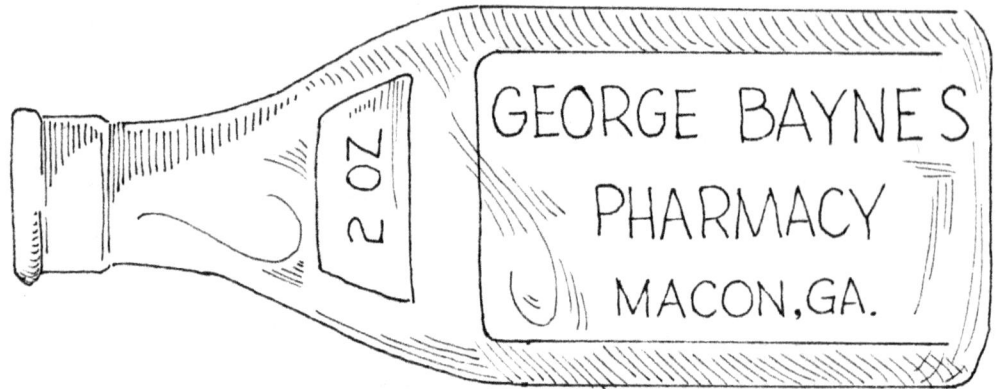

GEORGE BAYNES
PHARMACY
MACON, GA.

2 OZ

ALSO WITH BAYNE'S OPEN ALL NIGHT

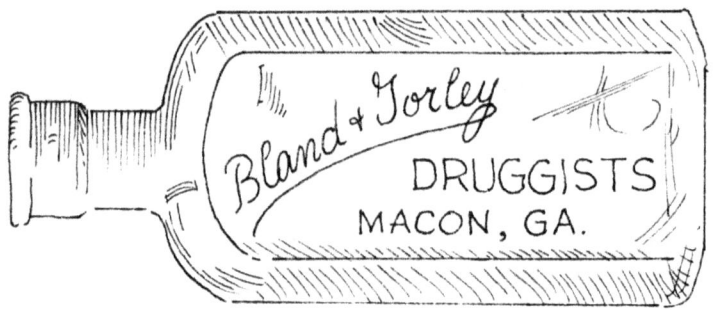

Bland & Torley
DRUGGISTS
MACON, GA.

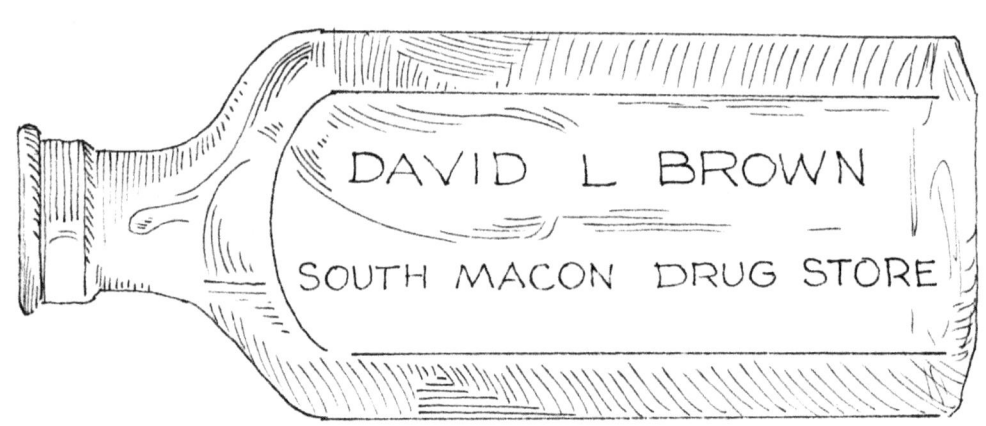

DAVID L BROWN

SOUTH MACON DRUG STORE

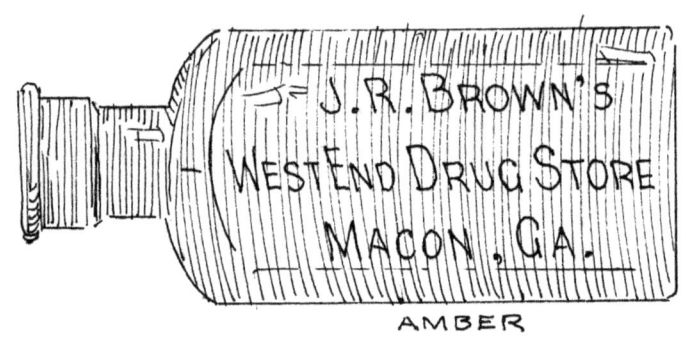

J. R. BROWN'S
WEST END DRUG STORE
MACON, GA.

AMBER

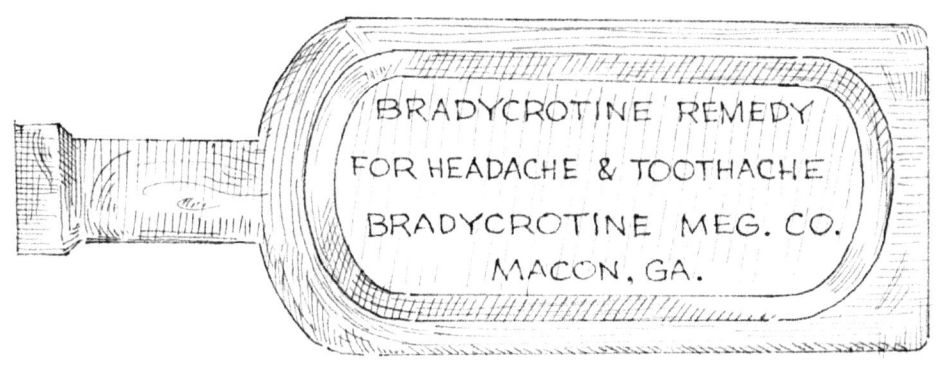

BRADYCROTINE REMEDY
FOR HEADACHE & TOOTHACHE
BRADYCROTINE MEG. CO.
MACON, GA.

AMBER - HICKS SHAPE

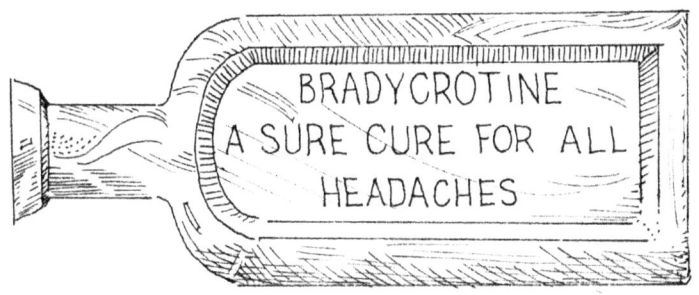

BRADYCROTINE
A SURE CURE FOR ALL
HEADACHES

CLEAR

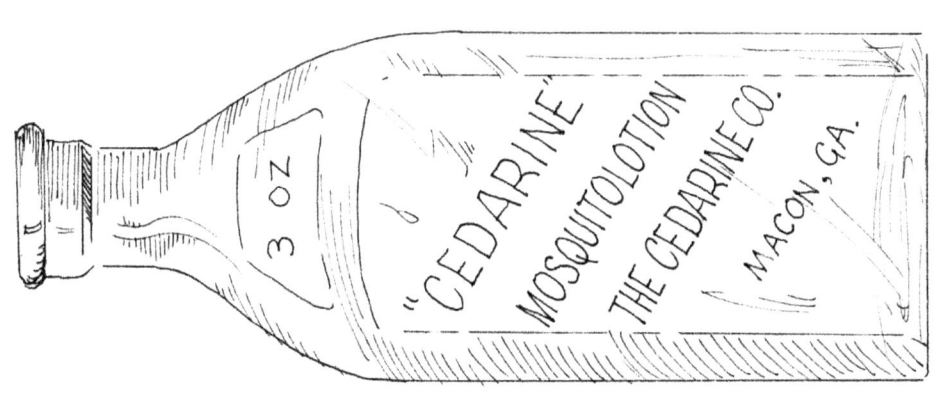

"CEDARINE" MOSQUITO LOTION THE CEDARINE CO. MACON, GA.

3 OZ

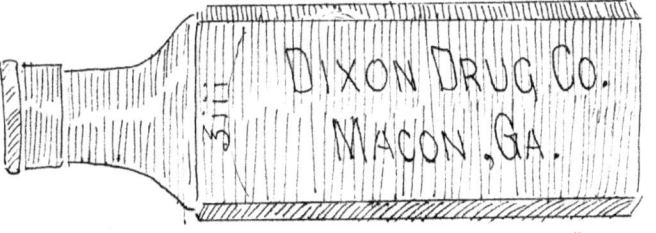

DIXON DRUG CO. MACON, GA.

7 up Green 5¼" & 4"

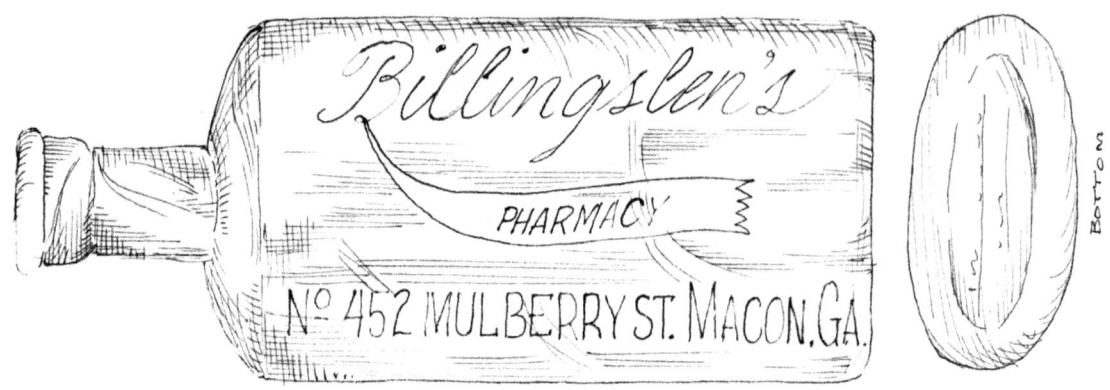

Billingslen's

PHARMACY

№ 452 MULBERRY ST. MACON, GA.

Bottom

CLEAR   5 3/8" long 2 7/8" wide BOTTOM PAT'D 6/25/89
CLC. CO.

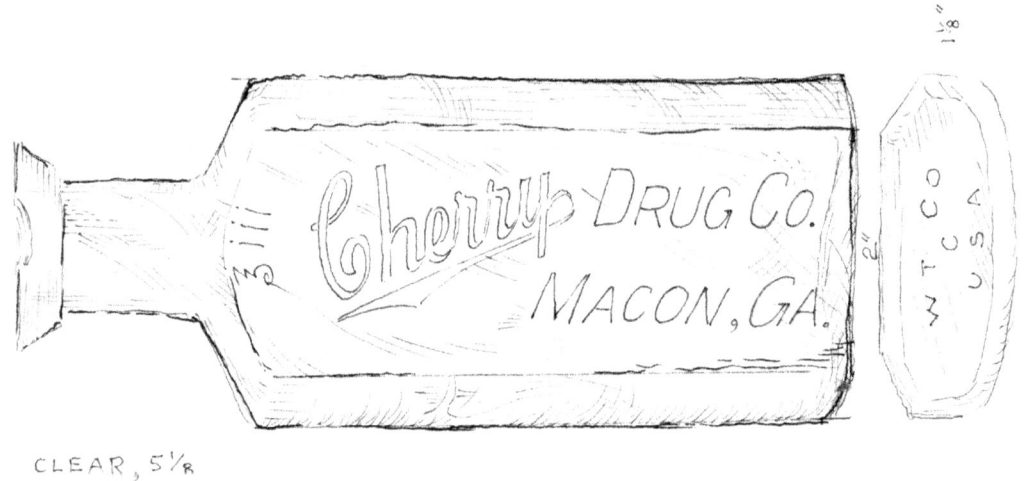

Cherry DRUG CO.
MACON, GA.

W T C CO U S A

1 1/8"

2"

3"

CLEAR, 5 1/8

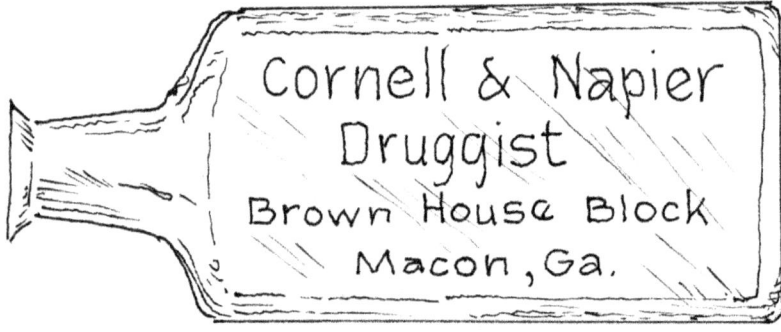

Cornell & Napier
Druggist
Brown House Block
Macon, Ga.

clear
May be in
Various Sizes

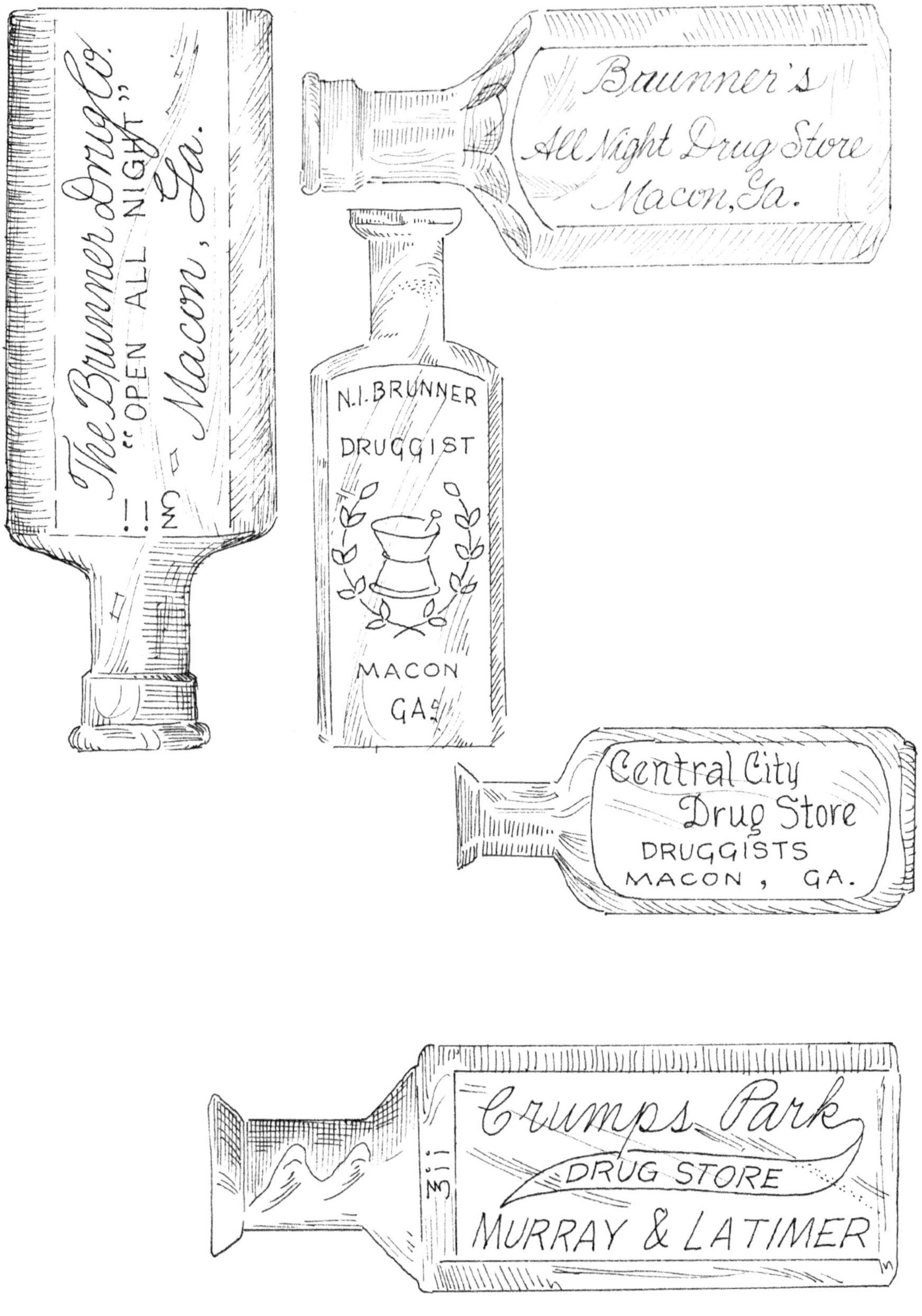

The Brunner Drug Co.
"OPEN ALL NIGHT"
Macon, Ga.

Brunner's
All Night Drug Store
Macon, Ga.

N.I. BRUNNER
DRUGGIST
MACON
GA.

Central City
Drug Store
DRUGGISTS
MACON, GA.

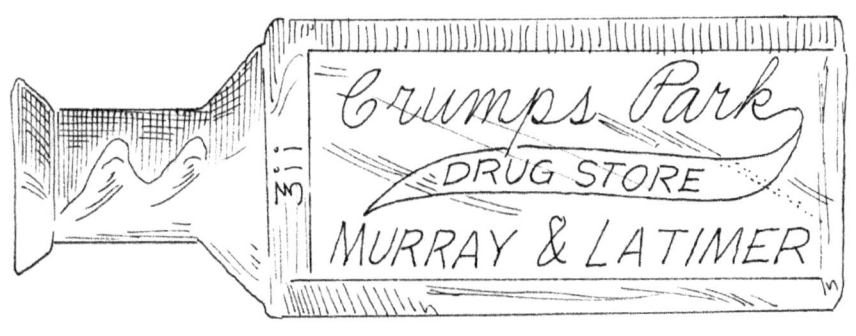

Crumps Park
DRUG STORE
MURRAY & LATIMER

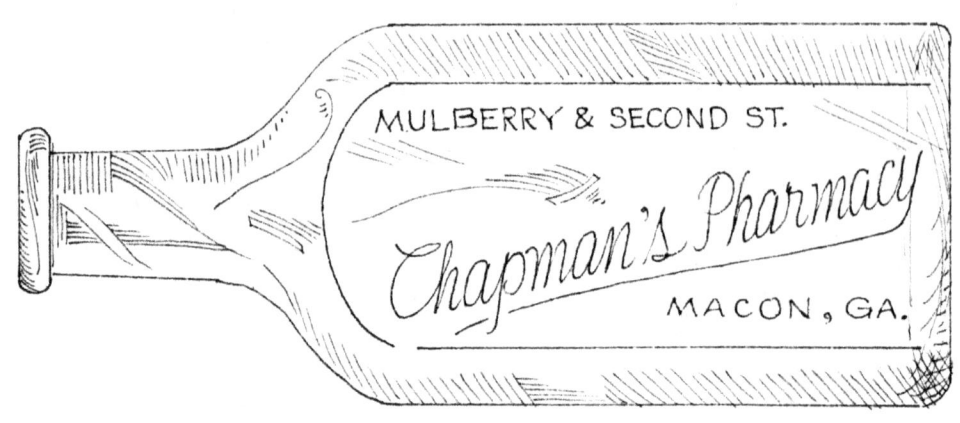

MULBERRY & SECOND ST.

Chapman's Pharmacy

MACON, GA.

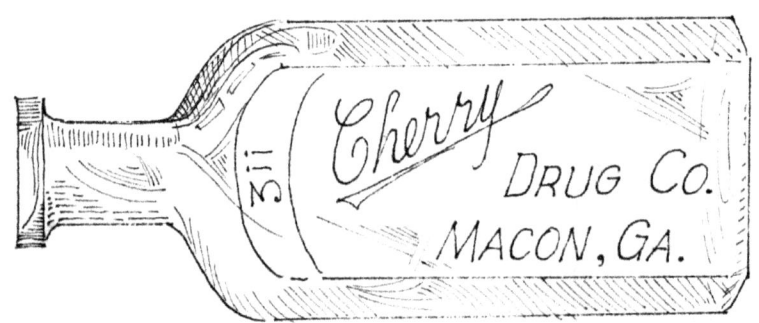

℥ii

Cherry DRUG CO.
MACON, GA.

ROSE & CHERRY IN THE REAR
SECTION

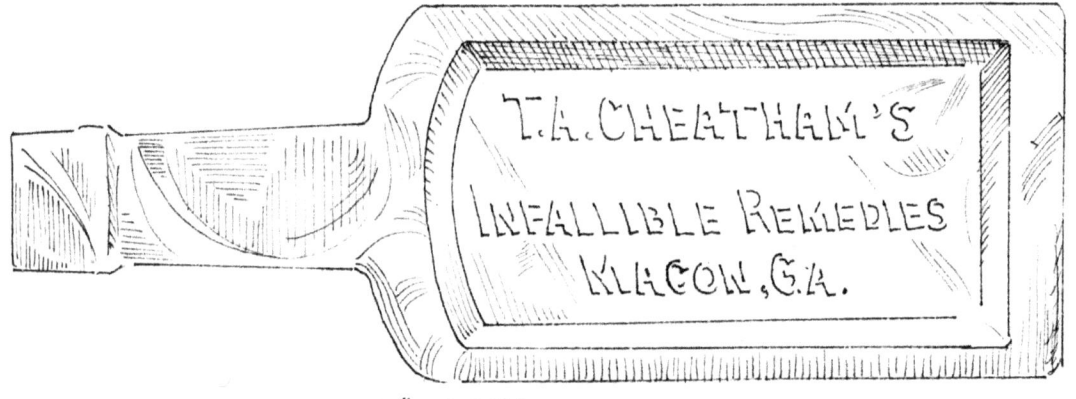

T.A. CHEATHAM'S

INFALLIBLE REMEDIES

MACON, GA.

7" AQUA

(ALSO)
CHEATHAM'S
INFALLIBLE COUGH SYRUP
MACON, GA.

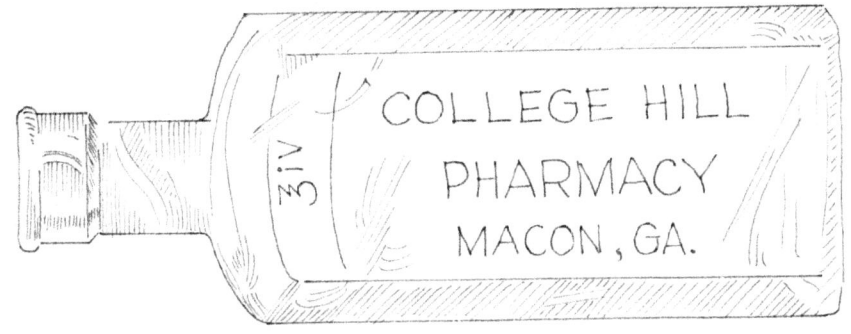

Also had a labled bottle that contained Gasoline
`keep away from flame or fire´ CLEAR - ROUND - Pt.

- -

2 x 5½ , paper lable, clear, paper type top, with a cork.
3 Fl.oz. STEAMBOAT CHILL & FEVER TONIC 25¢
Coleman Meadows Pate Drug Co. Distributor, Macon, Ga.
Recommended for all form of chills, Fever, W. Lagrippe &
all malarial diseases — has a drawing of a twin smoke stack
steam boat —

Coleman Meadows - Pate Drug Co
     Paper lable — Violet Toilet Ammonia
clear, barber shaped bottle. .

TOP

Silk Screen. Solution Magnesium Citrate
crown top bottle, light 7up Green 7oz.

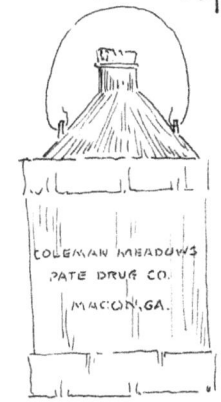

COLEMAN MEADOWS
PATE DRUG CO.
MACON, GA.

GAL. CONTANER, METAL WITH A
WOOD JACKET —

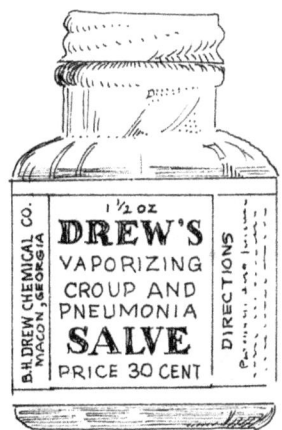

1½ OZ
DREW'S
VAPORIZING
CROUP AND
PNEUMONIA
SALVE
PRICE 30 CENT

B.H. DREW CHEMICAL CO.
MACON, GEORGIA

DIRECTIONS

```
DANELION TONIC CO
SOLE PROPIETORS
1003 Fourth St. Macon Ga.
```

LABLE ONLY

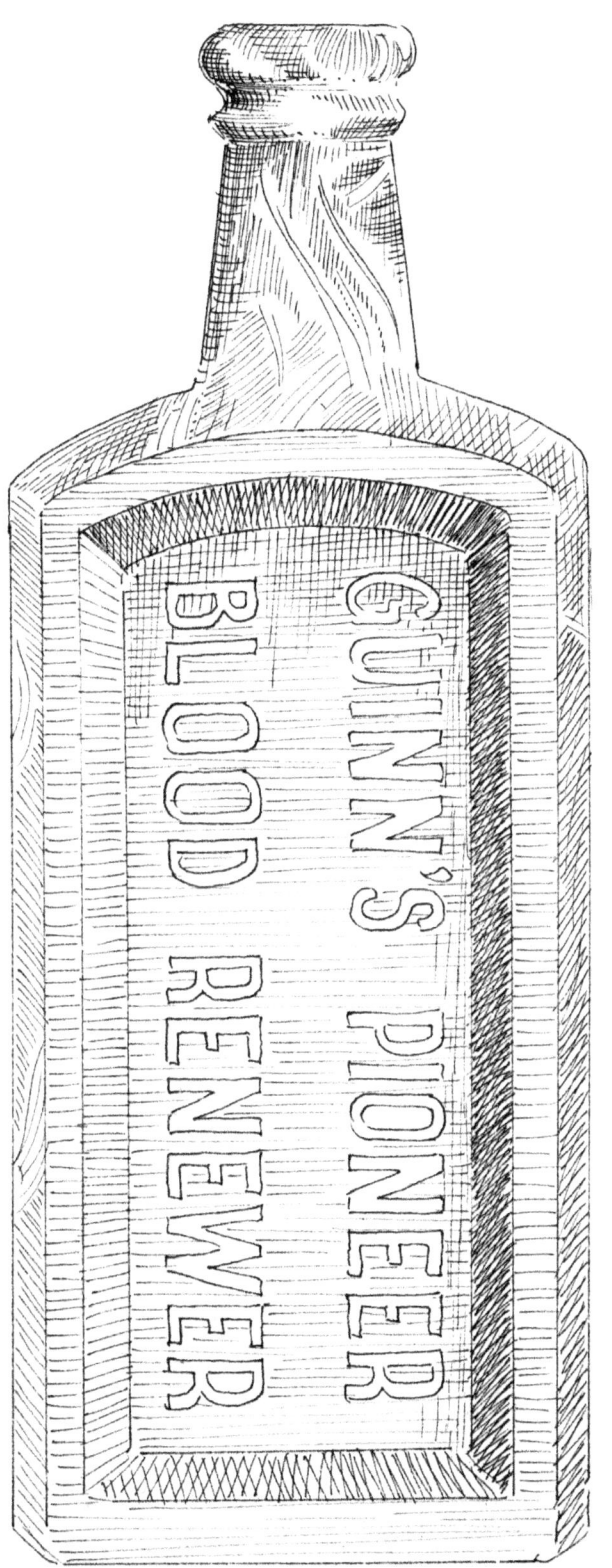

GUINN'S PIONEER
BLOOD RENEWER

MACON MEDICINE CO.

MACON, GA.

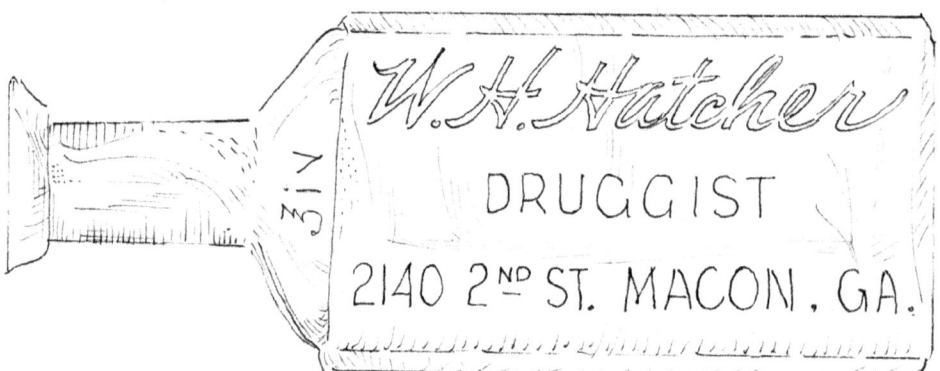

W. H. Hatcher

DRUGGIST

2140 2ND ST. MACON, GA.

S BRO'S
BALTO. MD

ℨiv

CLEAR 5 2/8

PHARMAGIST

SOL HOGE

MACON, GA.

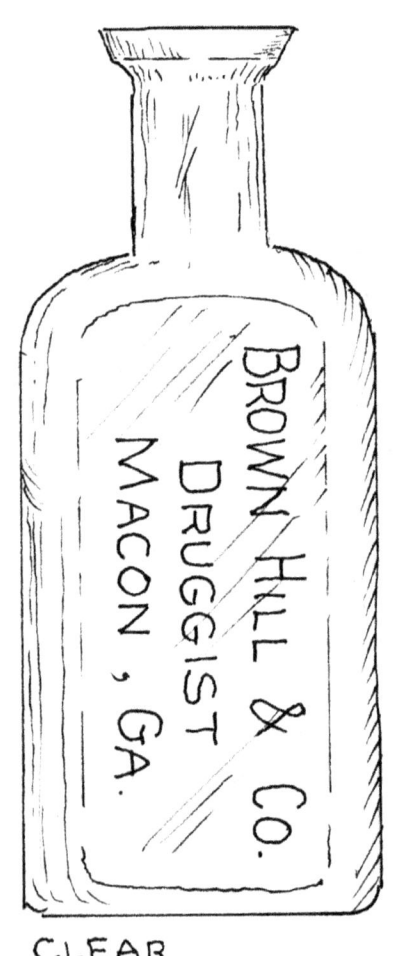

BROWN HILL & CO.
DRUGGIST
MACON, GA.

CLEAR

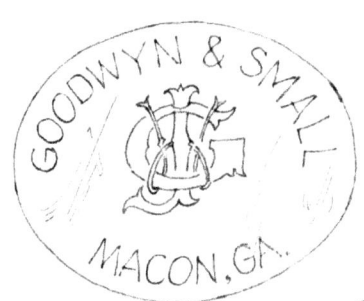

SAME WITH 'DRUGGIST'
INSTEAD OF MONOGRAM

GOODWYN & SMALL
PHARMACISTS
MACON , GA

CLEAR, 4¾

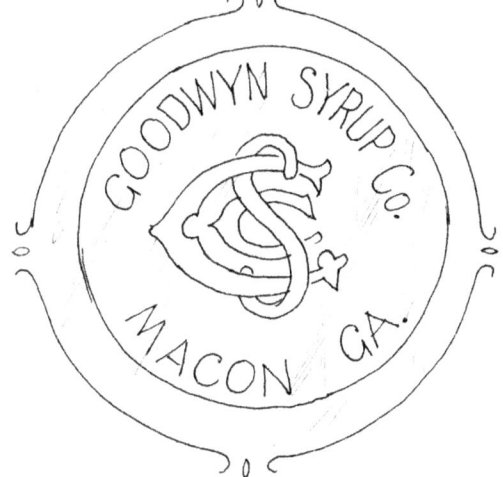

Sol Hog

Macon Ga

5⅛, CLEAR, 2" x 1½"

2%₆ SOL HODG
MACON . GA.

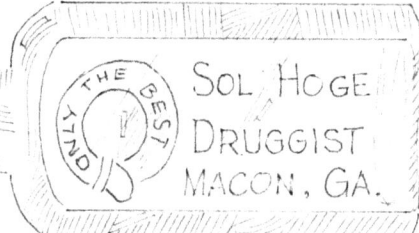

GEORGIA
TRIPOLI Co
MACON GEO

FROSTED CLASS, GROUND TOP

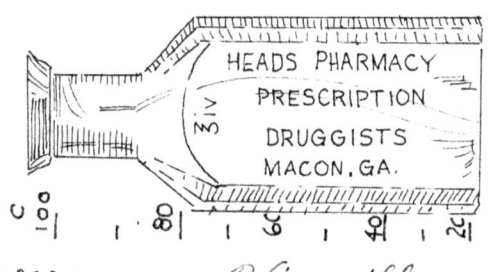

HEADS PHARMACY
PRESCRIPTION
DRUGGISTS
MACON. GA.

℥iv

Heads

*Vineville
Pharmacy
Macon, Ga.*

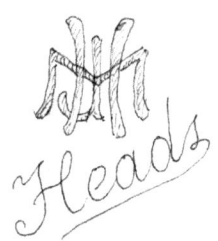

Heads

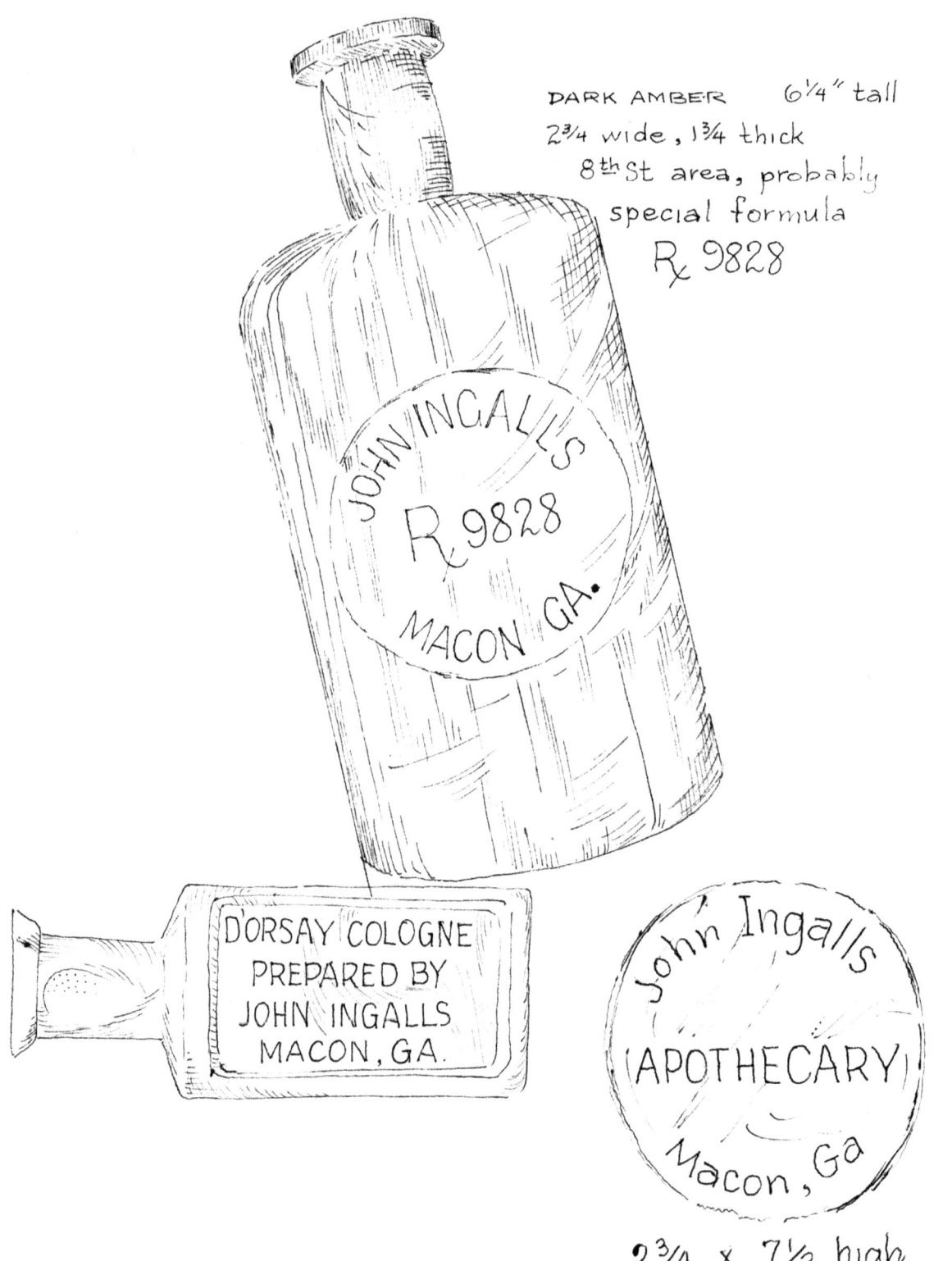

DARK AMBER   6¼" tall
2¾ wide, 1¾ thick
8th St area, probably
special formula
Rx 9828

JOHN INGALLS
Rx 9828
MACON GA.

D'ORSAY COLOGNE
PREPARED BY
JOHN INGALLS
MACON, GA.

John Ingalls
APOTHECARY
Macon, Ga

2¾ x 7½ high
may be in Teal green
or clear.

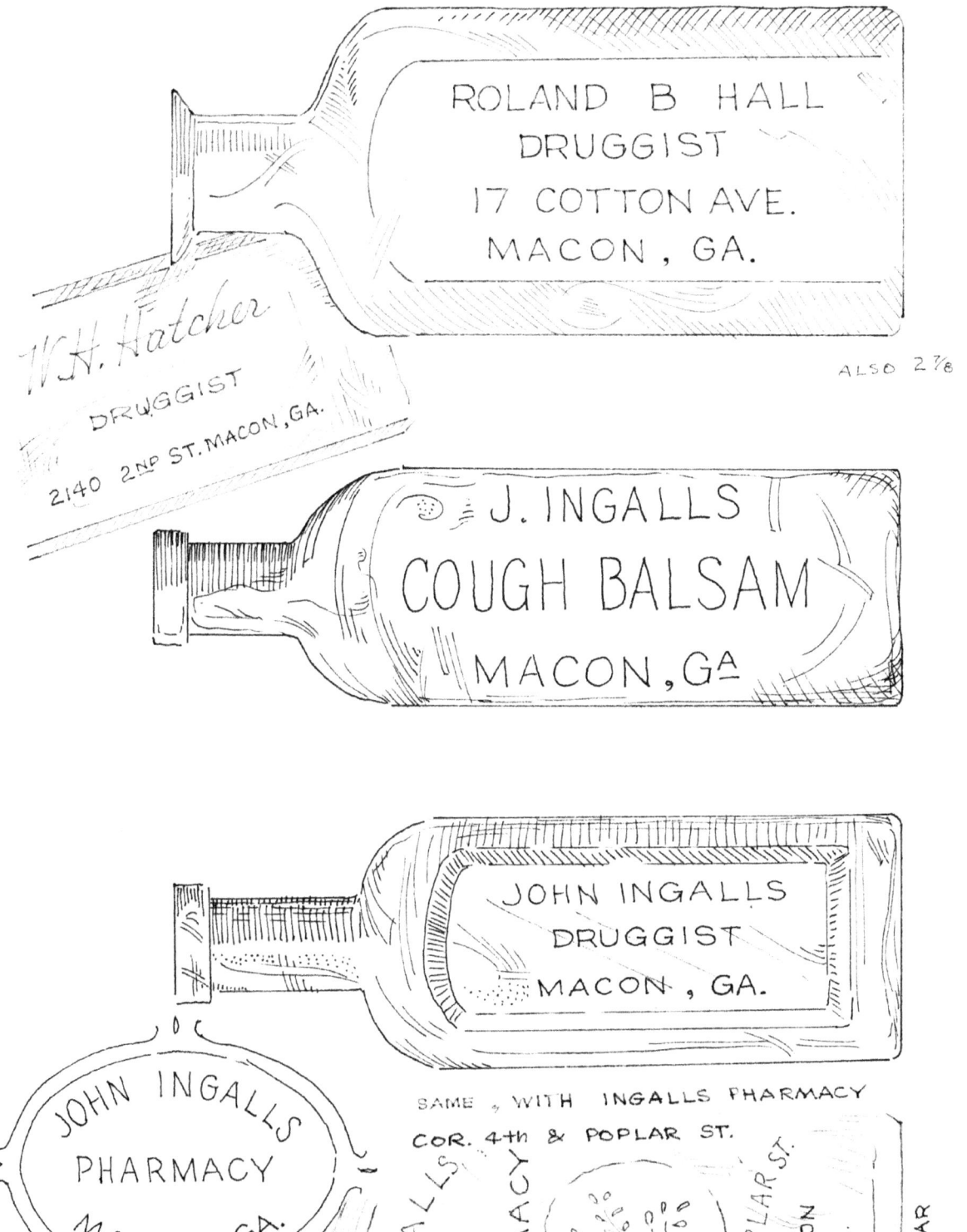

ROLAND B HALL
DRUGGIST
17 COTTON AVE.
MACON, GA.

ALSO 2⅞

W.H. Hatcher
DRUGGIST
2140 2ND ST. MACON, GA.

J. INGALLS
COUGH BALSAM
MACON, GA

JOHN INGALLS
DRUGGIST
MACON, GA.

JOHN INGALLS
PHARMACY
MACON, GA.

SAME WITH INGALLS PHARMACY
COR. 4th & POPLAR ST.

INGALLS PHARMACY

4th & POPLAR ST. MACON GA.

SQ CLEAR

Clear, maybe in Various Sizes --
Marked on one side _ HUNT, RANKIN & LAMAR _
other side _ DANFORTHS SANATIVE DENTIFRIC

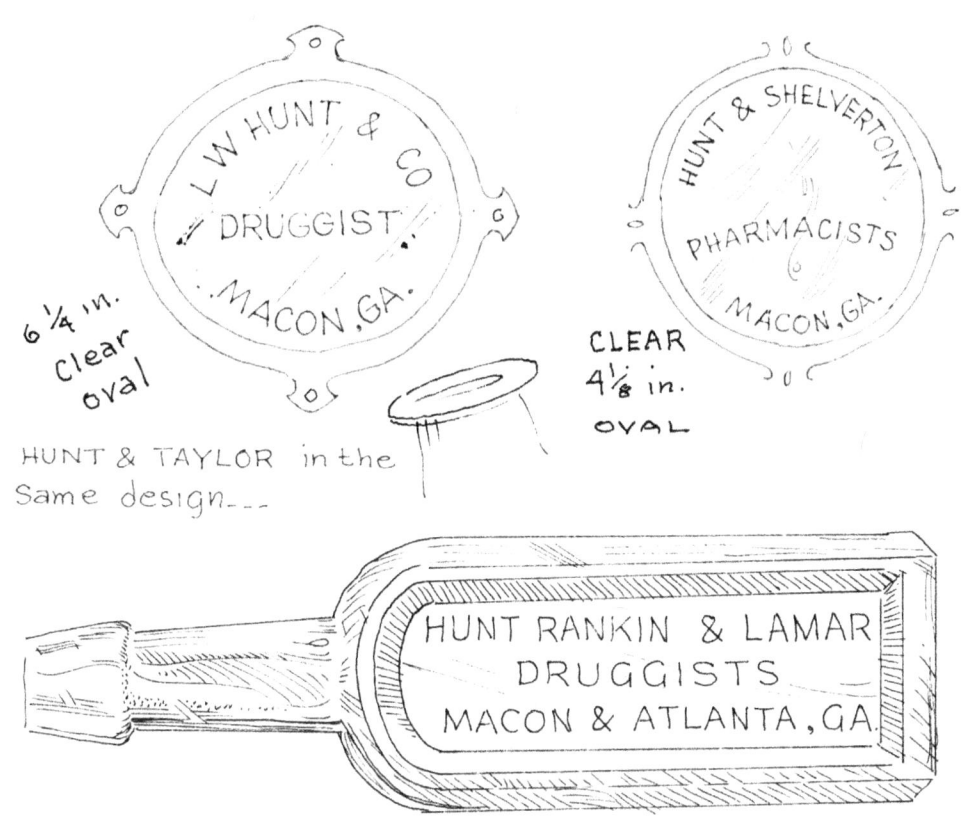

6¼ in.
Clear
oval

HUNT & TAYLOR in the
same design---

CLEAR
4⅛ in.
OVAL

Also a 8¾ by 2¾ AQUA, concave, 4 sides - on the
front - L.W. HUNT & Cº DRUGGIST'S. Left - MACON
RIGHT - GEORGIA - Shaped as the one above

GREEN'S BELVIDERE COLOGNE-HUNT RANKIN & LAMAR ATLANTA, GA.

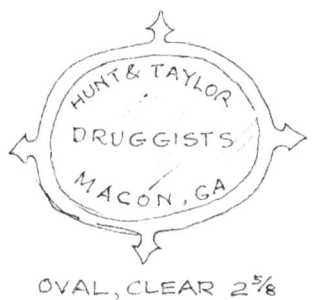

OVAL, CLEAR 2⅝

HUNT'S GERMAN COLOGNE - SHAPED LIKE HOYT'S COLOGNE SMALL POCKET
SIZE - CLEAR & TWO SIZES

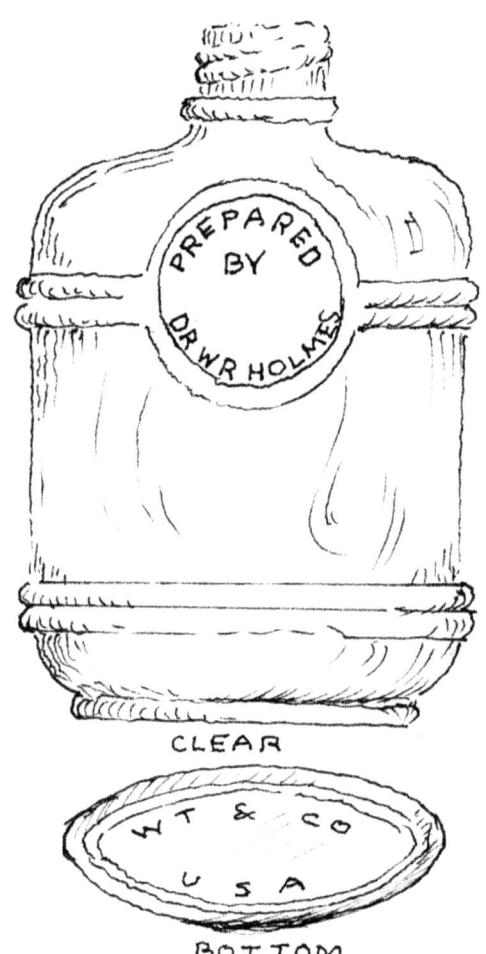

PREPARED BY DR W R HOLMES

CLEAR

WT & CO
U S A

BOTTOM

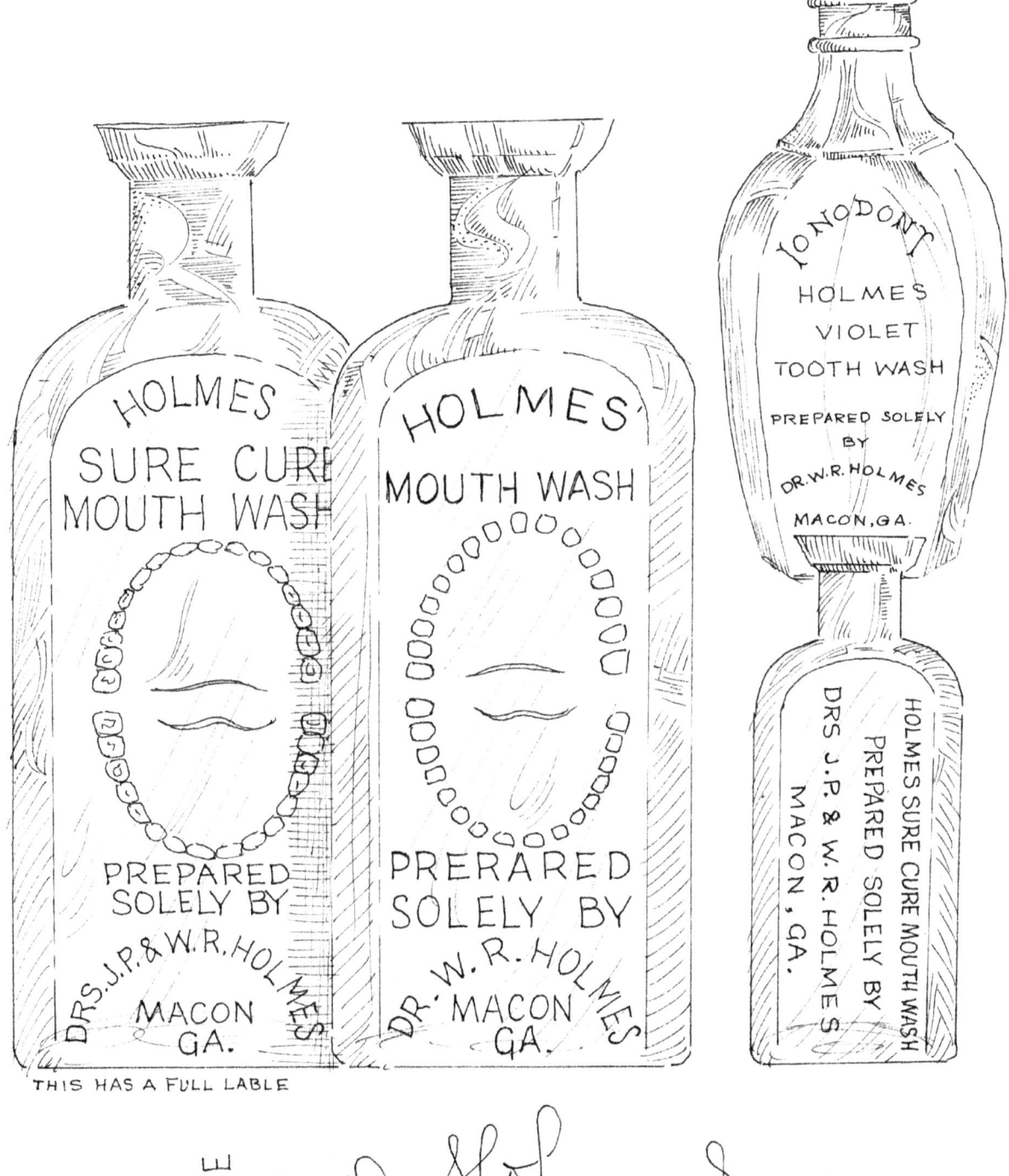

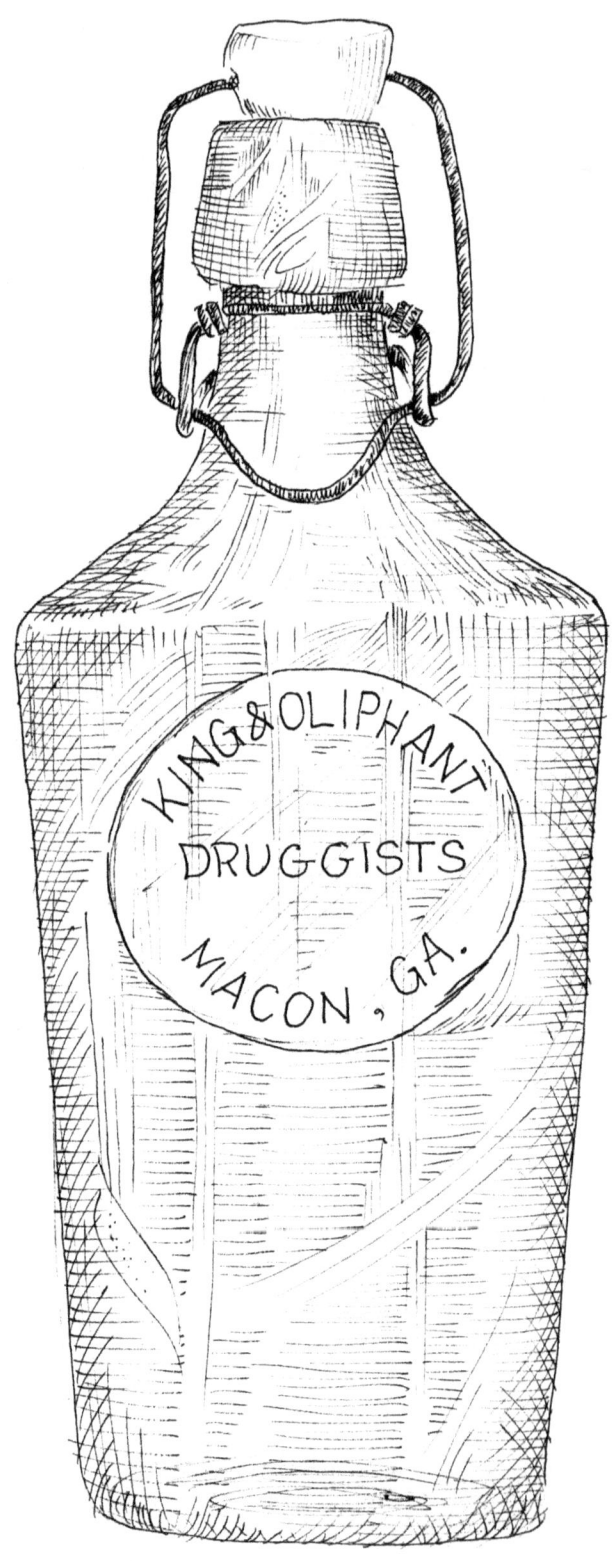

Med light 7up Green

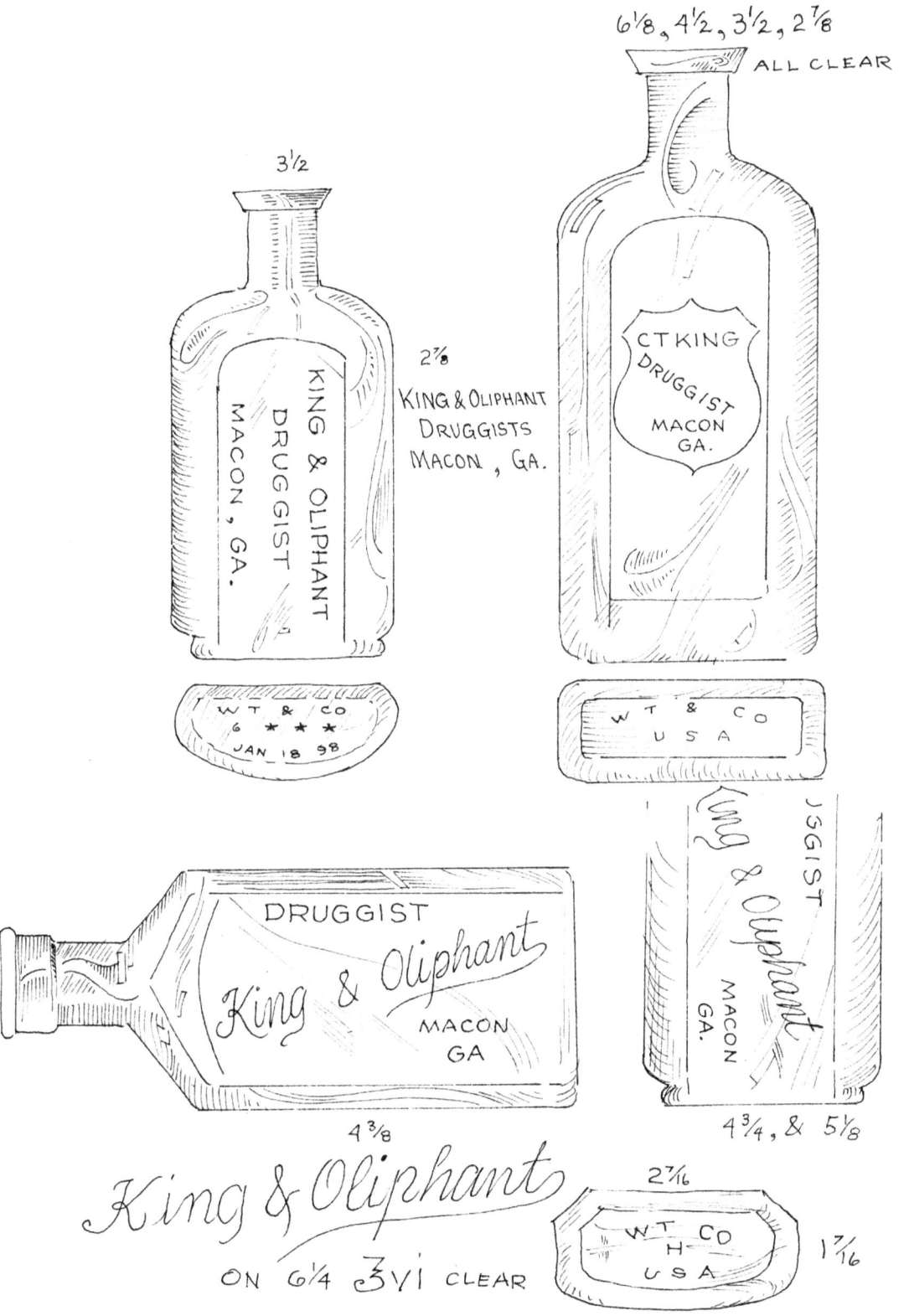

KING PHARMACY AT
FORSYTH RD. 9313_Ph.
1932

$6\frac{1}{8}$, $4\frac{1}{2}$, $3\frac{1}{2}$, $2\frac{7}{8}$

ALL CLEAR

$3\frac{1}{2}$

KING & OLIPHANT
DRUGGIST
MACON, GA.

$2\frac{7}{8}$

KING & OLIPHANT
DRUGGISTS
MACON, GA.

CT KING
DRUGGIST
MACON GA.

WT & CO
6 ✱✱✱
JAN 18 98

WT & CO
USA

DRUGGIST
King & Oliphant
MACON GA

King & Oliphant
MACON GA.

$4\frac{3}{8}$

$4\frac{3}{4}$, & $5\frac{1}{8}$

King & Oliphant

$2\frac{7}{16}$

ON $6\frac{1}{4}$ 3ⅵ CLEAR

WT CO
H
USA

$1\frac{7}{16}$

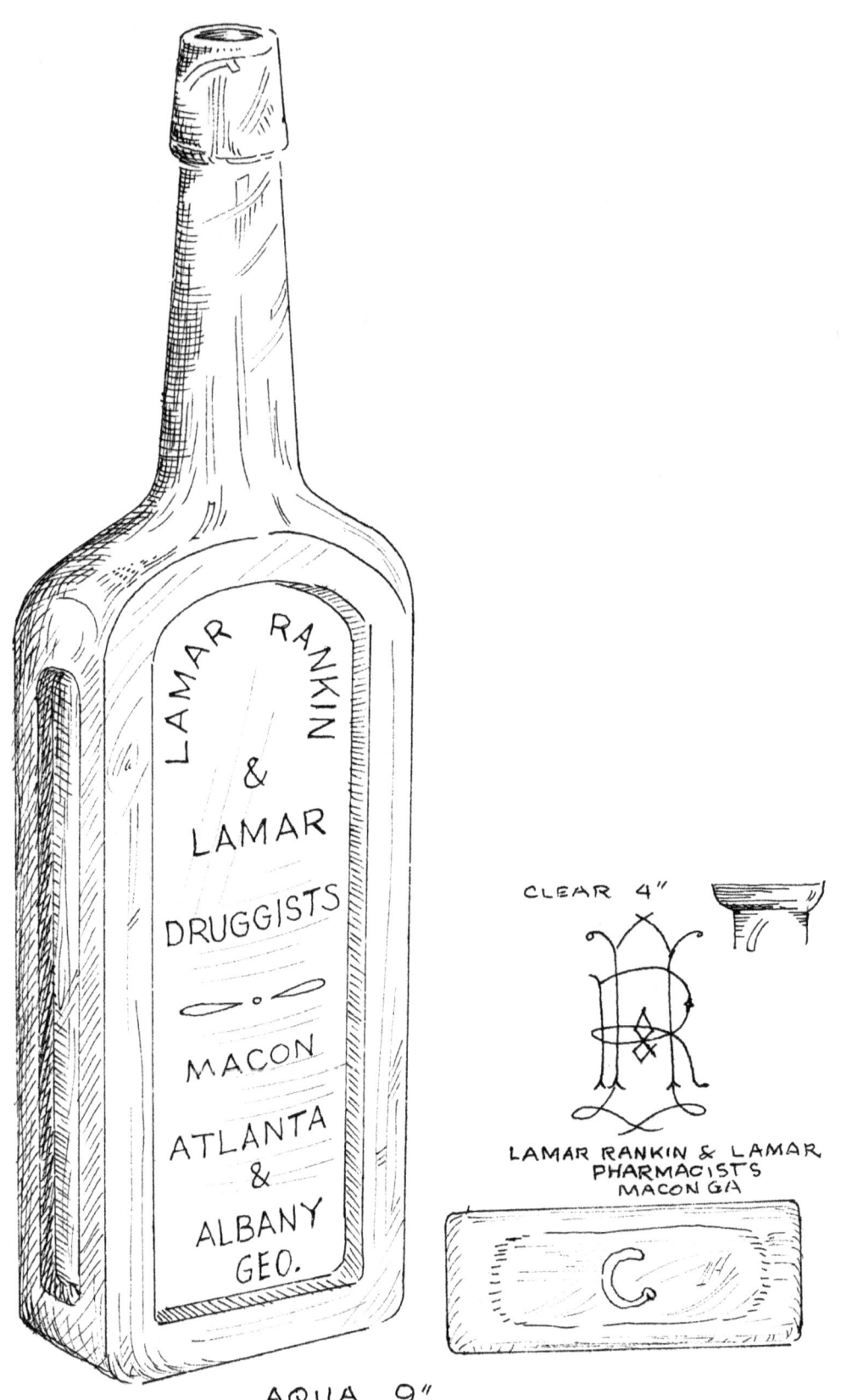

LAMAR RANKIN
&
LAMAR
DRUGGISTS
MACON
ATLANTA
&
ALBANY
GEO.

CLEAR 4"

LAMAR RANKIN & LAMAR
PHARMACISTS
MACON GA

C

AQUA 9"
ALSO SMALL 5¾

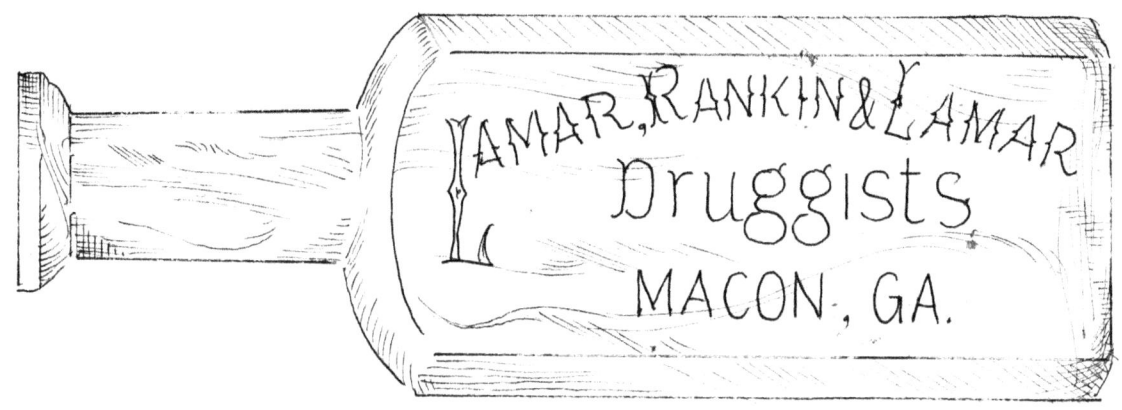

LAMAR, RANKIN & LAMAR
Druggists
MACON, GA.

4 SIZES 8" to   SQ. Clear.

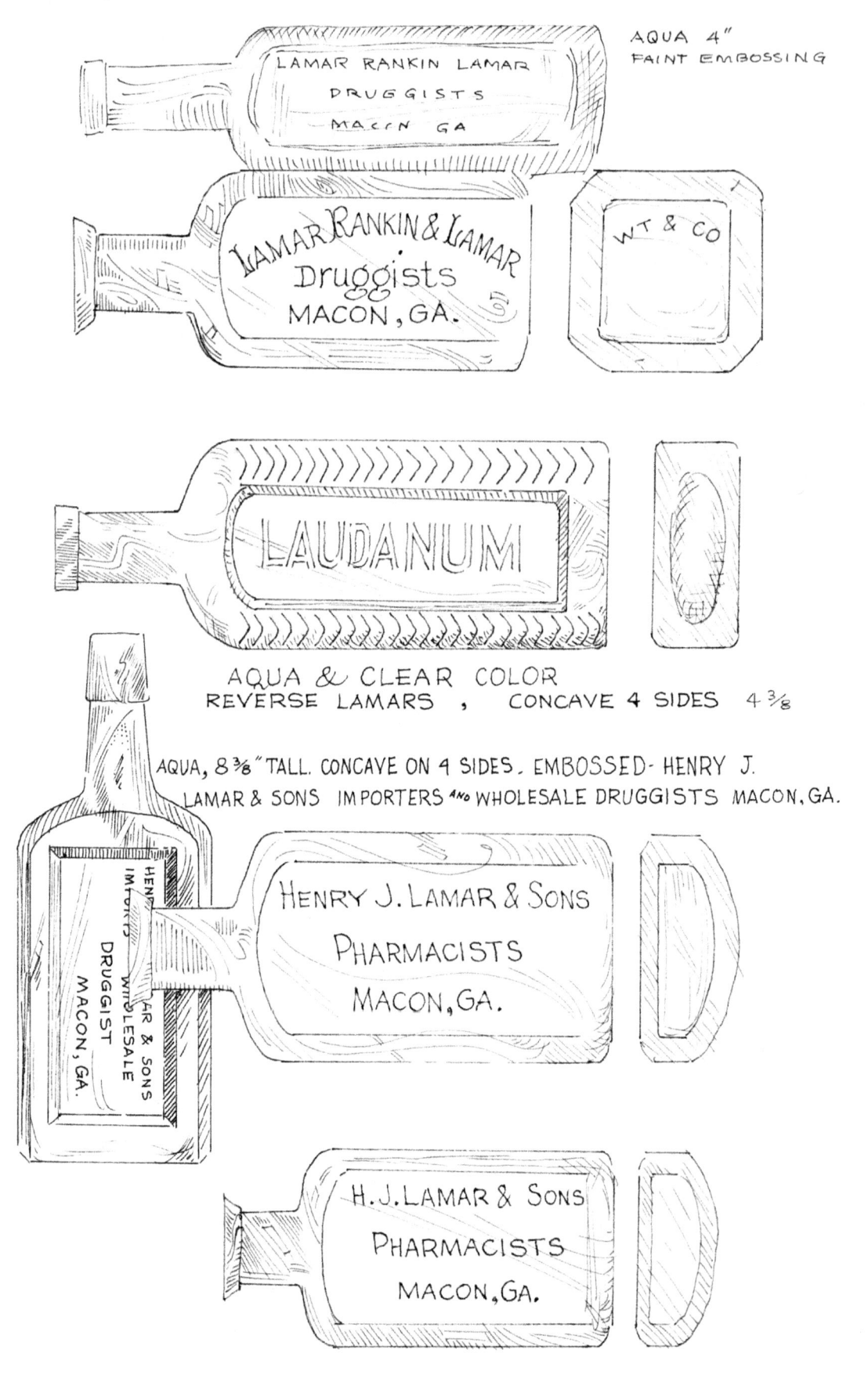

AQUA 4"
FAINT EMBOSSING

LAMAR RANKIN LAMAR
DRUGGISTS
MACON GA

Lamar Rankin & Lamar
Druggists
MACON, GA.

WT & CO

LAUDANUM

AQUA & CLEAR COLOR
REVERSE LAMARS , CONCAVE 4 SIDES 4 3/8

AQUA, 8 3/8" TALL. CONCAVE ON 4 SIDES. EMBOSSED - HENRY J.
LAMAR & SONS IMPORTERS AND WHOLESALE DRUGGISTS MACON, GA.

HENRY J. LAMAR & SONS
PHARMACISTS
MACON, GA.

HENRY J. LAMAR & SONS
IMPORTERS WHOLESALE
DRUGGIST
MACON, GA.

H. J. LAMAR & SONS
PHARMACISTS
MACON, GA.

HENRY J. LAMAR AND SONS
PHARMACISTS
MACON, GA.

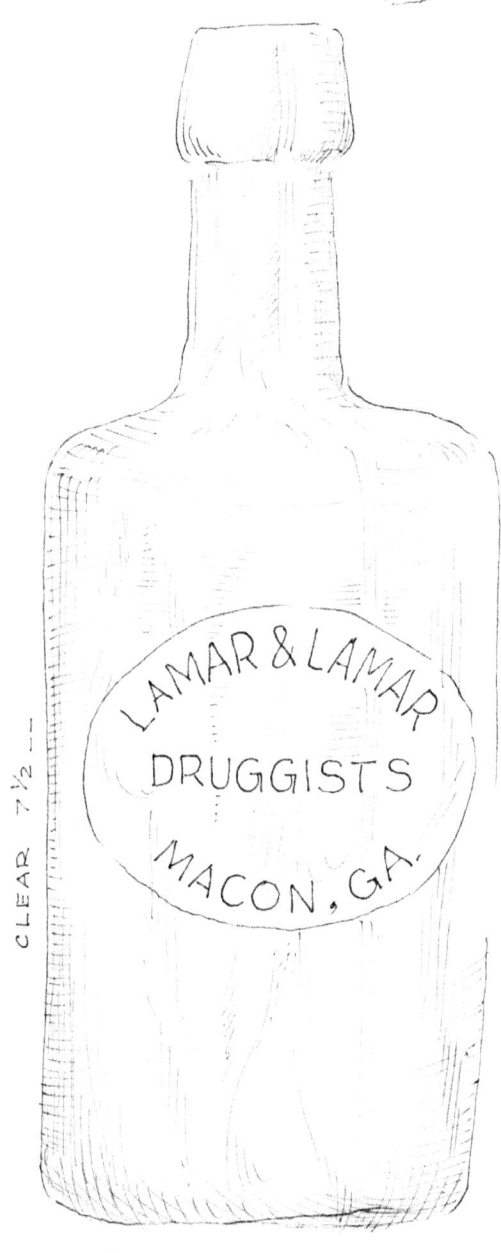

CLEAR 5⅜

CLEAR 7½ —

LAMAR & LAMAR
DRUGGISTS
MACON, GA.

paper lables - Lamar, Taylor & Riley - J.B. Riley Drug Co -

McKesson-Riley Drug Co - McKesson-Robins - Coleman-Meadows
Pate - all the above was Wholesale druggists -

A metal sign 10"x 2¼" Yellow, black lettering TRY LAMAR'S LEMON LAXATIVE for THE LIVER L.L.L.

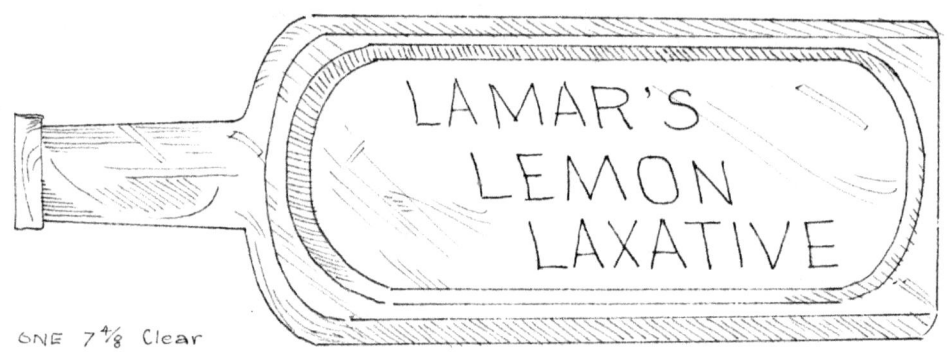

ONE 7⁴⁄₈ Clear

Also have a labled bottle from Lamar, Taylor & Riley Drug Co. brown, crown top, contain ASPHALTUM OR GRATE VARNISH.

ALSO 6'½" ALL CLEAR

LAMAR & CO.
DRUGGISTS
MACON, GA.

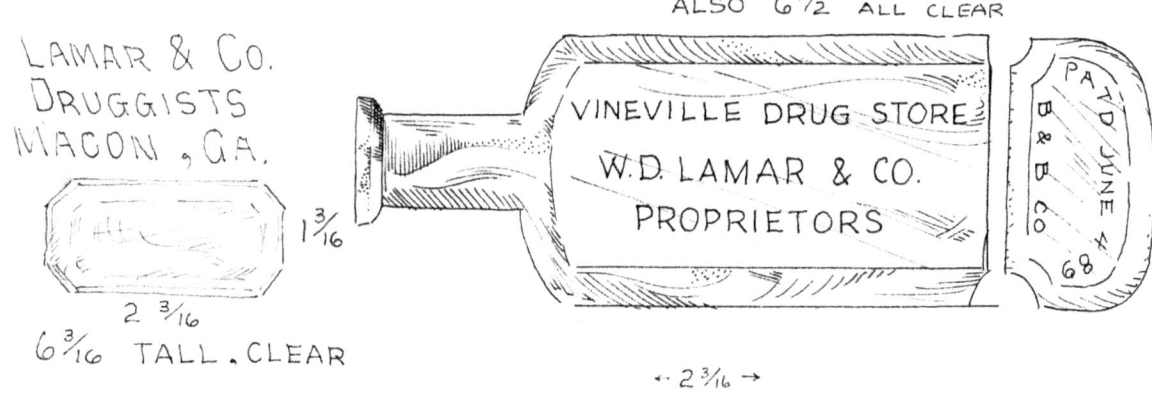

1 ³⁄₁₆

2 ³⁄₁₆

6 ³⁄₁₆ TALL. CLEAR

LAMAR & CO.
PRESCRIPTION DRUGGISTS
MACON, GA.

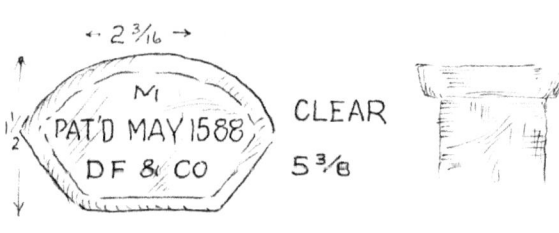

CLEAR
5 ³⁄₈

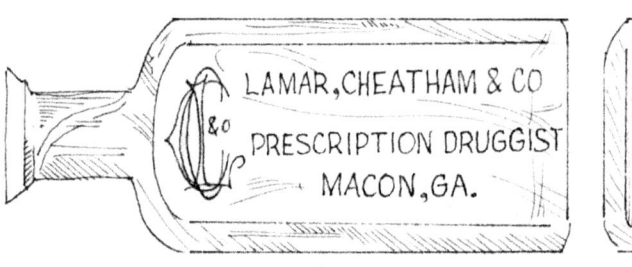

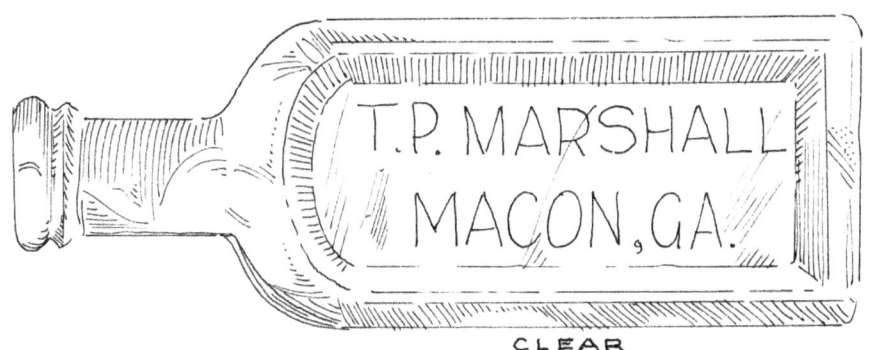

T.P. MARSHALL
MACON, GA.

CLEAR

ALSO AQUA WITH 'BABY EASE'

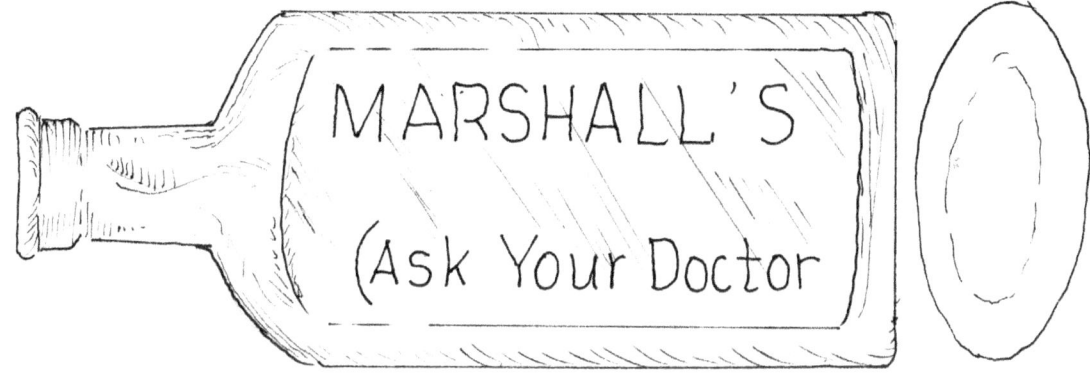

MARSHALL'S

(Ask Your Doctor

CLEAR 5¾

labled, crown top, amber bottle from McKesson-Riley
Drug Co. Wholesale Druggists, contain Citrate of
Magnesia — Machine made and embossed on back — top
shoulder in horseshoe shape — Compania Cervecera Inter
Nacional S.A.
HABANA

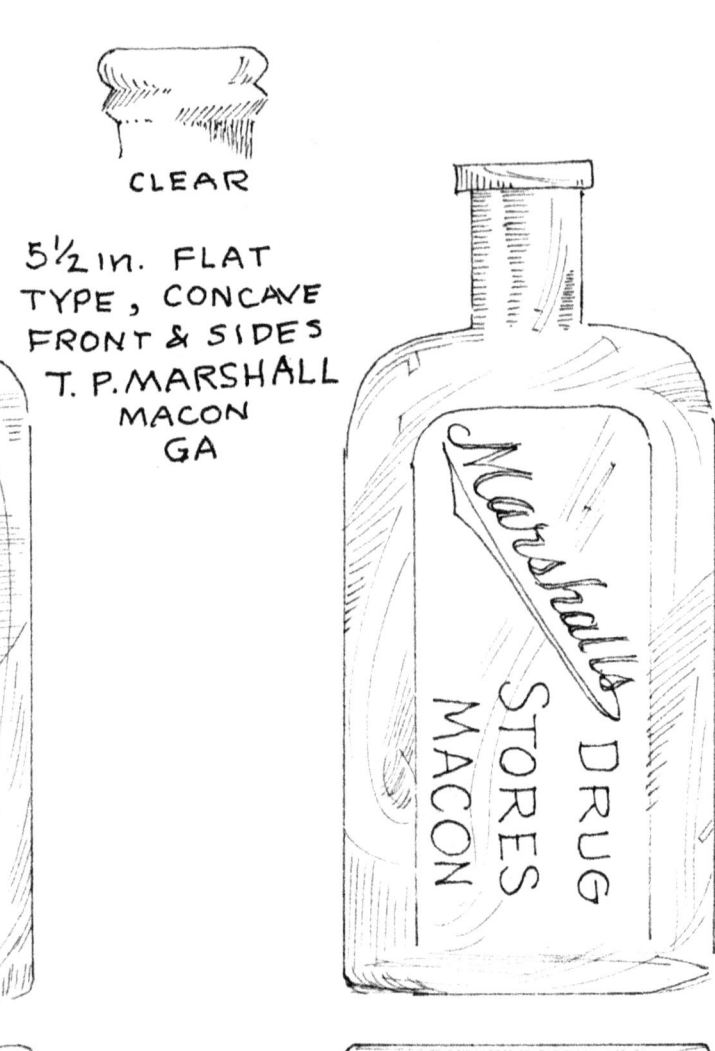

CLEAR

5½ in. FLAT
TYPE, CONCAVE
FRONT & SIDES
T. P. MARSHALL
MACON
GA

BENZOIN CREAM
FOR CHAPPED HANDS
T.P MARSHALL MACON, GA.

Marshall's DRUG
STORES
MACON

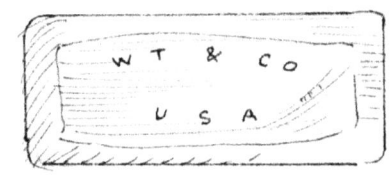

W T & C O
U S A

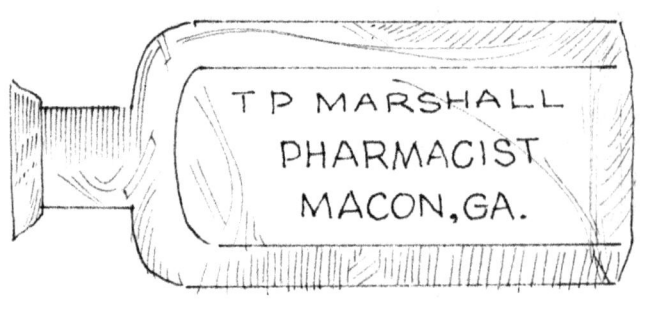

W T & C O
U S A

T P MARSHALL
PHARMACIST
MACON, GA.

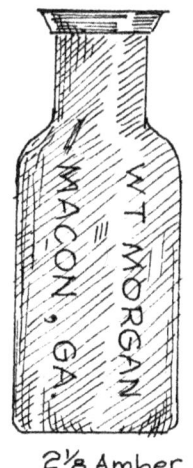

2⅛ Amber

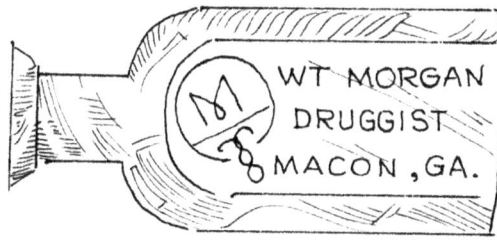

WT MORGAN
DRUGGIST
MACON, GA.

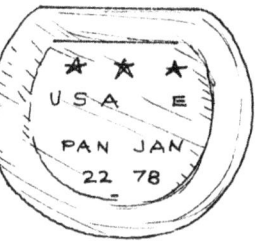

★ ★ ★
U S · A   E
PAN JAN
22 78

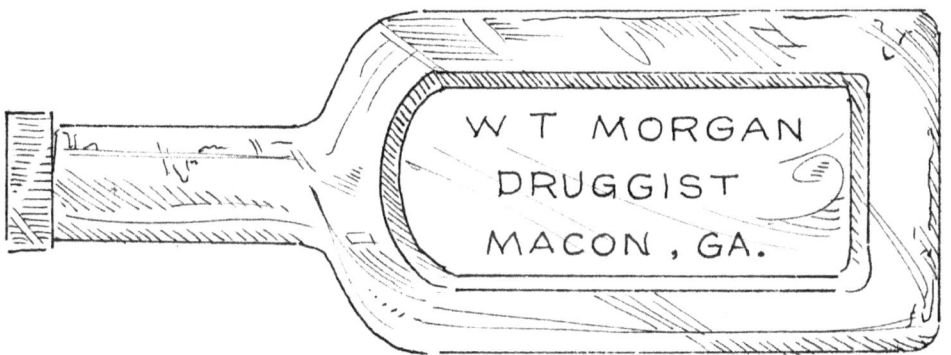

W T MORGAN
DRUGGIST
MACON, GA.

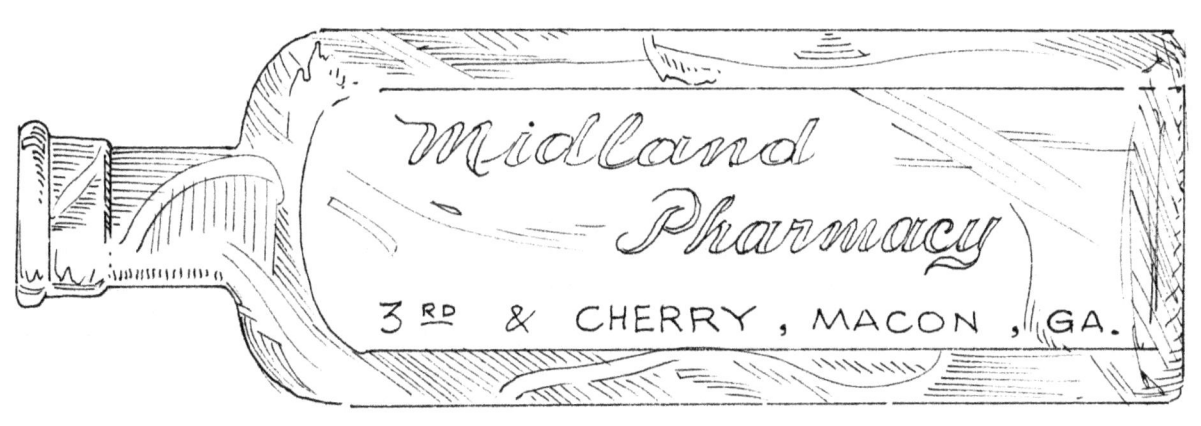

Midland
Pharmacy
3RD & CHERRY, MACON, GA.

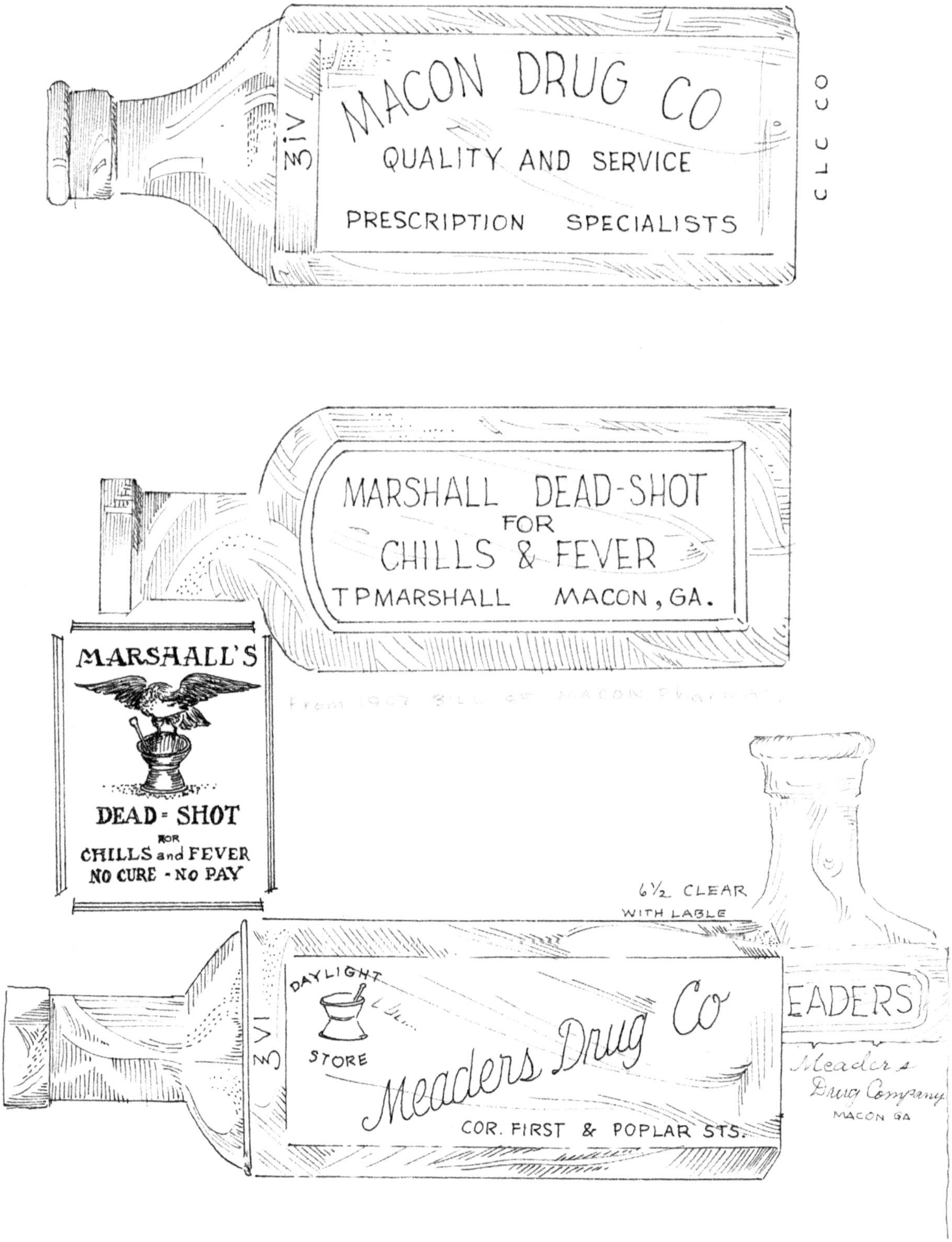

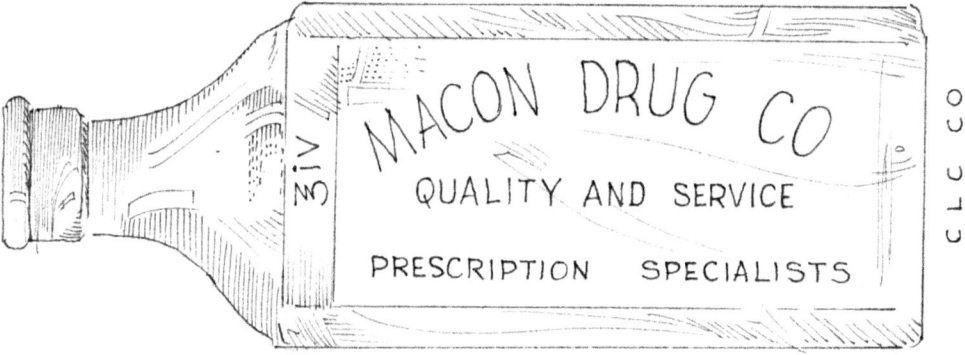

℥iv
MACON DRUG CO
QUALITY AND SERVICE
PRESCRIPTION SPECIALISTS
CLC CO

MARSHALL DEAD-SHOT
FOR
CHILLS & FEVER
T.P.MARSHALL   MACON, GA.

From 1907 Bill of Macon Druggist

MARSHALL'S
DEAD = SHOT
FOR
CHILLS and FEVER
NO CURE - NO PAY

6½ CLEAR
WITH LABLE

EADERS

℥VI
DAYLIGHT
STORE
Meaders Drug Co
COR. FIRST & POPLAR STS.

Meaders
Drug Company
MACON GA

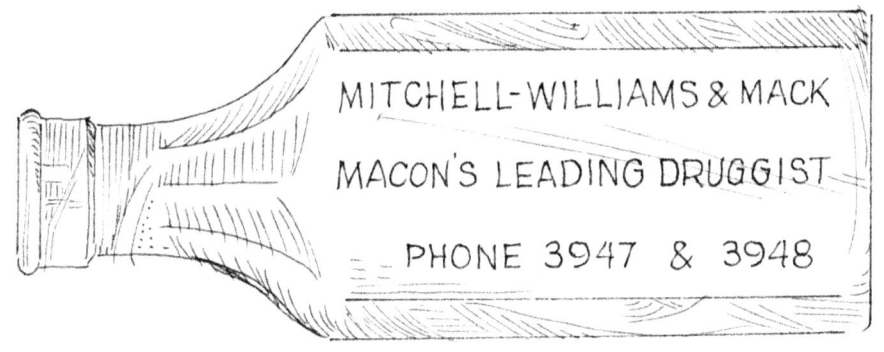

MITCHELL-WILLIAMS & MACK

MACON'S LEADING DRUGGIST

PHONE 3947 & 3948

ALSO 8⅞ SCALES ALONG BOTH SIDES OF EMBOSSING
3 LEFT SIDE, CC ON RIGHT - CLEAR_ _ _ _ _ _ _ _ _ _ _ _

ALF MACK'S PHARMACY Ph. 1941-1942
401 Cherry St. BIBB Building- LABEL ONLY

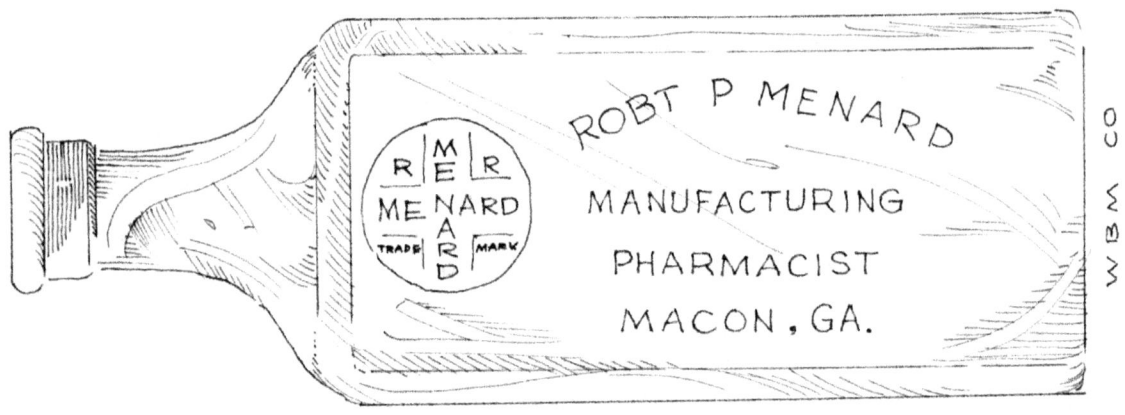

ROBT P MENARD

MANUFACTURING

PHARMACIST

MACON, GA.

W B M CO

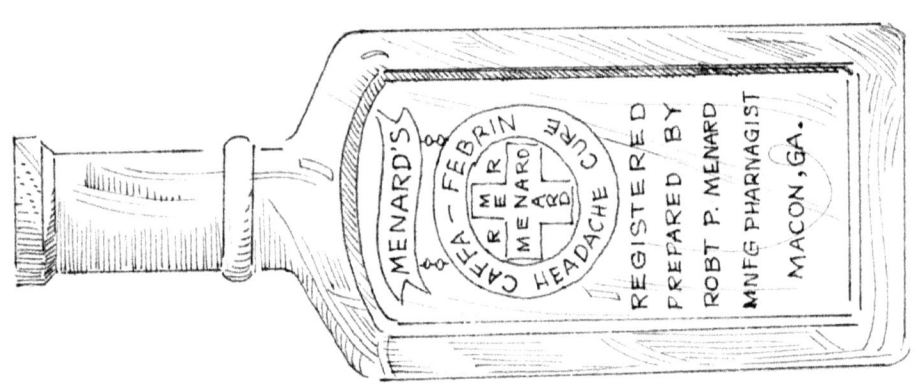

MENARD'S CAFFEA – FEBRIN HEADACHE CURE

REGISTERED
PREPARED BY
ROBT. P. MENARD
MNFG PHARNAGIST
MACON, GA.

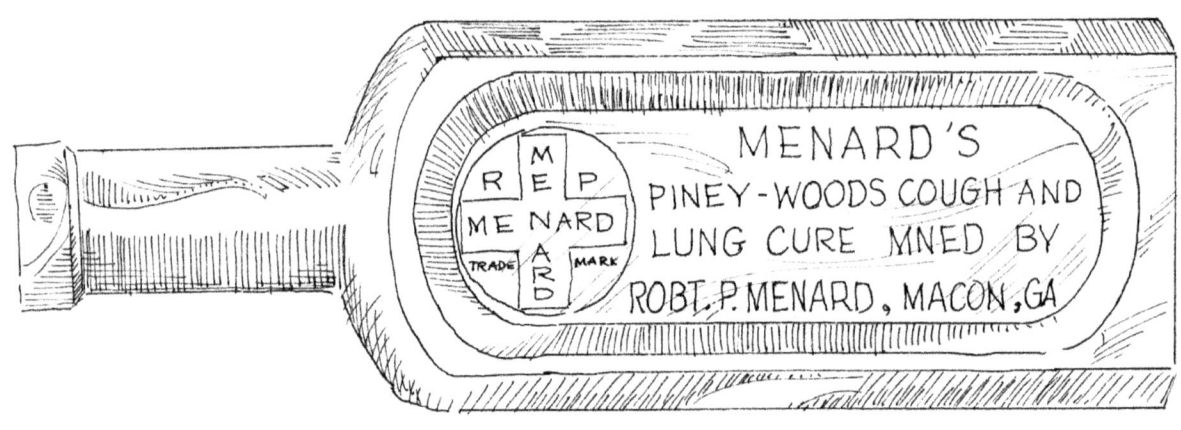

MENARD'S
PINEY-WOODS COUGH AND
LUNG CURE MNED BY
ROBT. P. MENARD, MACON, GA

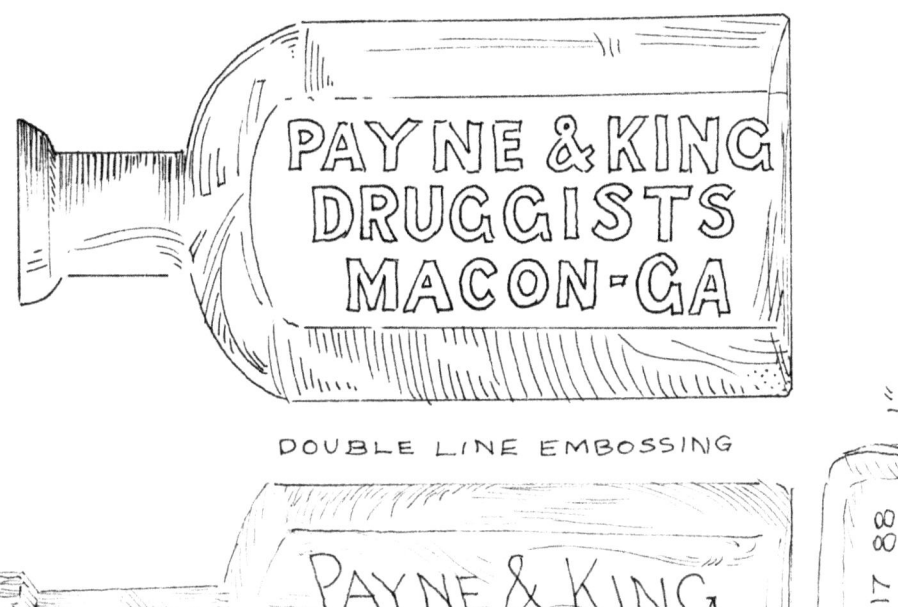

PAYNE & KING
DRUGGISTS
MACON - GA

DOUBLE LINE EMBOSSING

PAYNE & KING
DRUGGISTS
MACON , GA.

PAT JUN. 17 88
S B

1"

1·3/4"

4²/8 CLEAR

GEO F. PAYNE PhG
DRUGGISTS
MACON, GA.
2¾ CLEAR

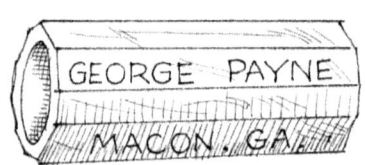

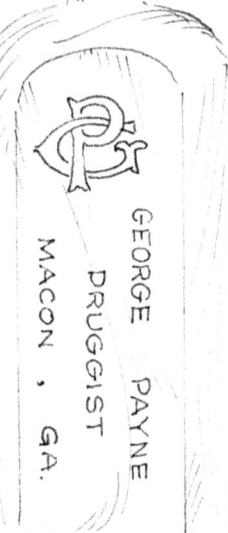

GEORGE PAYNE
MACON. GA.

CLEAR - 2¹⁄₁₆ IN. TALL - TAPPERS
OFF ⅛" FROM TOP TO BOTTOM —
10 SIDED

GEORGE PAYNE
FEVER & AGUE
PILLS
MACON, GA.

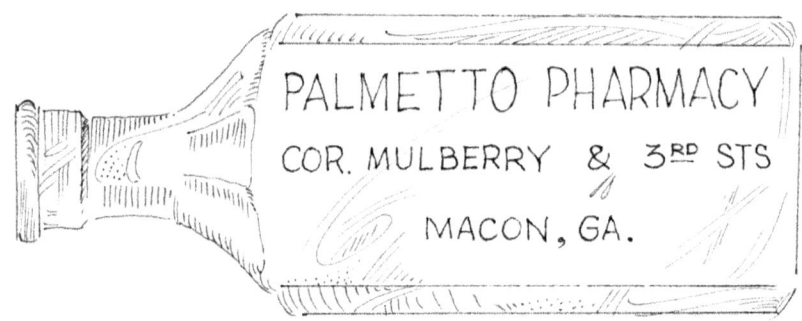

PALMETTO PHARMACY
COR. MULBERRY & 3ᴿᴰ STS
MACON, GA.

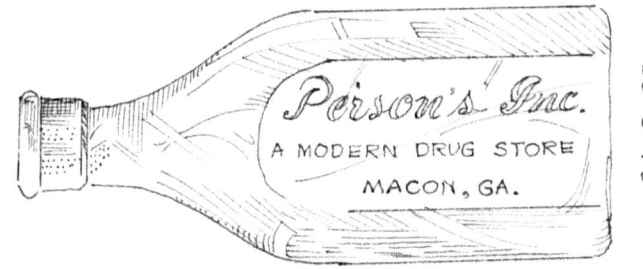

Person's Inc.
A MODERN DRUG STORE
MACON, GA.

CLC CO

TOP

SPIRITS OF TUPPENTINE, PERSONS PHARMACY, 7739 College
paper lable, cork stopper, clear, 5¾ tall — 1⅞ wide
"From 5 to 20 drops on sugar."

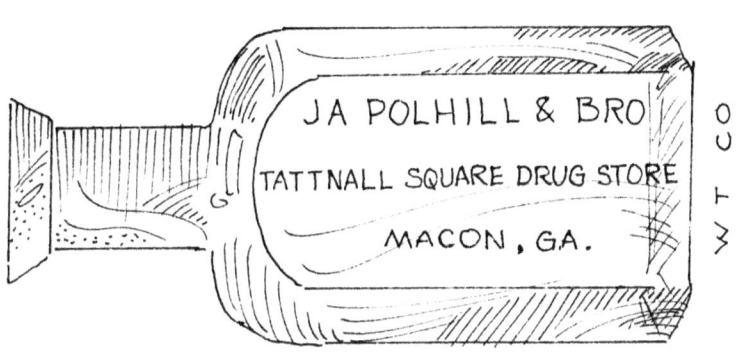

JA POLHILL & BRO

TATTNALL SQUARE DRUG STORE

MACON, GA.

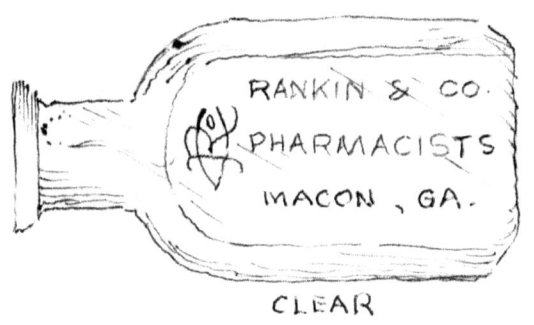

RANKIN & CO.
PHARMACISTS
MACON, GA.

CLEAR

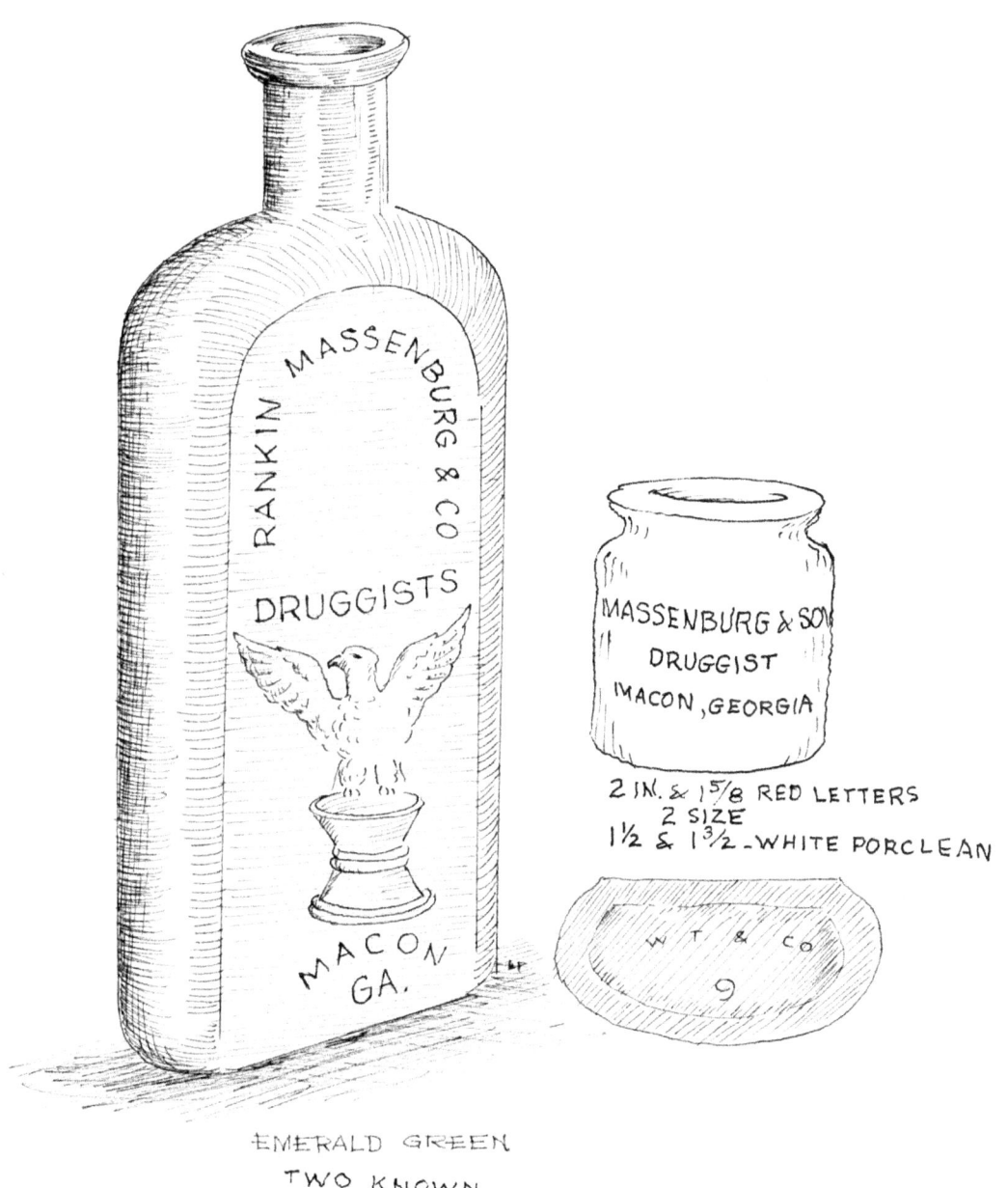

RANKIN MASSENBURG & CO

DRUGGISTS

MACON
GA.

EMERALD GREEN
TWO KNOWN

MASSENBURG & SON
DRUGGIST
MACON, GEORGIA

2 IN. & 1⁵/₈ RED LETTERS
2 SIZE
1½ & 1³/₂ - WHITE PORCLEAN

W T & CO
9

Also in emerald green. RANKIN MASSENBURG & CO
various SIZES   DRUGGISTS
                            MACON, GA

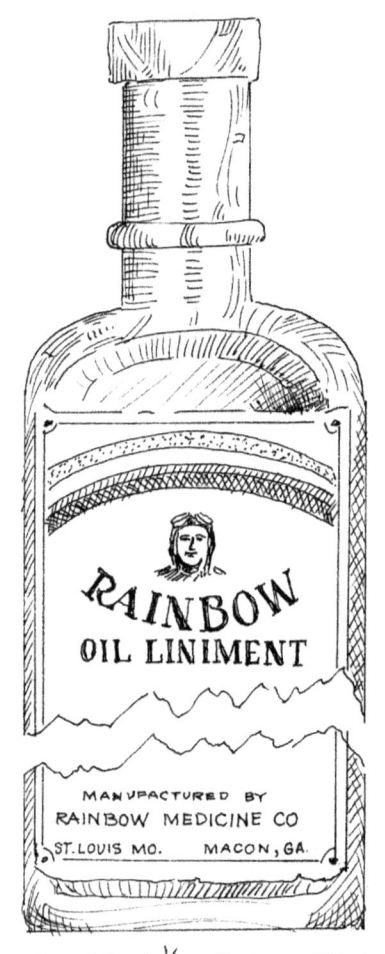

CLEAR 6½ x 2 MACHINE
MADE. LABEL ONLY

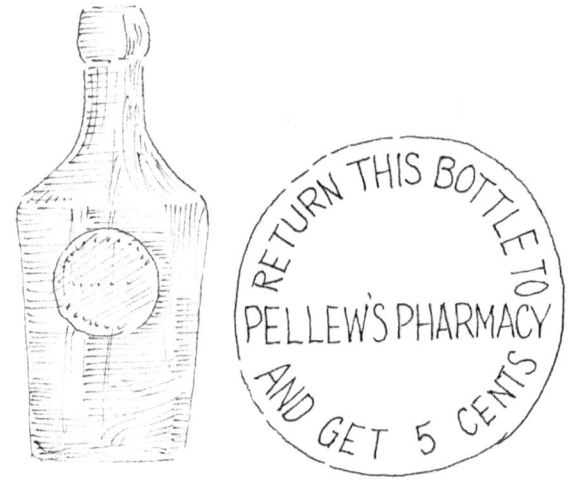

light 7 UP Green. 7¼ in.
Maybe a soda water drink.

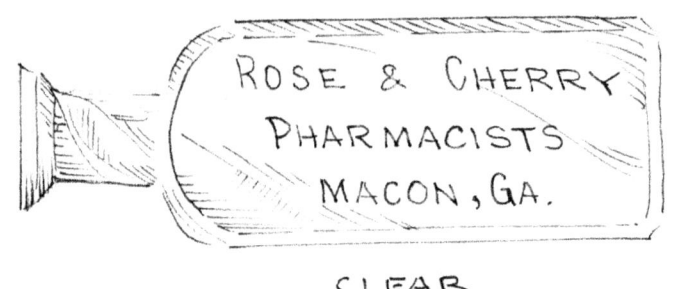

CLEAR

J.B. Riley Drug Co.(WHOLESALE) lables only
Solution Sodium Silicate. for preserving eggs.. light
aqua, Phillips Milk Mag. shape —

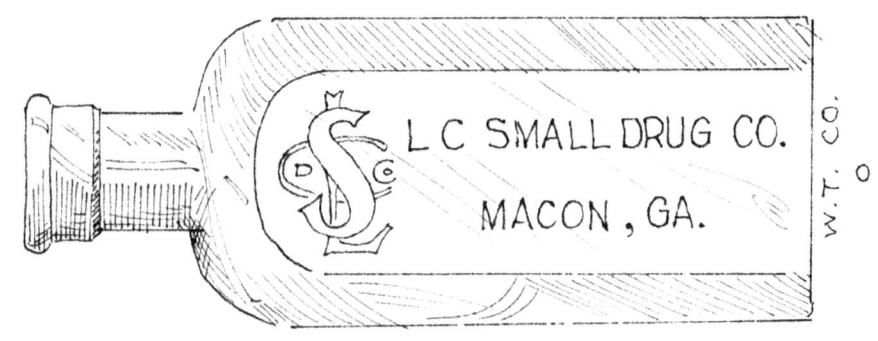

L C SMALL DRUG CO.

MACON, GA.

W.T. CO.

ALSO 7" ALL CLEAR, 4¼, 3⅝

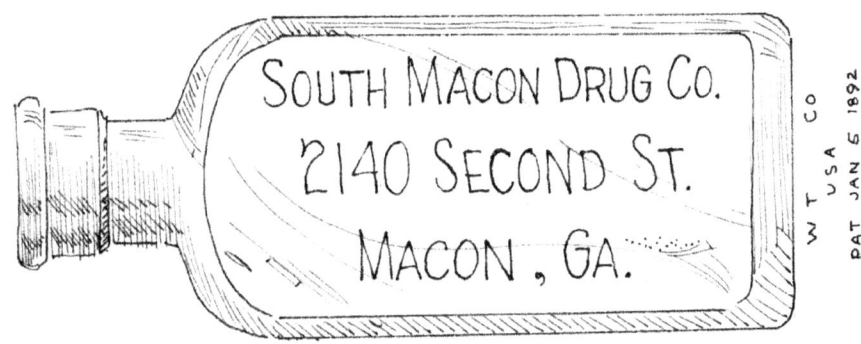

SOUTH MACON DRUG CO.

2140 SECOND ST.

MACON, GA.

W T CO USA
PAT JAN 5 1892

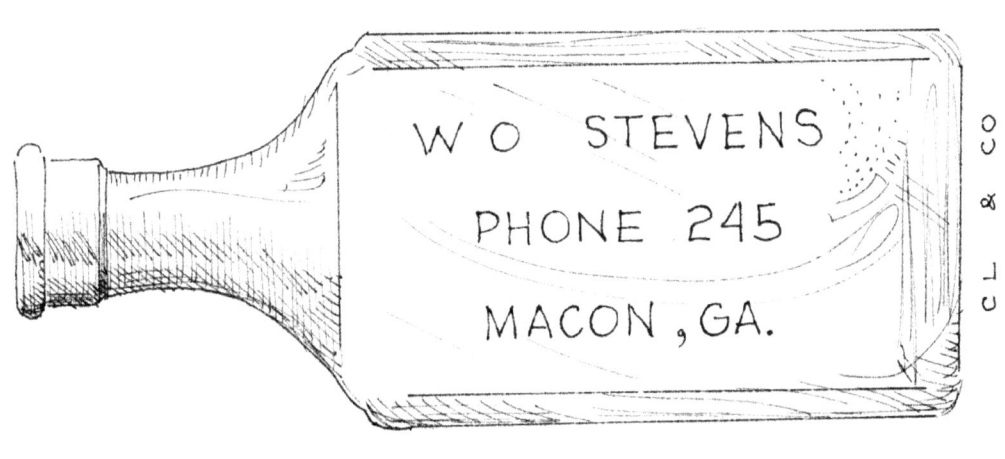

W O STEVENS

PHONE 245

MACON, GA.

C L & CO

ALSO PHONE 1236

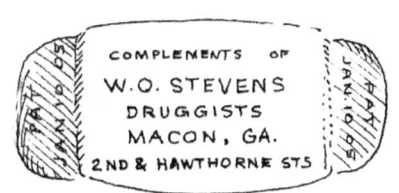

COMPLEMENTS OF
W.O. STEVENS
DRUGGISTS
MACON, GA.
2ND & HAWTHORNE STS

PAT JAN 05   PAT JAN 10 05

PENCIL SHARPNER & ERASER

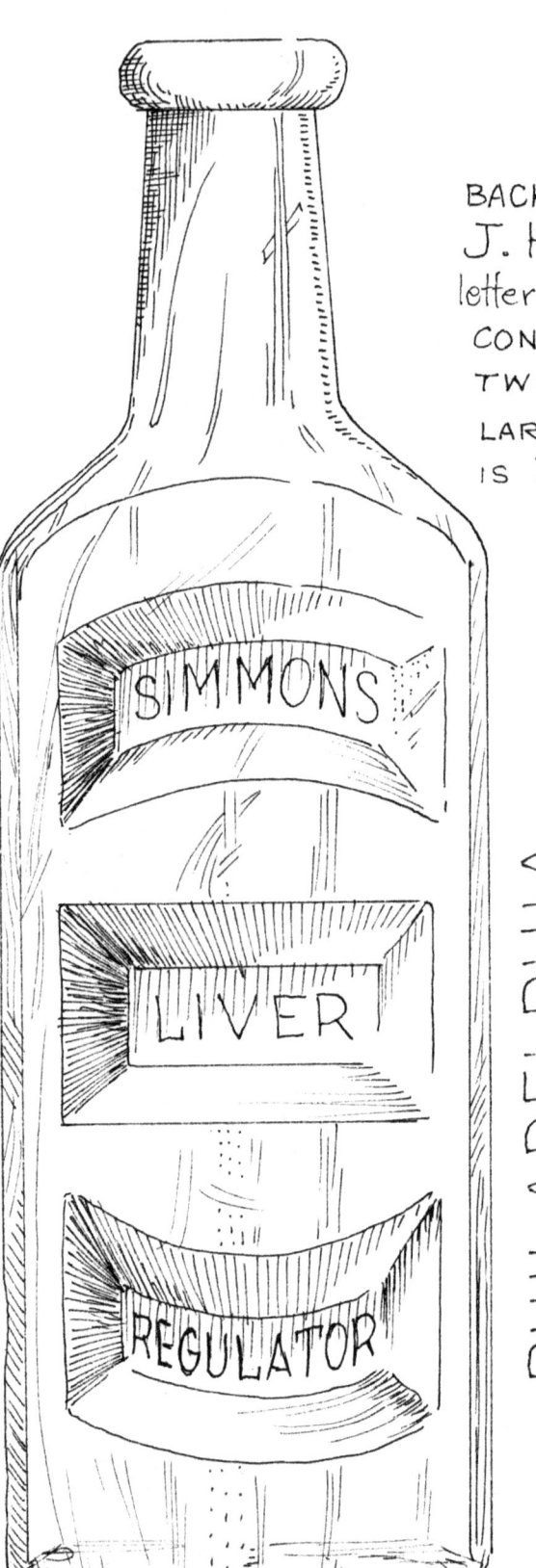

BACK—
J. H. ZEILIN & CO
lettering on 8¾" is ⁷⁄₁₆ – 9½" is ¹⁰⁄₁₆
CONCAVE ON 4 SIDES
TWO SIZES THIS IS THE
LARGE SIZE. SMALL SIZE
IS 7³⁄₁₆ & 7²⁄₁₆—

MACON, GA

PHILADELPHIA

SIMMONS

LIVER

REGULATOR

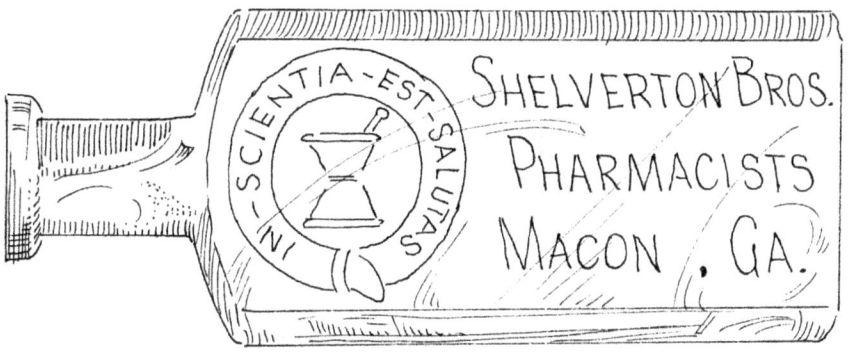

SHELVERTON BROS.
PHARMACISTS
MACON, GA.

IN · SCIENTIA · EST · SALUTAS

MEDICINES

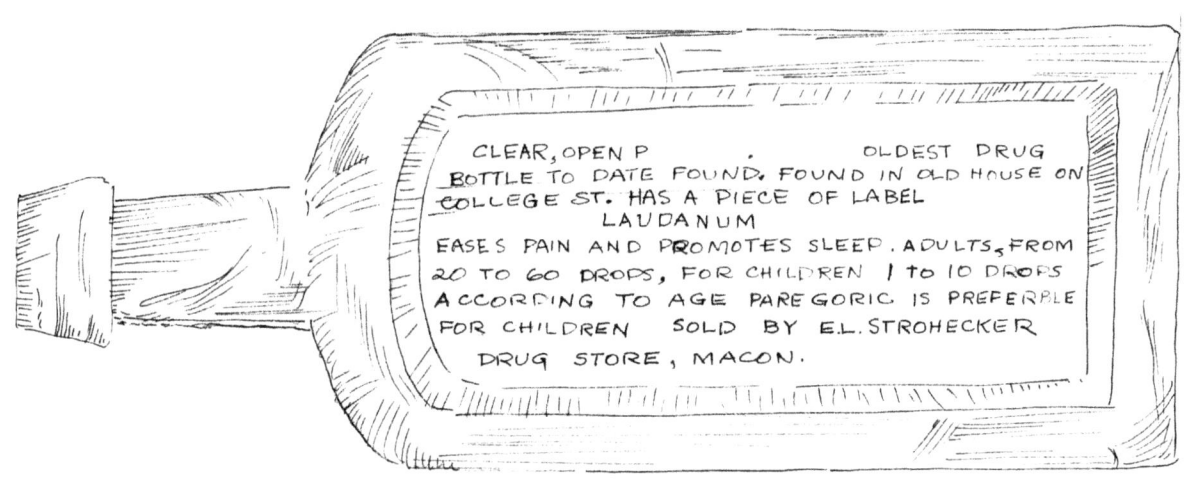

CLEAR, OPEN P   OLDEST DRUG
BOTTLE TO DATE FOUND. FOUND IN OLD HOUSE ON
COLLEGE ST. HAS A PIECE OF LABEL
          LAUDANUM
EASES PAIN AND PROMOTES SLEEP. ADULTS, FROM
20 TO 60 DROPS, FOR CHILDREN 1 to 10 DROPS
ACCORDING TO AGE PAREGORIC IS PREFERBLE
FOR CHILDREN   SOLD BY E.L. STROHECKER
   DRUG STORE, MACON.

E.L. STROHECKER
& C°
MACON
DRUGS &

ℨviii—7"— ℨi 3⅝"—

ℨiv

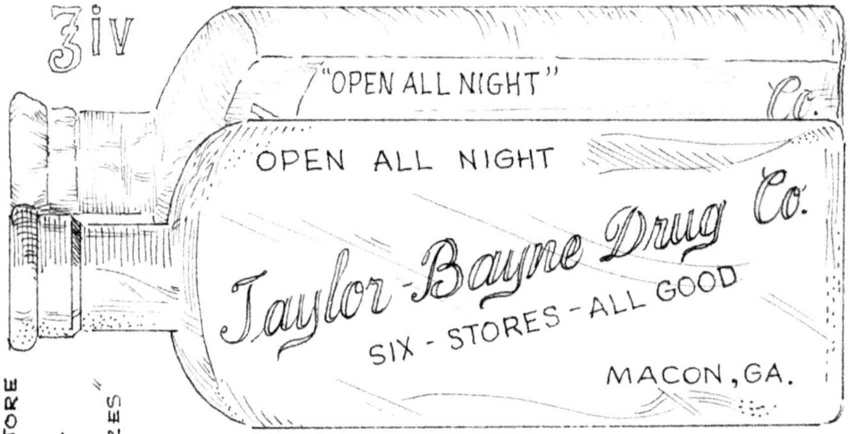

"OPEN ALL NIGHT"

Co.

OPEN ALL NIGHT

Taylor-Bayne Drug Co.

SIX — STORES — ALL GOOD

MACON, GA.

W. T. CO.
N.
U. S. A. 7".

5⅝, 5³⁄₈, 6⅝

REVERSE SIDE ⟶   TAYLOR-BAYNE

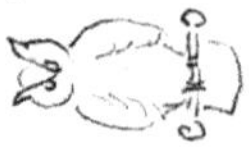

OPEN ALL NIGHT

TAYLOR-BAYNE DRUG CO.   4½ Tall, Clear   ℨii

MACON, GA.   3½ "   "   ℨi

3 — STRIGHT LINE LETTERING   2⅞ "   "   ℨiv

MALLORY H. TAYLOR

PHARMACIST

OPEN ALL NIGHT - MACON, GA.

ℨiii

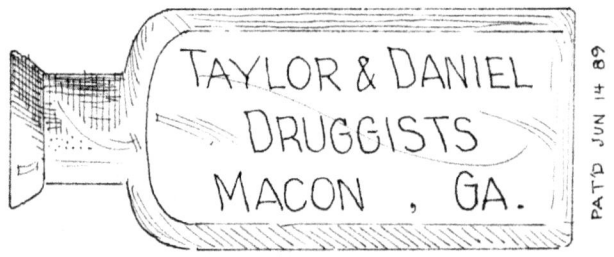

TAYLOR & DANIEL

DRUGGISTS

MACON   ,   GA.

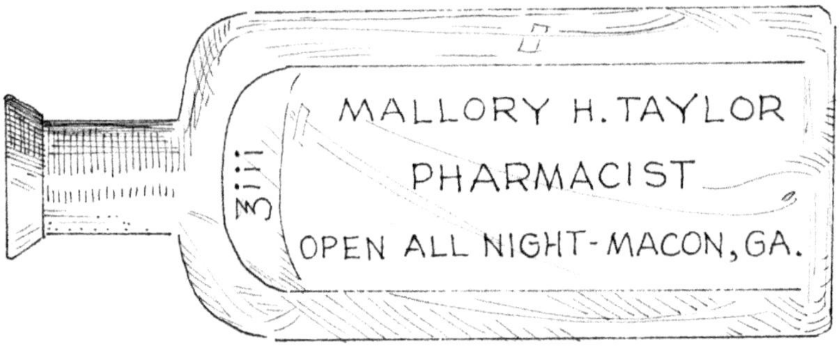

PAT'D JUN 14 89
B. B. & CO.

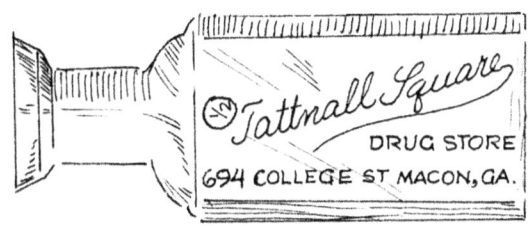

Tattnall Square
DRUG STORE
694 COLLEGE ST MACON, GA.

ALSO SIZE ①, ④

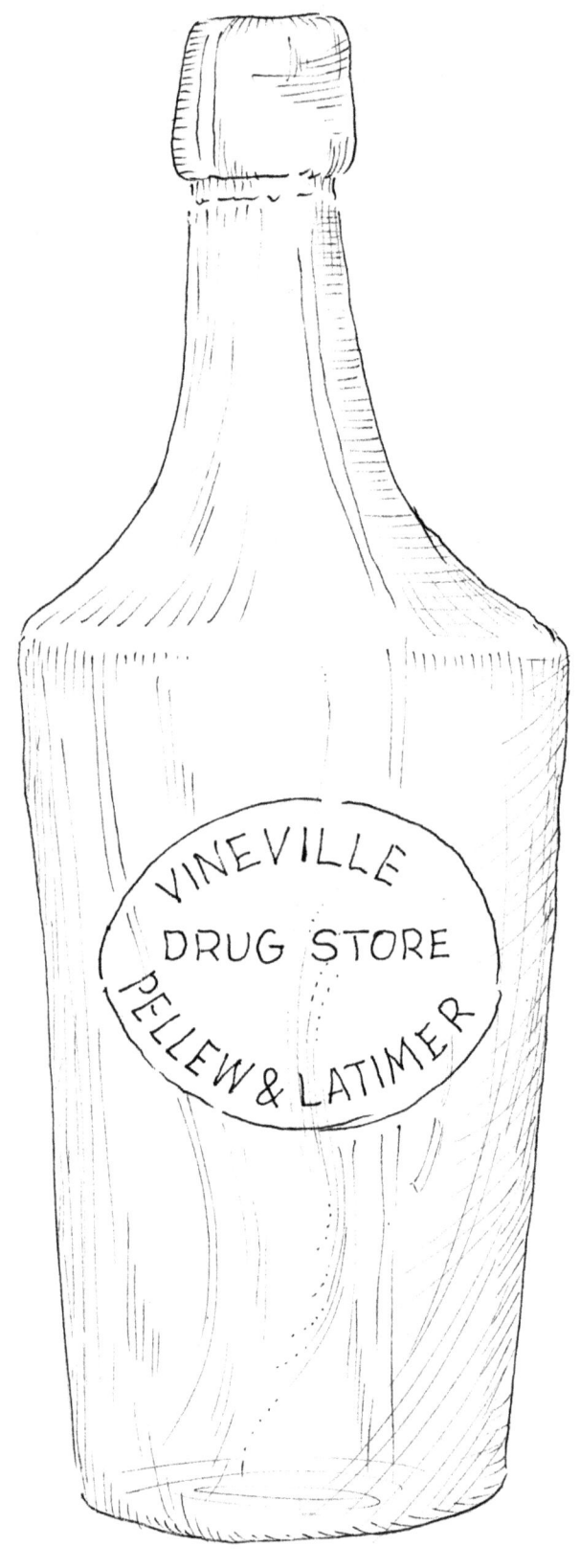

CLEAR

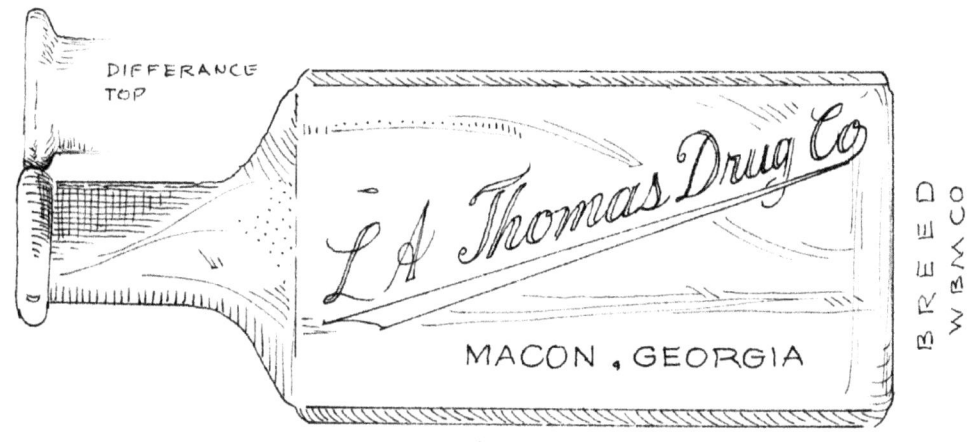

DIFFERANCE TOP

L A Thomas Drug Co

MACON , GEORGIA

BREED W B M CO

5" tall clear — 1⅞" x 2"

ALSO WITH PHONE # IN THE FLAG UNDER THE NAME,
NAME FANCIER — FINGER GRIPS ON SIDE OF BOTTLE
OVAL SHAPE TOO —

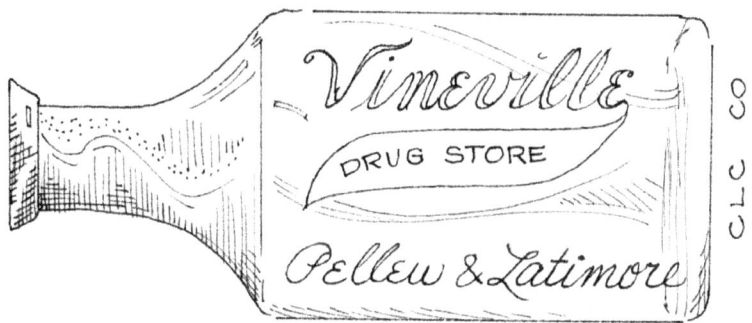

Vineville

DRUG STORE

Pellew & Latimore

CLC CO

ALSO 5⅜ CLEAR

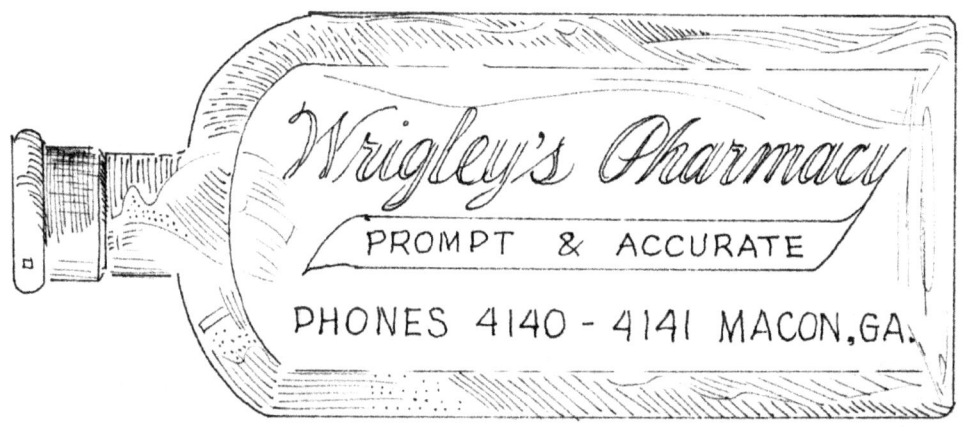

Wrigley's Pharmacy

PROMPT & ACCURATE

PHONES 4140 - 4141 MACON, GA.

ALSO EMBOSSING IN RIBBON "OPP PHONE EXCHANGE
& PHONES 4141 - 4151 4⅞ ABOVE

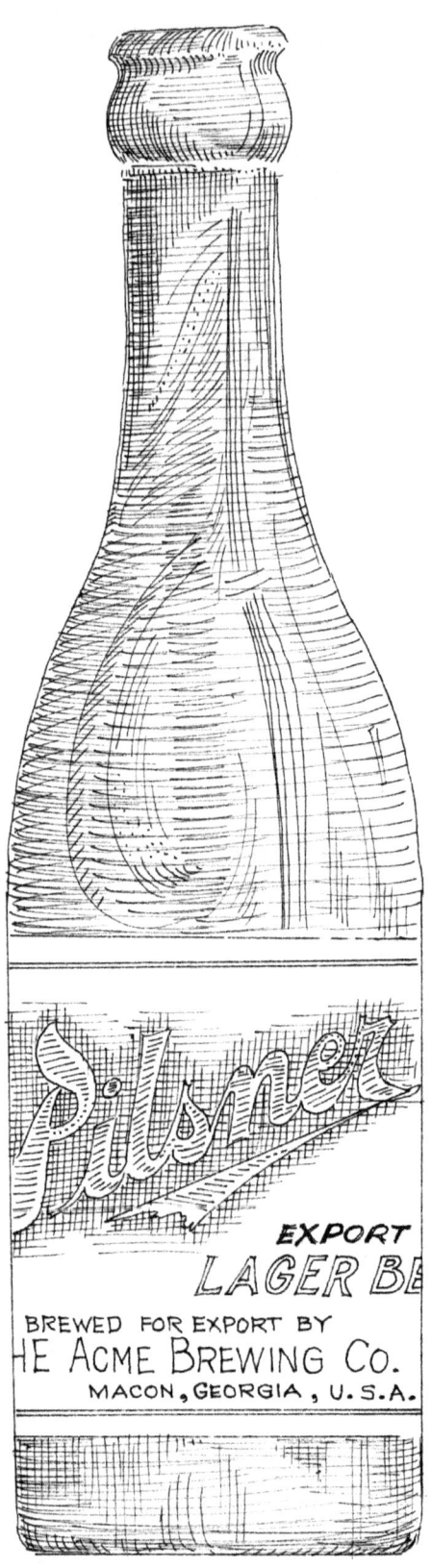

Pilsner

EXPORT
LAGER BE

BREWED FOR EXPORT BY
HE ACME BREWING Co.
MACON, GEORGIA, U.S.A.

AMBER
WHITE LABLE WITH
BLUE PRINTING

ALSO IN LIGHT BLUE
GLASS – WHITE LABLE
WITH BLACK PRINTING

S B & G CO.
BOTTOM

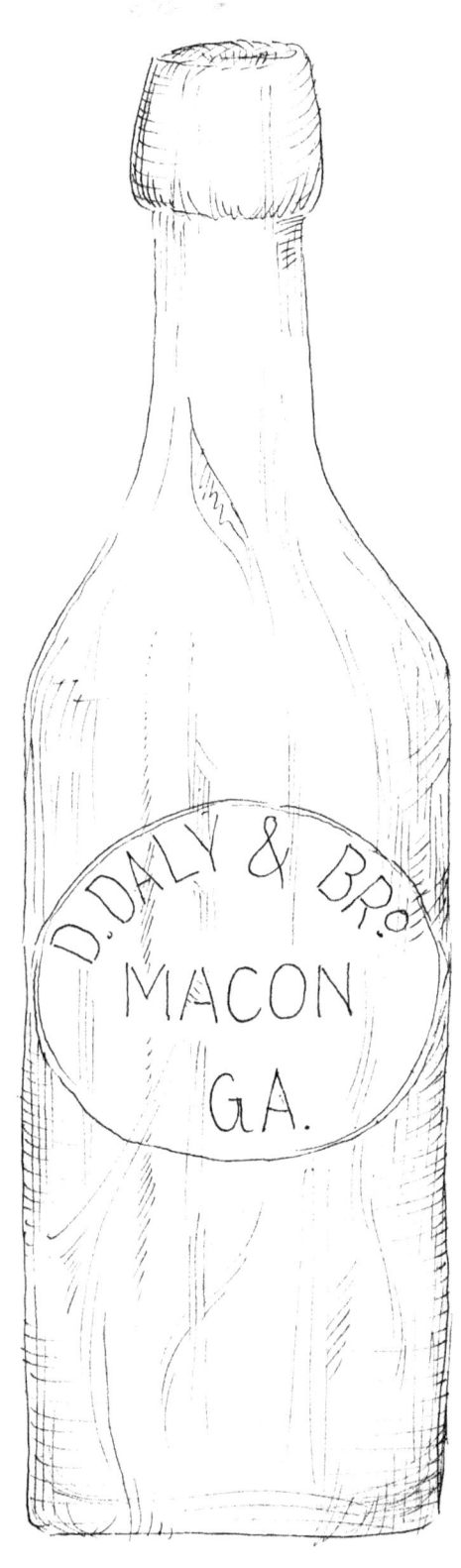

9½ × 2¾ AQUA – BACK – THIS
BOTTLE NOT TO BE SOLD

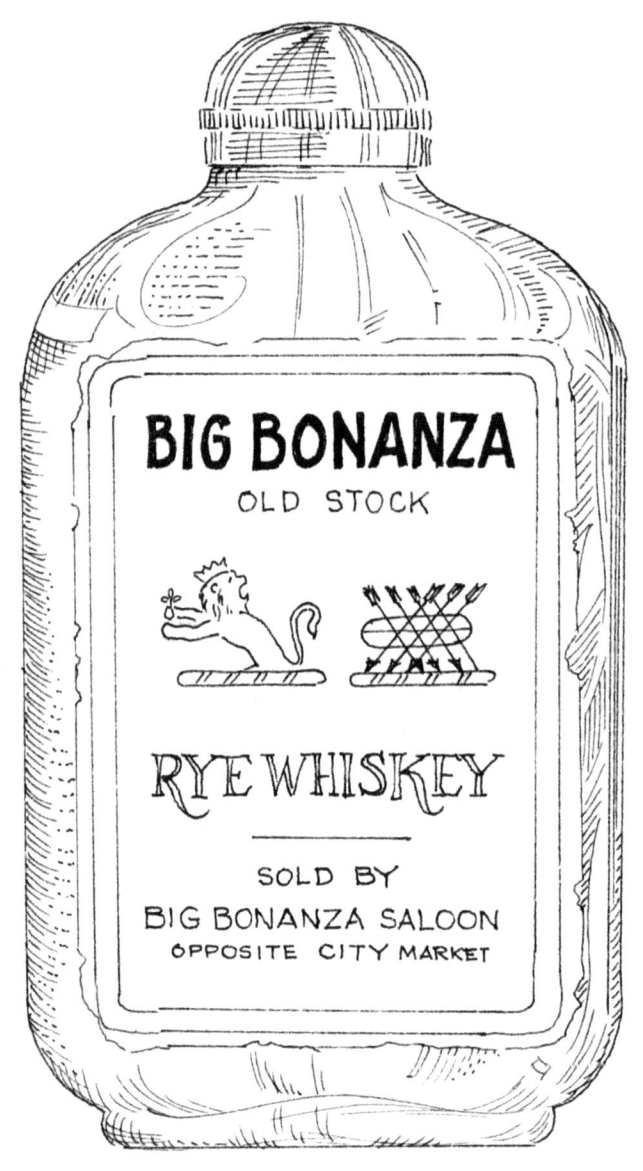

5 7/8 CLEAR
METAL CAP
NO EMBOSSING

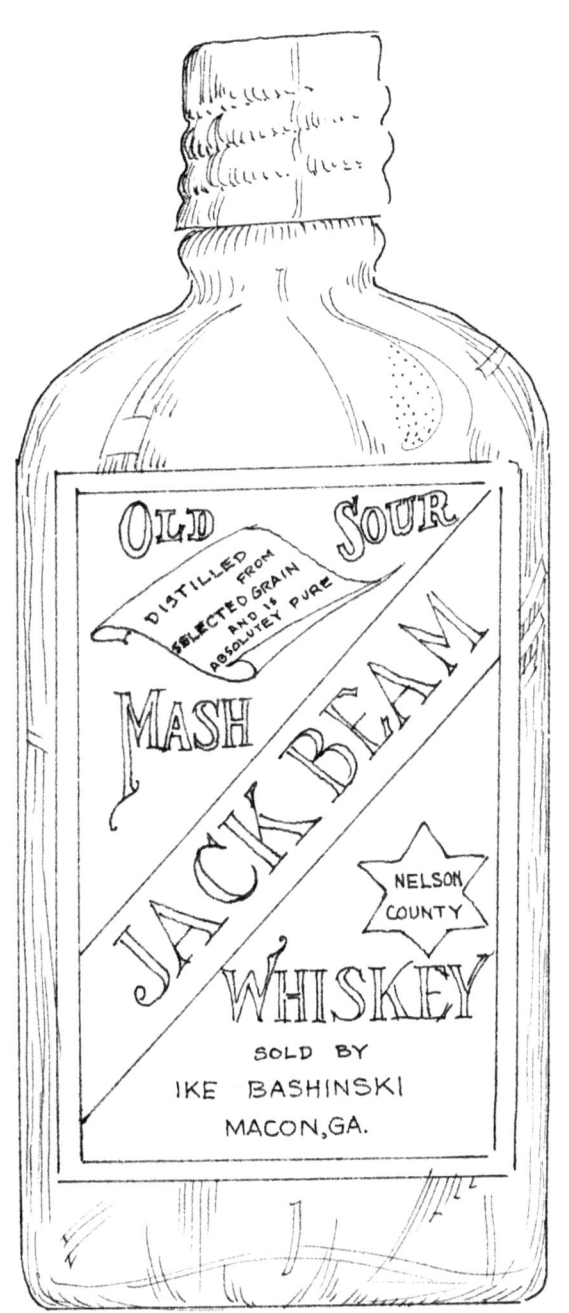

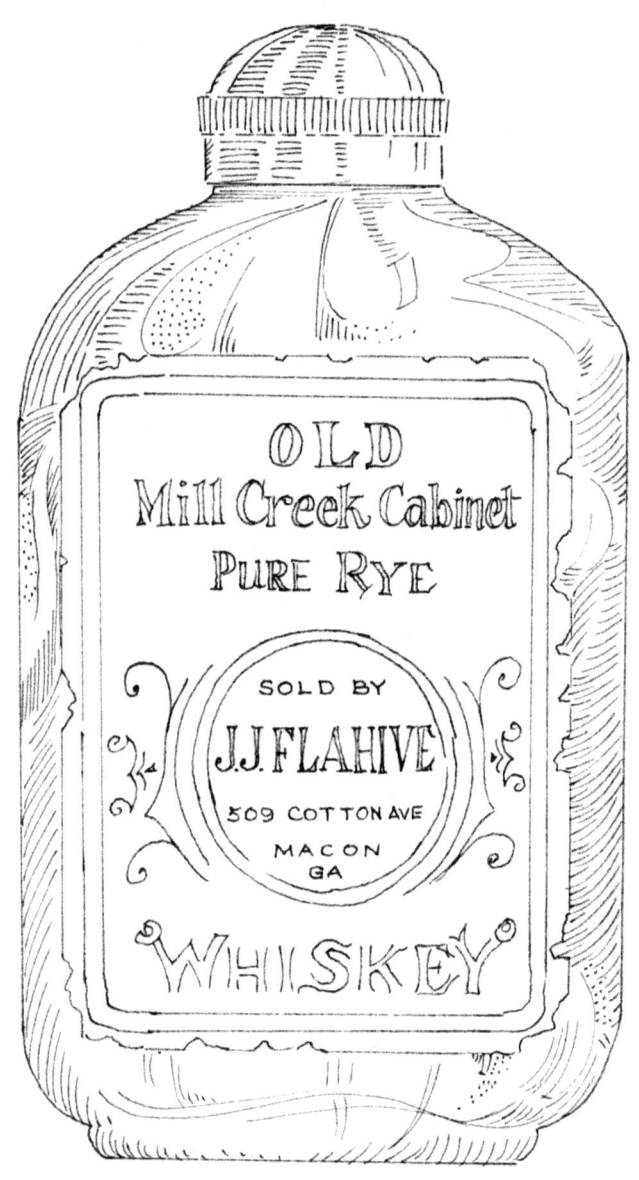

OLD
Mill Creek Cabinet
Pure Rye

SOLD BY
J.J. FLAHIVE
509 COTTON AVE
MACON
GA

WHISKEY

CLEAR   5⅞
METAL CAP NO
EMBOSSING

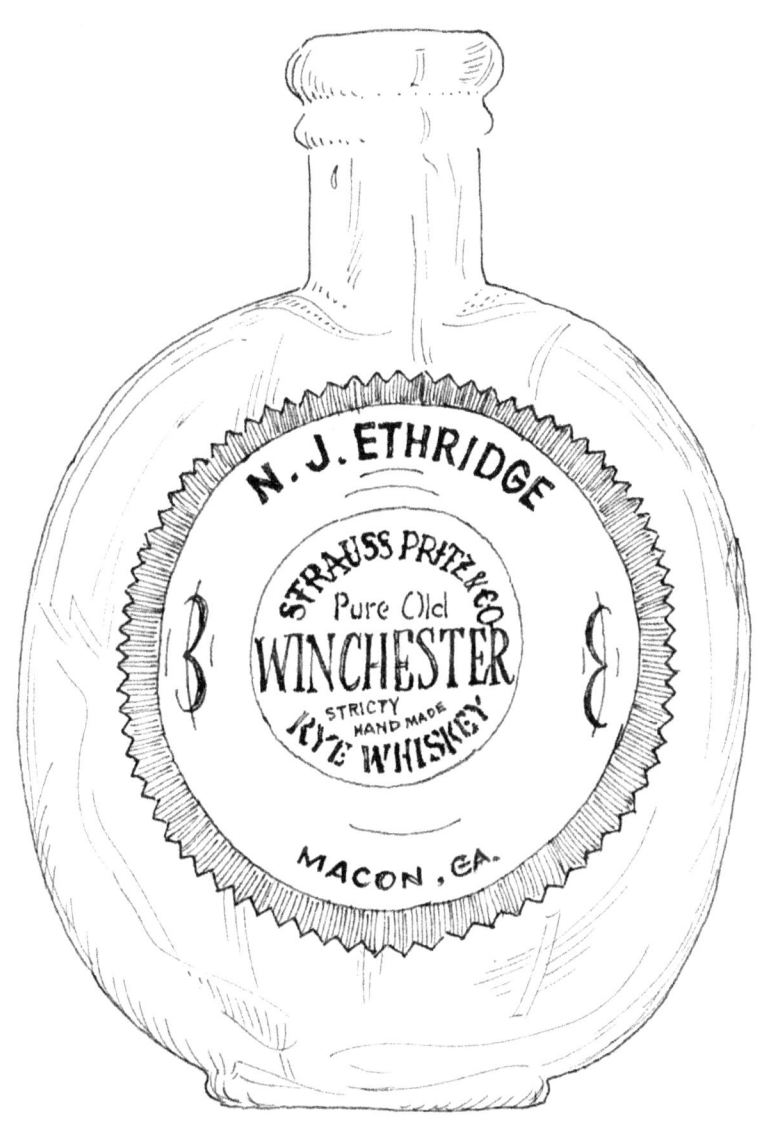

CLEAR 5½ Punkinseed
LABLE WHITE with Dark BLUE

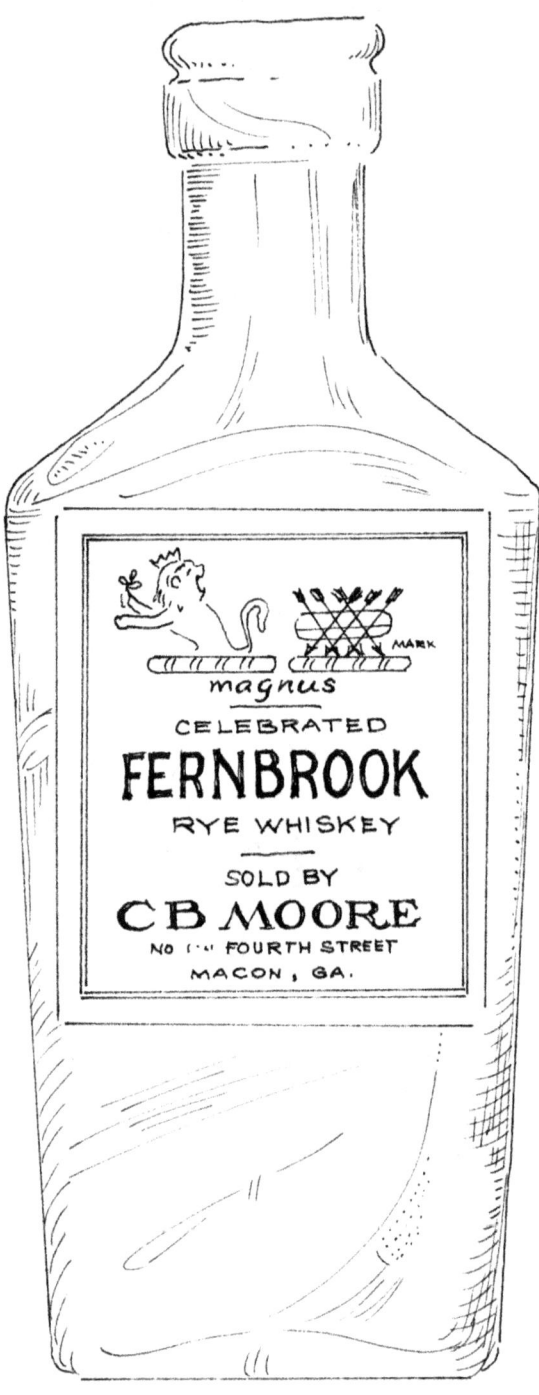

FERNBROOK

magnus

CELEBRATED

RYE WHISKEY

SOLD BY

CB MOORE

NO 1 FOURTH STREET

MACON, GA.

DESIGN PATENTED

IGCO

7ᴵⁿ. CLEAR

LABLE - BLACK, GOLD,

BLUE on WHITE

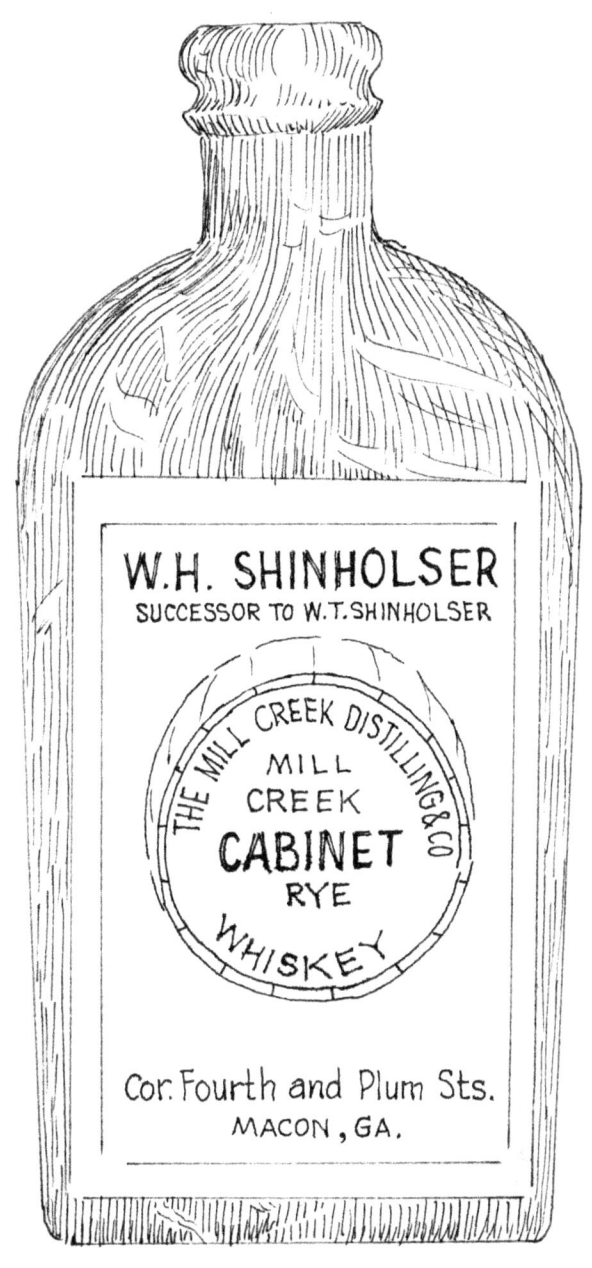

W.H. SHINHOLSER

SUCCESSOR TO W.T. SHINHOLSER

THE MILL CREEK DISTILLING & CO

MILL
CREEK
CABINET
RYE

WHISKEY

Cor. Fourth and Plum Sts.
MACON, GA.

AMBER 6⅜
SIDE STRAPS
paper lable

Also Pt. in clear 6⅛ and 7¼ clear . long neck, pt.
and inside threads, stopper wood painted black

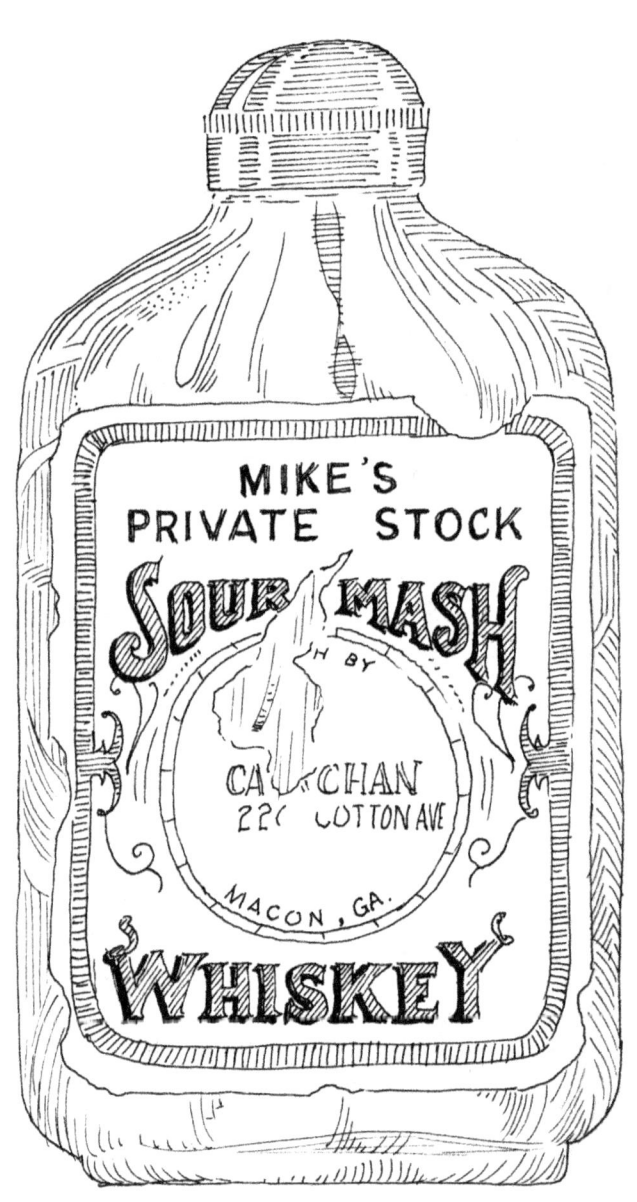

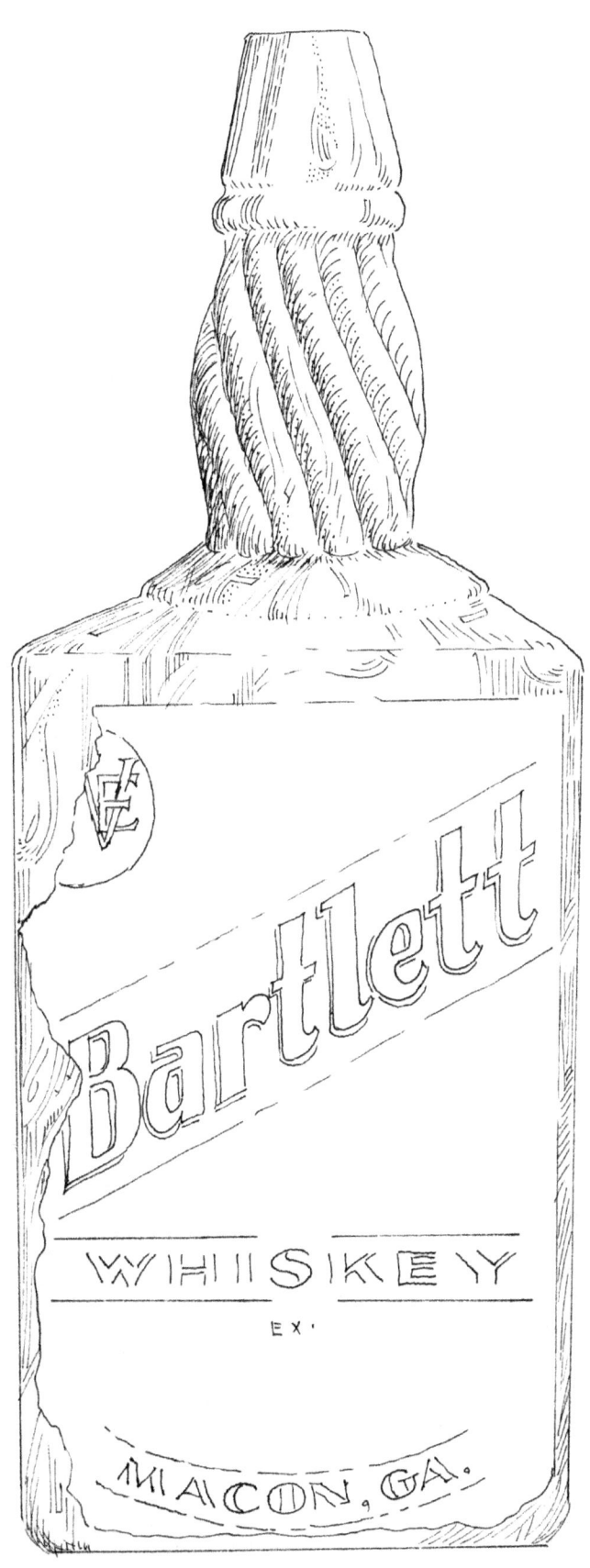

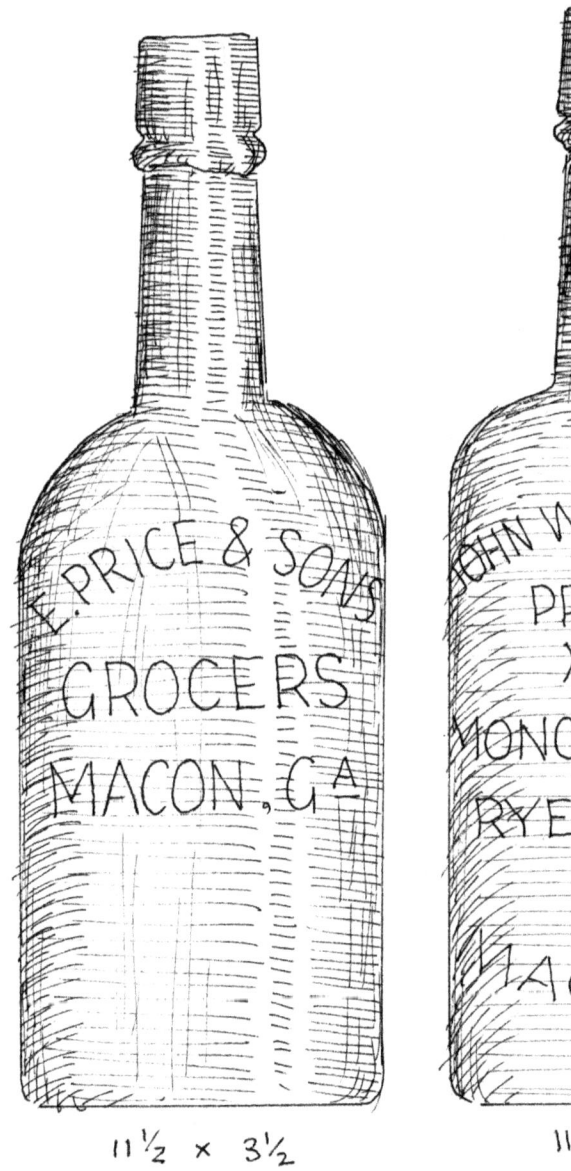

E. PRICE & SONS
GROCERS
MACON, GA

11½ × 3½
AMBER

JOHN W. O'CONNOR
PREMIUM
XXXX
MONONGAHELA
RYE WHISKEY
MACON, GA

11½ × 3½
AMBER

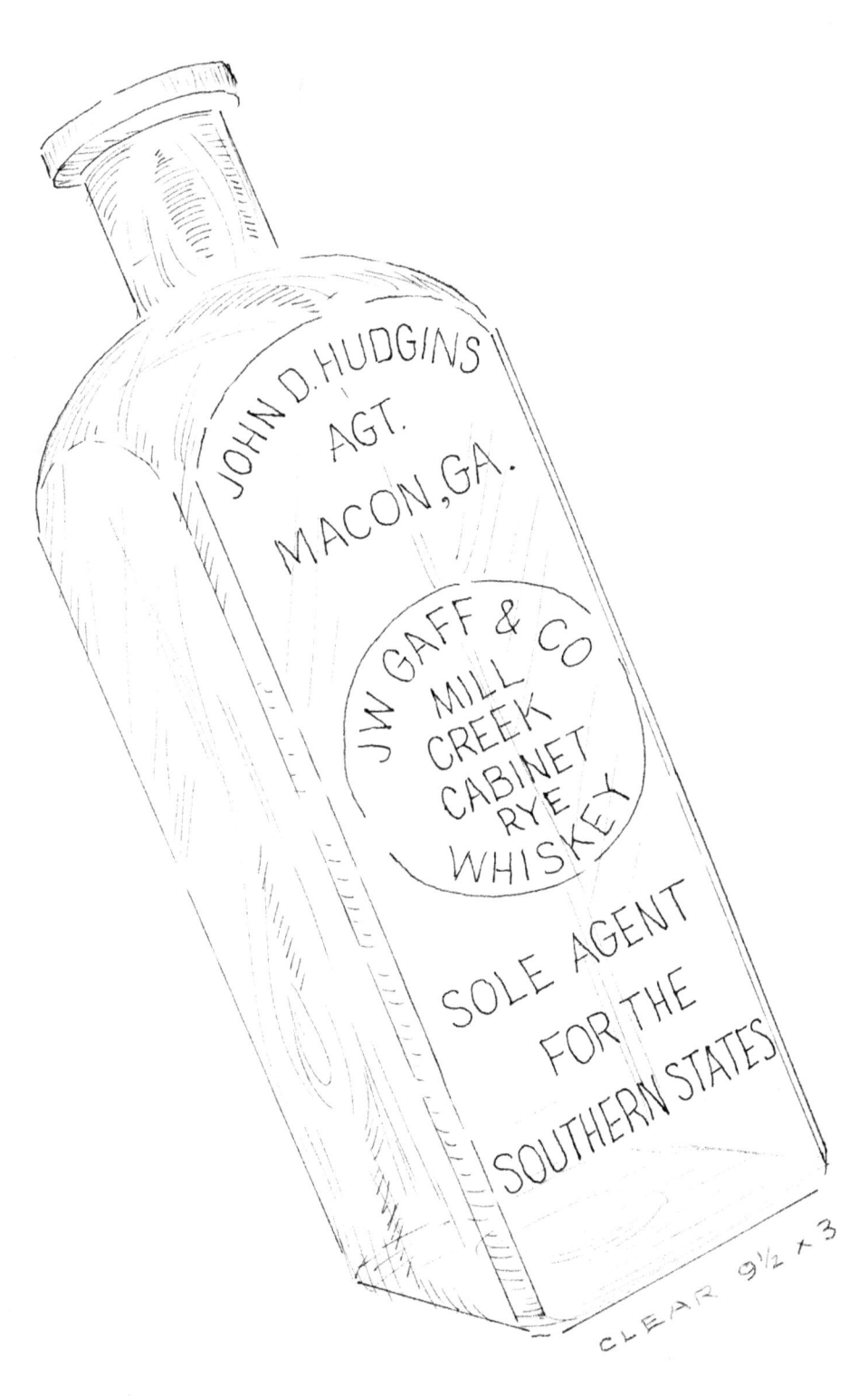

JOHN D. HUDGINS AGT. MACON, GA.

JW GAFF & CO MILL CREEK CABINET RYE WHISKEY

SOLE AGENT FOR THE SOUTHERN STATES

CLEAR 9½ x 3

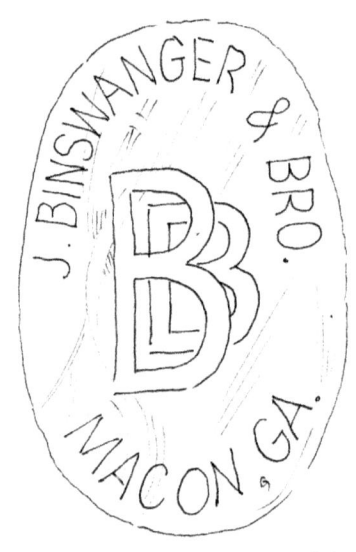

GLOB TOP, AQUA-BACK
THIS BOTTLE NOT TO BE SOLD
BOTTOM C 9½" TALL --------
5

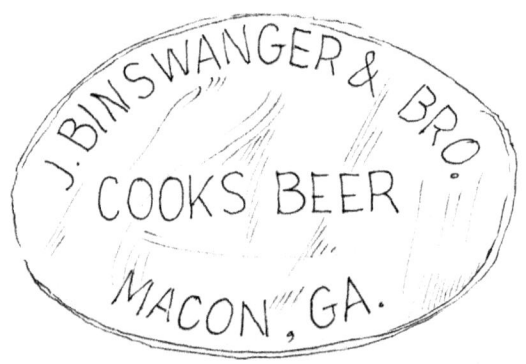

GLOB TOP - AQUA - BACK   THIS
BOTTLE NOT TO BE SOLD - 9½"

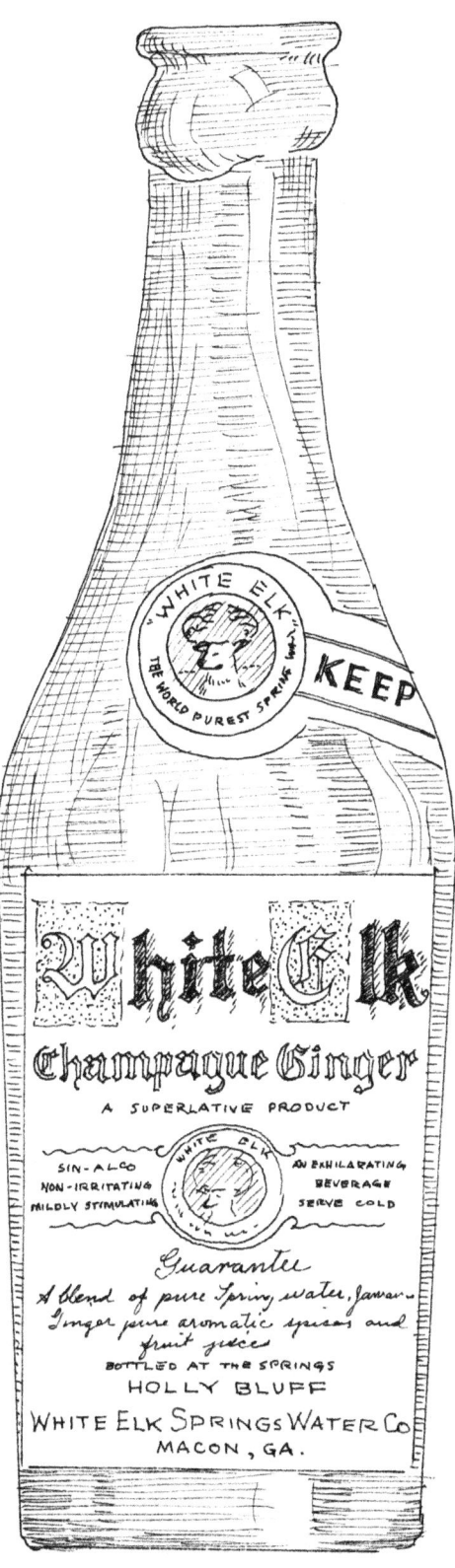

OLIVER AMBER

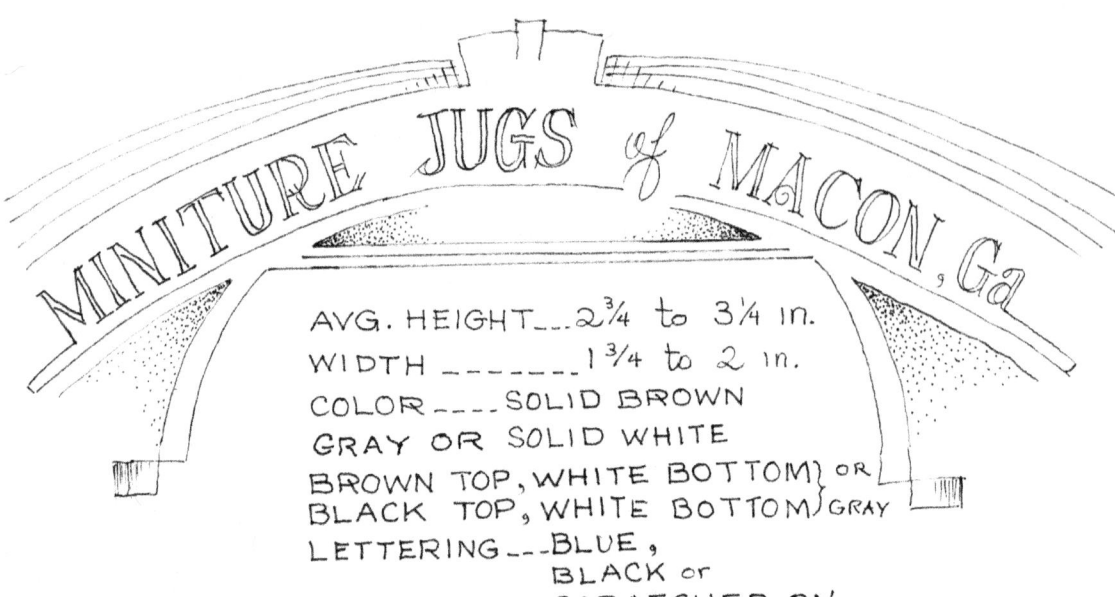

MINITURE JUGS of MACON, Ga

AVG. HEIGHT --- 2¾ to 3¼ in.
WIDTH _____ 1¾ to 2 in.
COLOR ---- SOLID BROWN
GRAY OR SOLID WHITE
BROWN TOP, WHITE BOTTOM} OR
BLACK TOP, WHITE BOTTOM} GRAY
LETTERING --- BLUE,
          BLACK or
          SCRATCHED ON

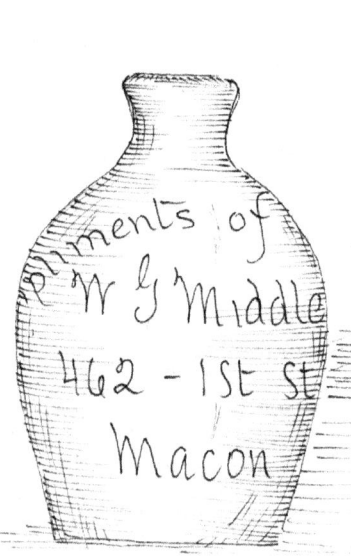

BROWN, SCRATCHED

Compliments of
W. G. Middlebrooks
462 1st. St.
Macon

W.A. MASON'S
FORT HAWKINS
CORN WHISKEY
420 POPLAR STREET
MACON, GA.

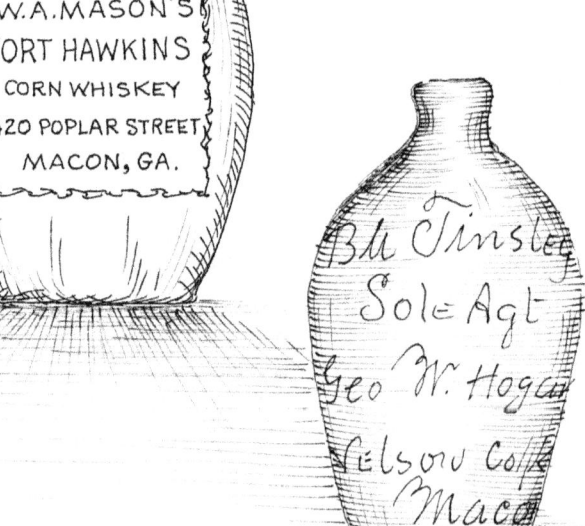

BROWN, SCRATCHED

BA Tinsley & Co.
SOLE AGT.
Geo. W. Hogan
Nelson Co. Ky.
Macon
Ga.

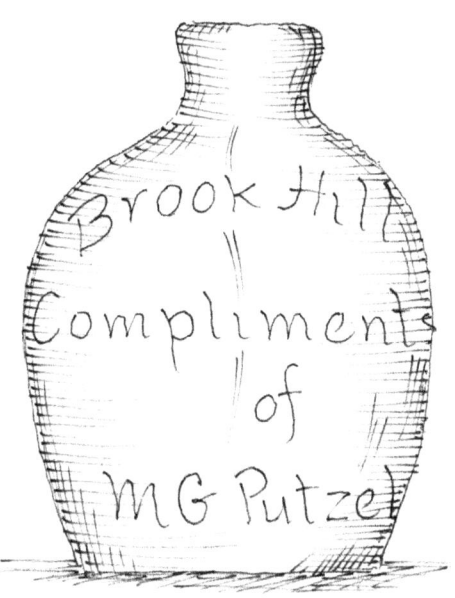

SCRATCHED , BROWN
BROOK HILL
Compliments of
M.G PUTZEL

$2\frac{7}{8}$ in high
$2\frac{1}{8}$ — wide

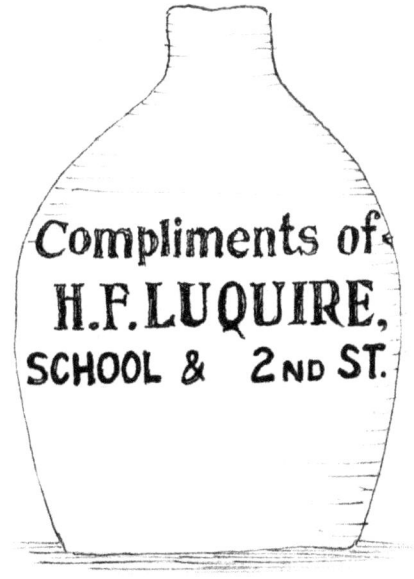

Compliments of
H.F. LUQUIRE,
SCHOOL & 2ND ST.

OFF WHITE
$2\frac{7}{8}$ High - 2 Wide
BLUE LETTERING

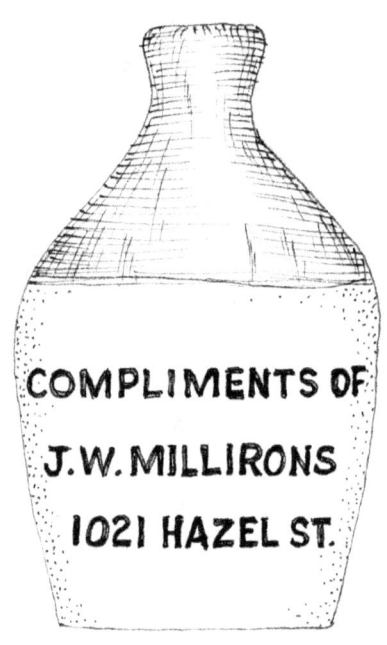

COMPLIMENTS OF

J.W. MILLIRONS

1021 HAZEL ST.

3¼ high - 2 wide
BROWN & GRAY
BLUE LETTERING

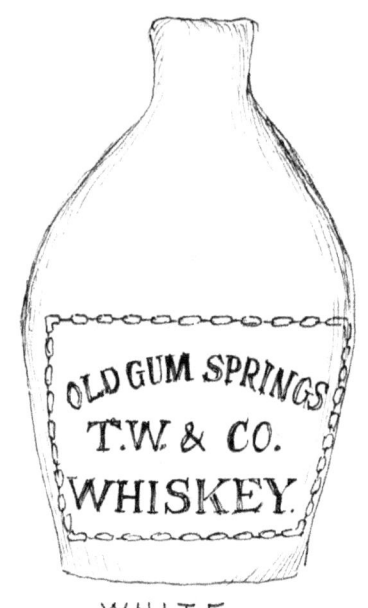

OLD GUM SPRINGS

T.W. & CO.

WHISKEY.

WHITE
BLUE LETTERING

LONG BROS. BROWN TOP, WHITE BOTTOM
W.T. WOMACK - SOLID OFF WHITE
D.F. LONG - SOLID GRAY
J.J. BROXTON - SOLID OFF WHITE
ALL BLUE LETTING ---

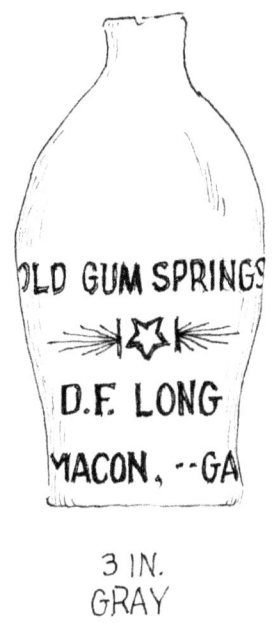

3 IN.
GRAY

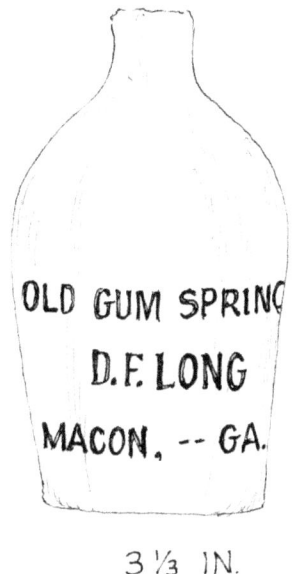

3 ⅓ IN.
OFF WHITE

W.M. ARMSTRONG & Co. 1602 4th St off White, Blue letters

J.W. Amason - Nelson Co. Macon, Ga. Gray-Blue block letters same, with Nelson Co. Whiskey - Gray bottom Brown top same as top - smaller letters, off white color, smaller

C.F. Collier -Compliments of C.F. Collier & Bro. 216 Cotton Ave. Gray -Blue lettering

W.O. Fretwell - Compliments of W.O. Fretwell 1120 Elm St. Gray bottom - Brown top

J.S. Frink - Compliments of J.S. Frink 410 Mulbery St off white. misspelling the street name Mulberry

R.C. Keen Compliments of R.C. Keen 212 Cotton Ave. off white color.

H.F. Luquire -Compliments of H.F. Luquire School & 2ND St. light gray School St. is now Bowden St.

W.M. Marshall- Compliments of W.M. Marshall- Columbus Rd. Brown top Gray bottom.

Scratched, with dark brown glaze

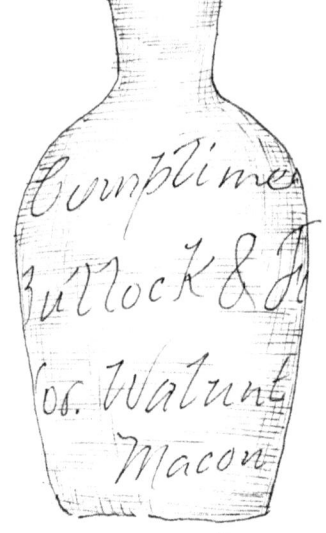 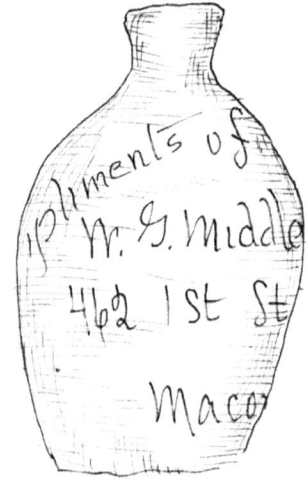 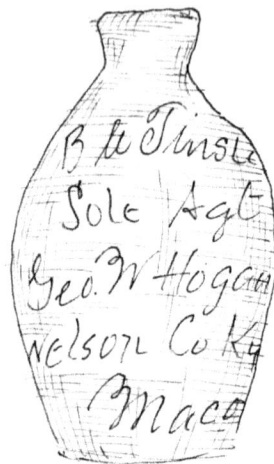

Compliments of
Bullock & Frink   Cor
Walnut & New St.
Macon, Ga. 3½

Compliments of
W.G. Middlebrooks
462 1st St.
Macon, Ga.   3

B.A. Tinsley & Co.
Sole Agt. Geo W. Hogan
Nelson Co. Ky.
Macon, Ga.   2⅞

J.F. May - Compliments of J.F. May 228 W Oglethorpe Ave.
off white

J.W. Millirons - Compliments of J.W. Millirons 1021 Hazel St.
dark gray bottom - brown top.

J.S. Mims - Compliments of J.S. Mims - Vineville Branch. OFF WHITE

N.L. Parr - Compliments of N.L. Parr - 271 Ocmulgee St.
off white bottom, brown top.

W.H. Reynolds - Compliments of W.H. Reynolds 312 3RD
St. off white -

O.R. Thorpe - Compliments of O.R. Thorpe Macon, Ga.
off white bottom, brown top -

W.T. Shinholster & Ray Pure Vingar Macon. Ga. Stratched
B.W. GLOVER Compliments of 872 Hazel - Macon, Ga Scratched
Old Gum Springs Whiskey 2¾ - 1¾ scratched. Slick brown

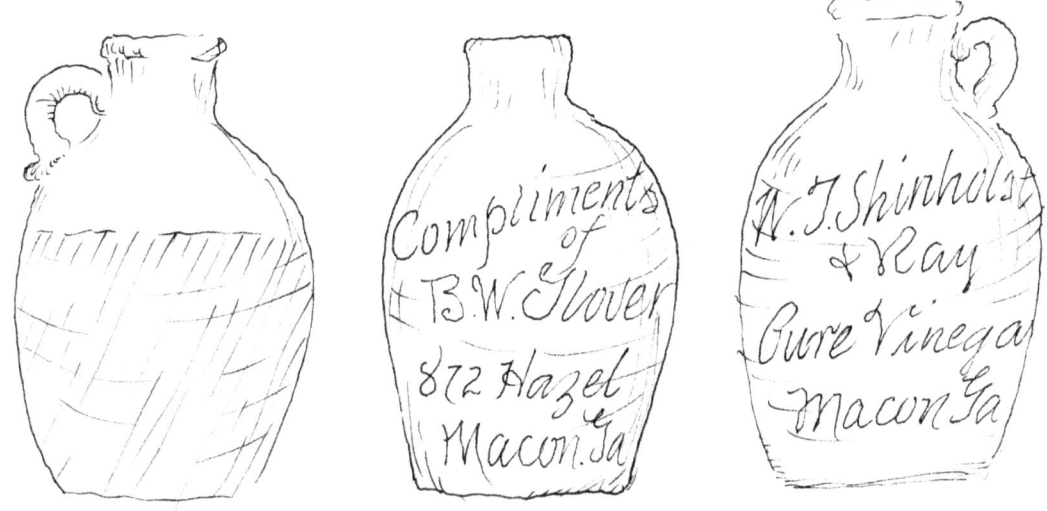

ED. DEVLIN Compliments of Victoria Rye Whiskey BROWN & WHITE BLUE LETTERS

N.J. ETHRIDGE _ Winchester Rye   Brown & White

Mrs. O.L. COOK Compliments of _ Macon, Ga. Brown & White

F. DISROOM Compliments of _ 117 Spring St Brown & White

W.H CASTELLO Compliments South Macon, Ga LITE BROWN & WHITE

J. T. & C.P. LONG _ Old Gum Springs Macon, Ga. White & off White

MURPHY & CASSIDY. Compliments of. Victoria Rye Whiskey Bro. & White

W.B. BULLOCK & Co. Compliments of _ Macon, Ga.

HAL WALTERS. Sole agts. Nelson Co. Ky. Whiskey. Fleetwood & Co. BROWN scratched

WALKER & LITTLE Co. Compliments of _ Slick dark br. scratched

these last two did not have MACON on them.

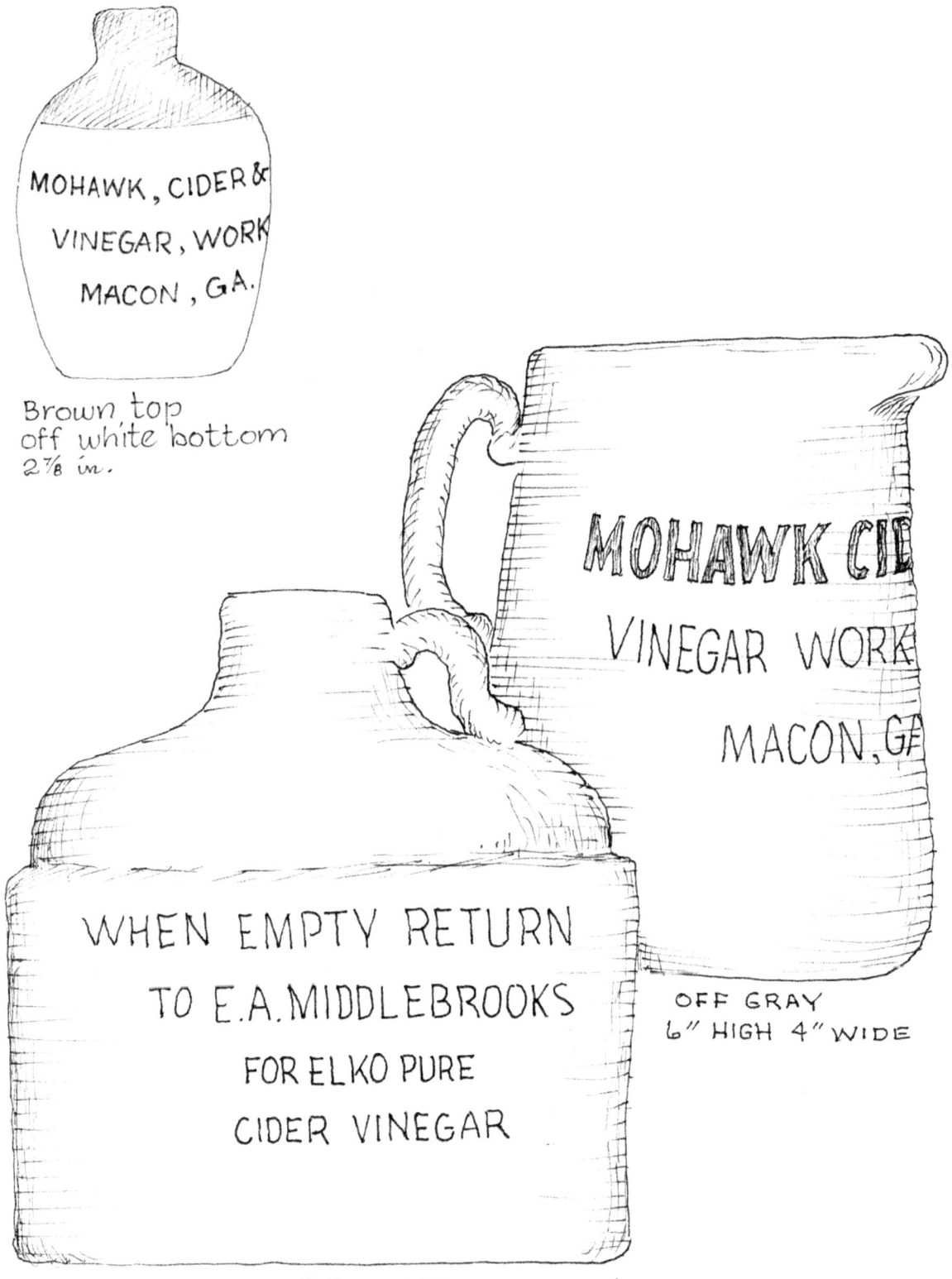

MOHAWK , CIDER &
VINEGAR , WORK
MACON , GA.

Brown top
off white bottom
2⅞ in.

MOHAWK CIE
VINEGAR WORK
MACON, GA

WHEN EMPTY RETURN
TO E.A. MIDDLEBROOKS
FOR ELKO PURE
CIDER VINEGAR

OFF GRAY
6" HIGH 4" WIDE

7" X 11" high Blue letters, OFF white

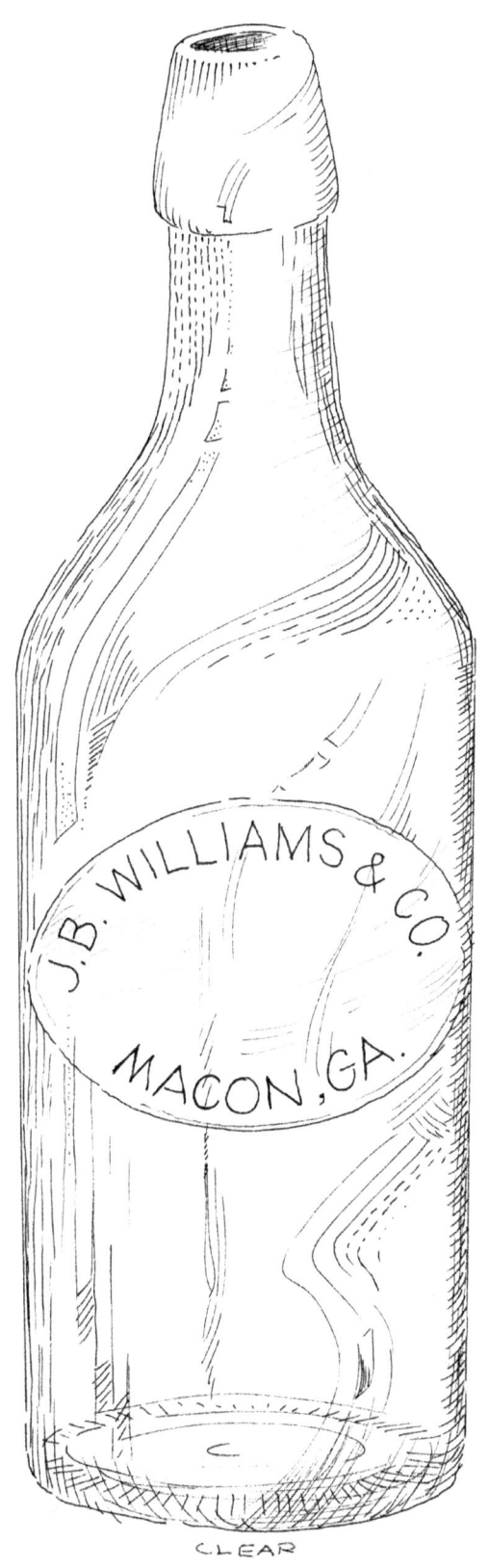

CLEAR

Reverse   THIS BOTTLE NOT TO BE SOLD

ALSO AQUA _

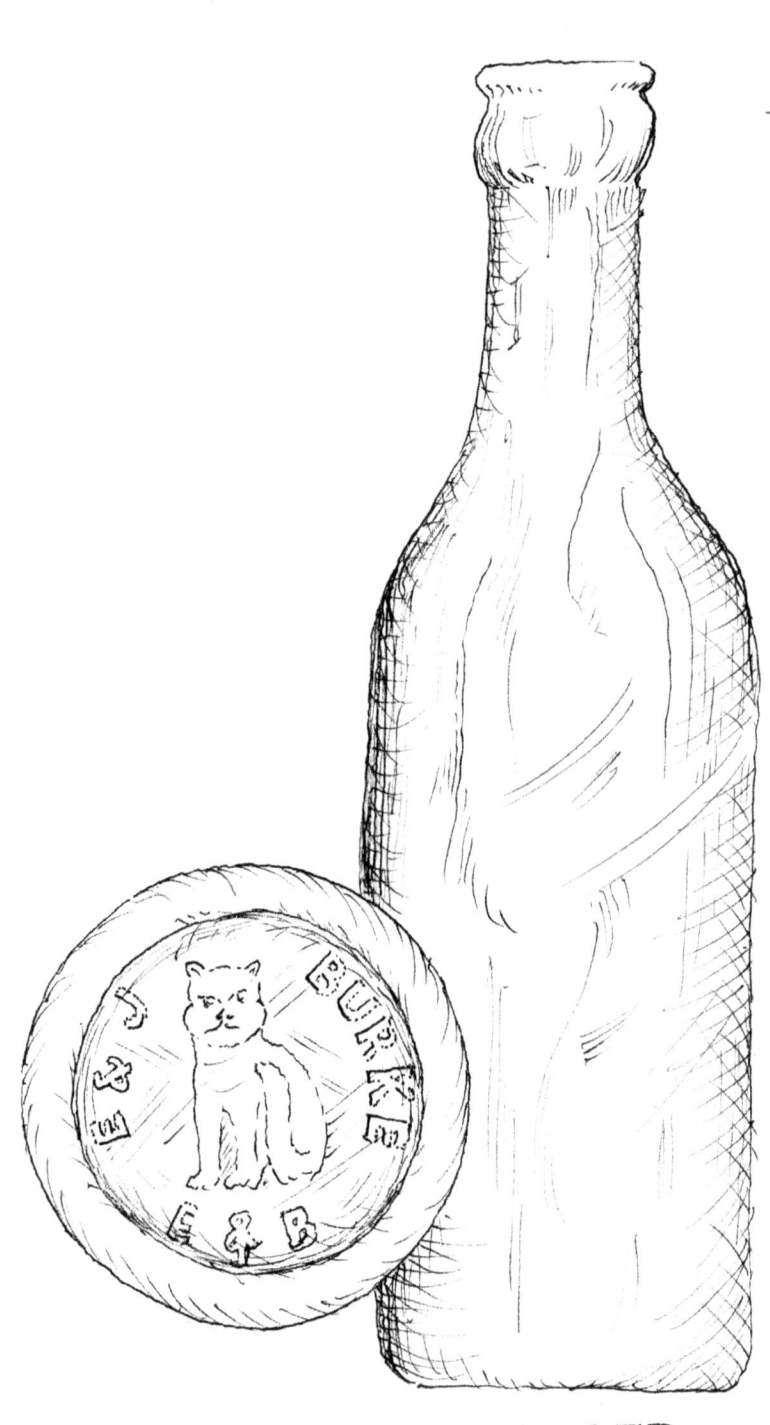

AMBER

E.J. BURKE ALSO HAD A HUTCHERSON BOTTLE Marked MACON, GA.

N.M. BLOCK
STEAM BEER
B
BOTTLING WORKS

CROWN TOP, AQUA, BACK
THIS BOTTLE NOT TO BE SOLD
9 3/8"

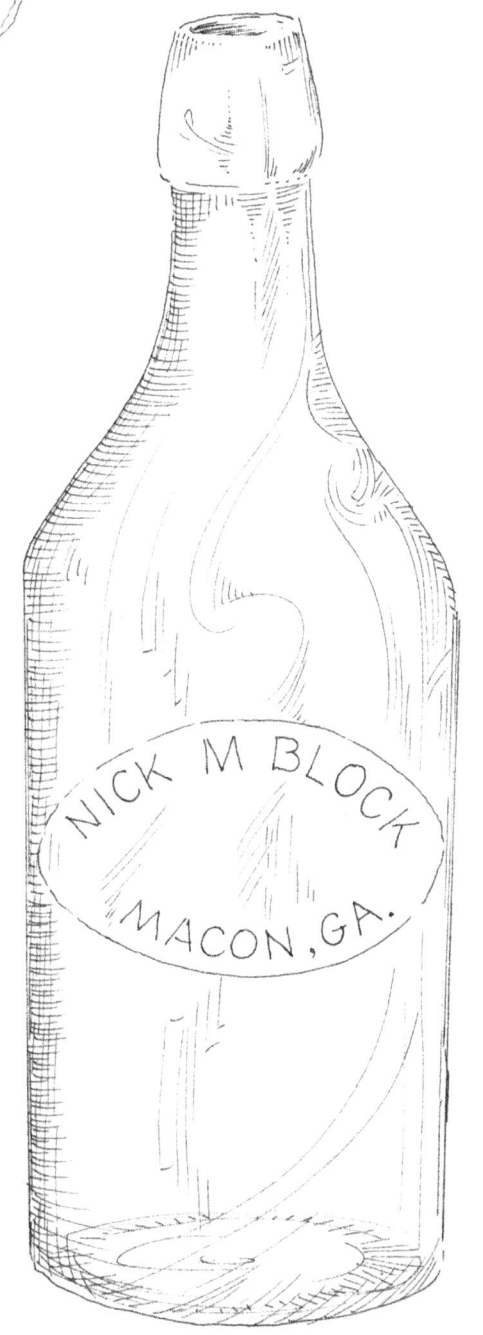

NICK M BLOCK
MACON, GA.

REVERSE THIS BOTTLE NOT TO BE SOLD
ALSO GLOB TOP WITH EMBOSSING IN ROUND
CIRCLE AQUA & BROWN

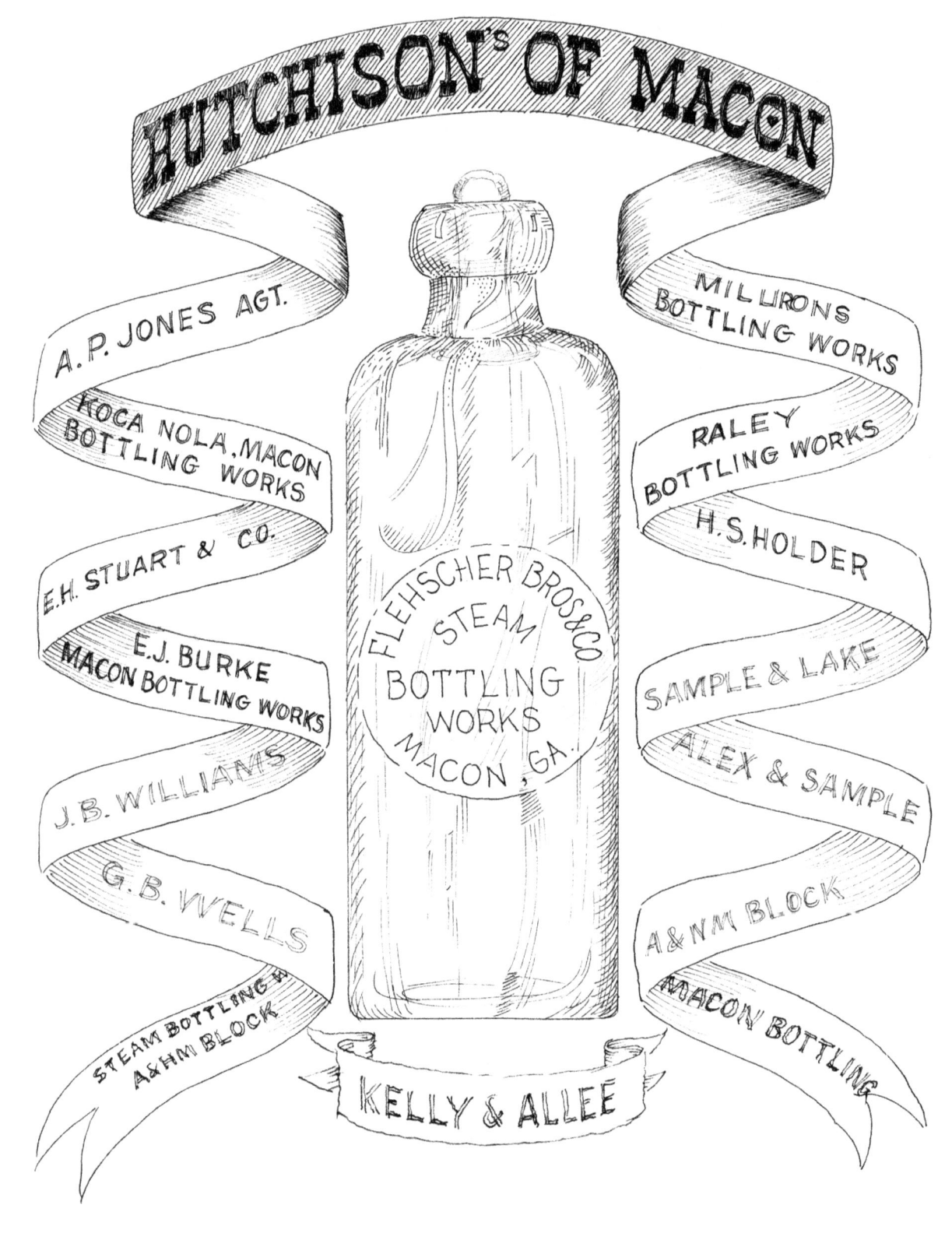

A & N.M. BLOCK Consolidated Steam bottling works Macon Ga. This bottle not to be Sold. Aqua.

E.J. BURKE Macon Bottling works 4 Styles - clear and aqua - one with *Koca Nola*

FLEISCHER BROS & CO Works (steam) Macon Ga. Aqua

H.S. HOLDER Macon, Ga Aqua This bottle never sold

AP JONES AGT. Macon, Ga - Aqua

RALEY BOTTLING WORKS - Macon - Clear, 2 Styles

SAMPLE & LAKE Macon Ga.

E.H. STUART & CO Macon Ga 4 Styles

G.B. WELLS Macon Ga

J.B. WILLIAMS Macon - Aqua - round slug plate

ALEX SAMPLE

KELLY & ALLEE

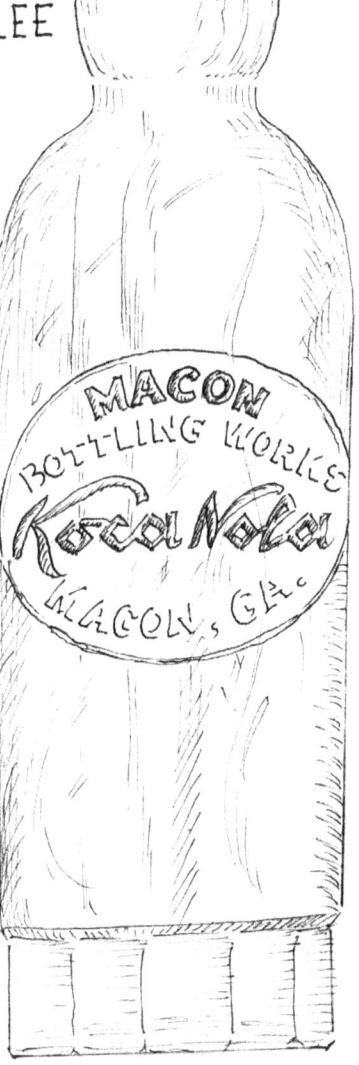

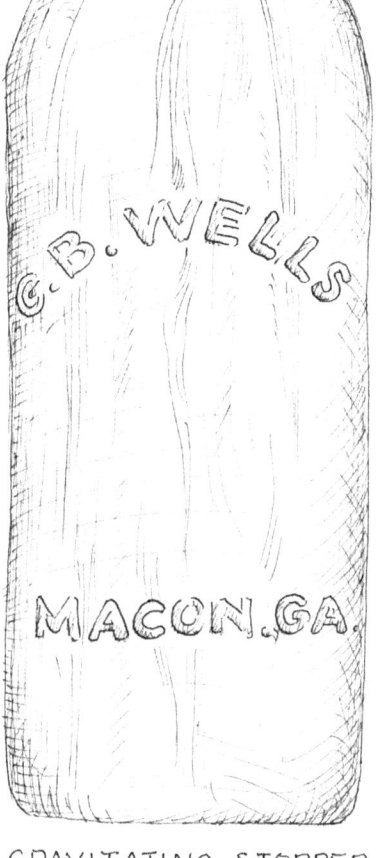

GRAVITATING STOPPER
MADE BY JOHN MATTHEWS
NEW YORK - PAT OCT 11 1884
· on the bottom — AQUA

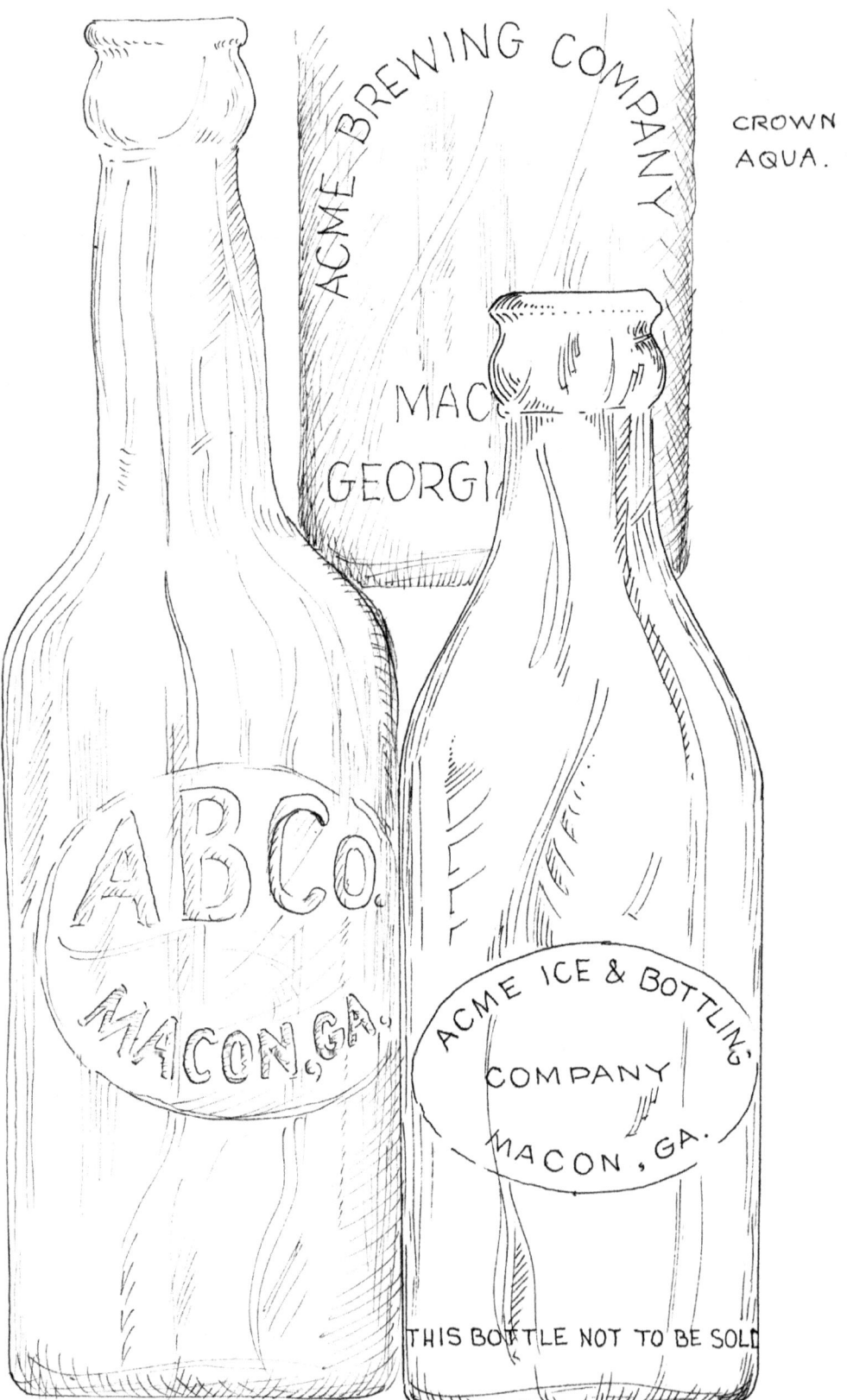

ACME BREWING COMPANY

MAC...
GEORGI...

CROWN TOP
AQUA. 9⅜"

ABCo.
MACON, GA.

ACME ICE & BOTTLING
COMPANY
MACON, GA.

THIS BOTTLE NOT TO BE SOLD

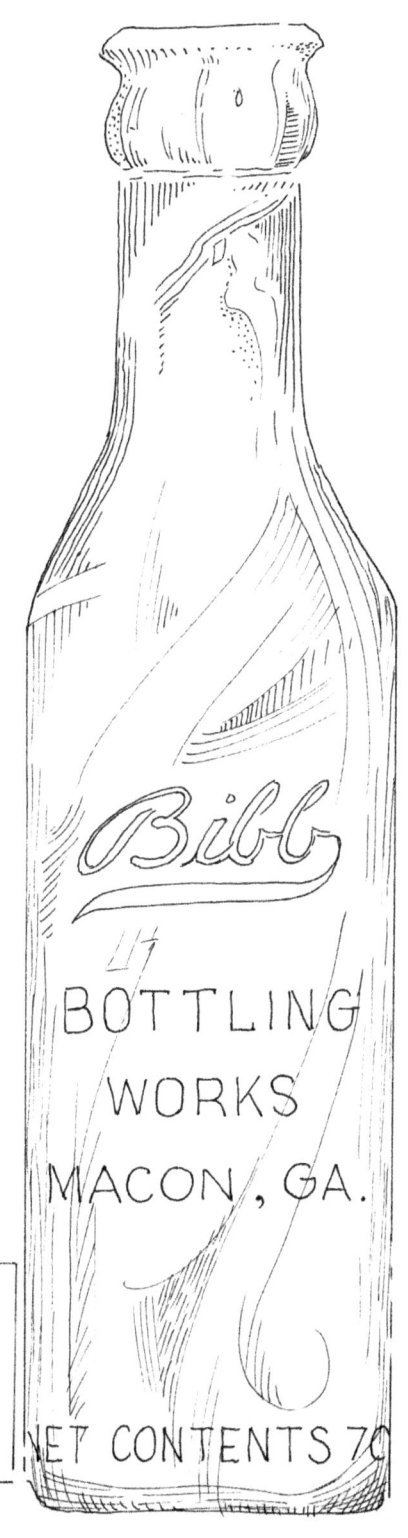

Bibb Bottling Works

MACON , GA.

CLEAR - SLUG PLATE ¾" FROM
BOTTOM

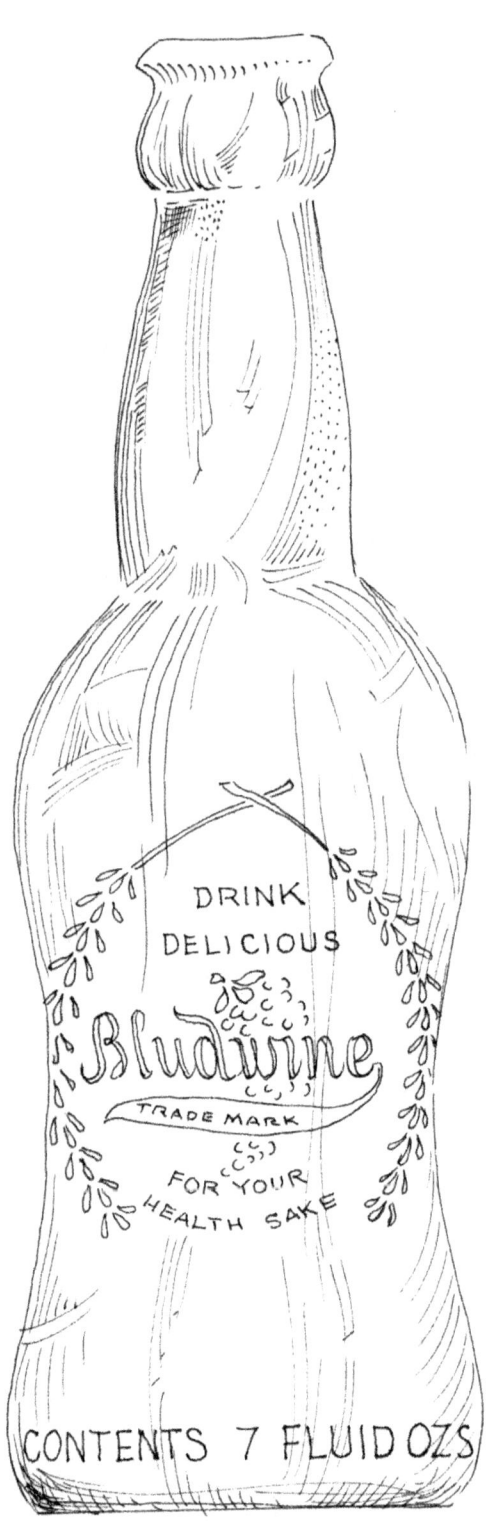

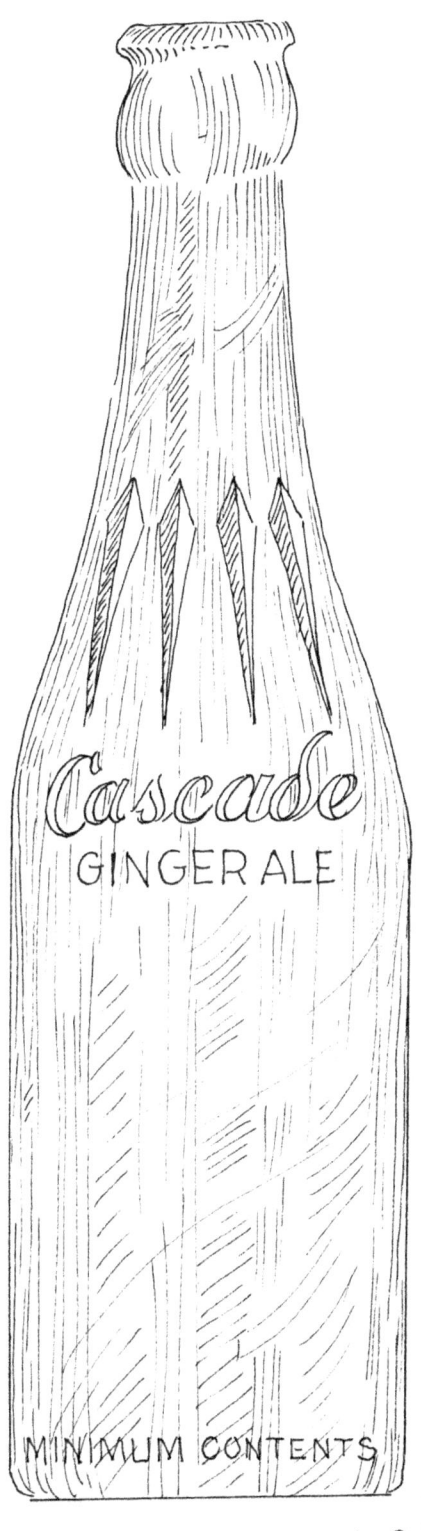

Cascade
GINGER ALE

MINIMUM CONTENTS

BOTTOM - MACON , GA.
7up Green
BACK 7 FLUID OZS
MACHINE MADE

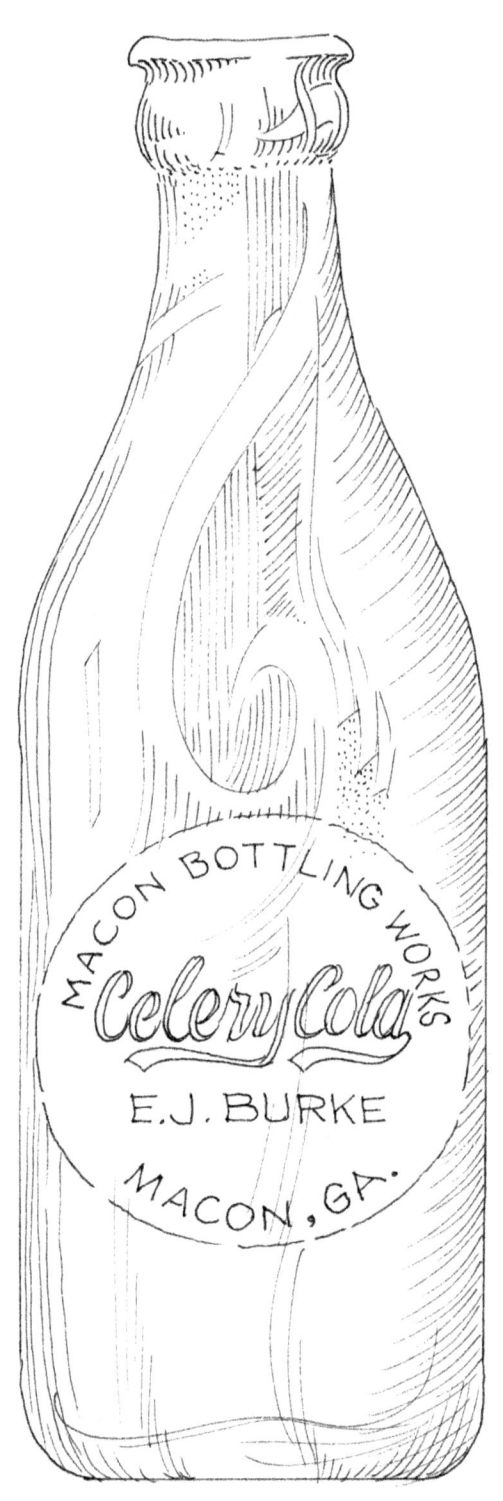

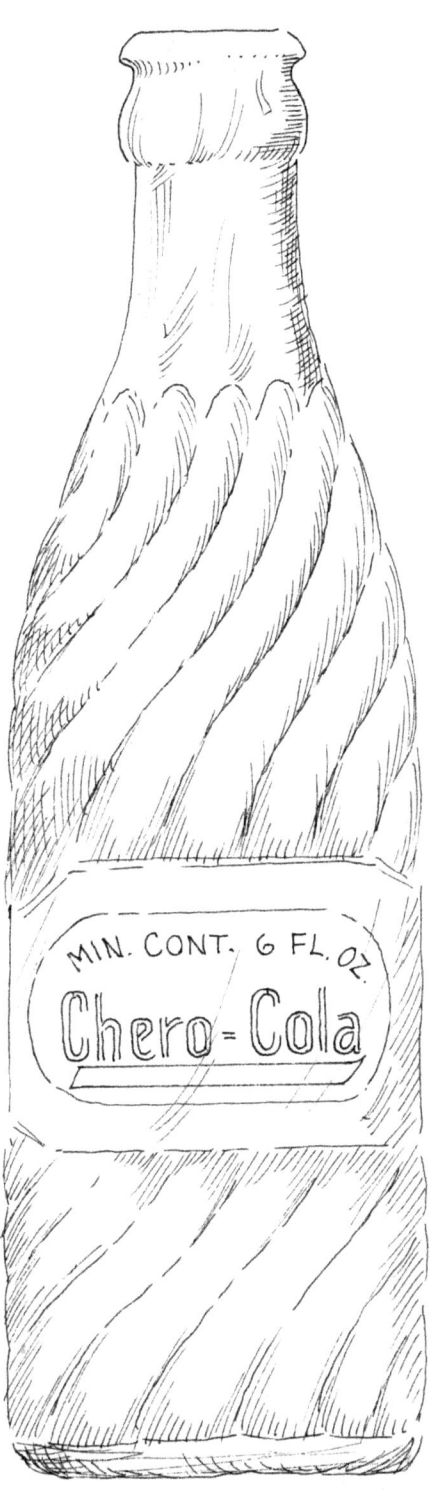

MIN. CONT. 6 FL. OZ.

Chero - Cola

BACK MACON GA - SLUG
PLATE - BOTTOM - PAT
PENDING - MACHINE MADE

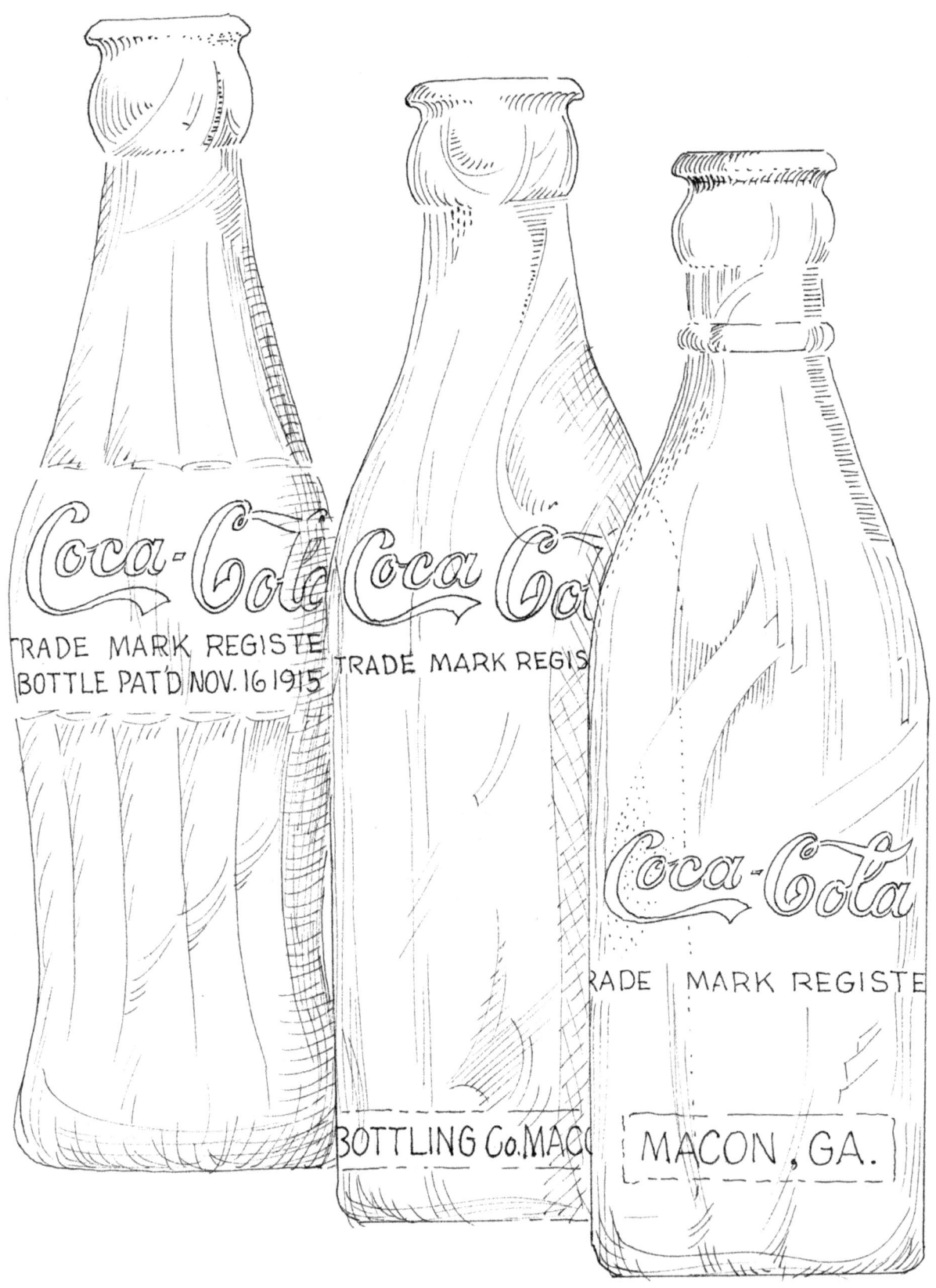

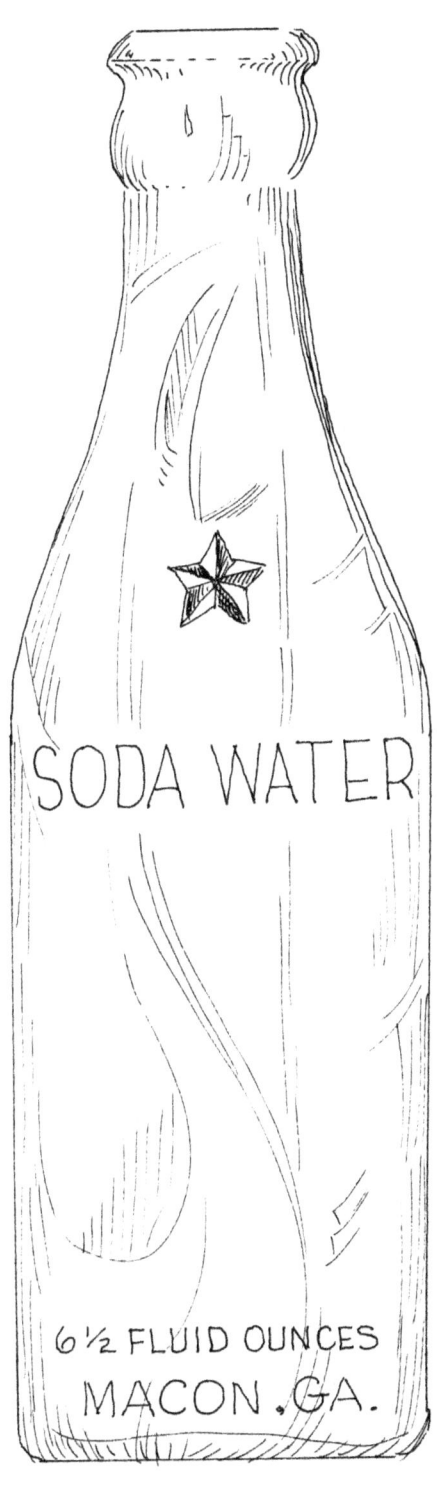

SODA WATER

6 ½ FLUID OUNCES

MACON . GA .

REVERSE _ SODA WATER + STAR-
PROPERTY OF COKE COCA
BOTTLING CO. HAS A STAR ON
BOTTOM

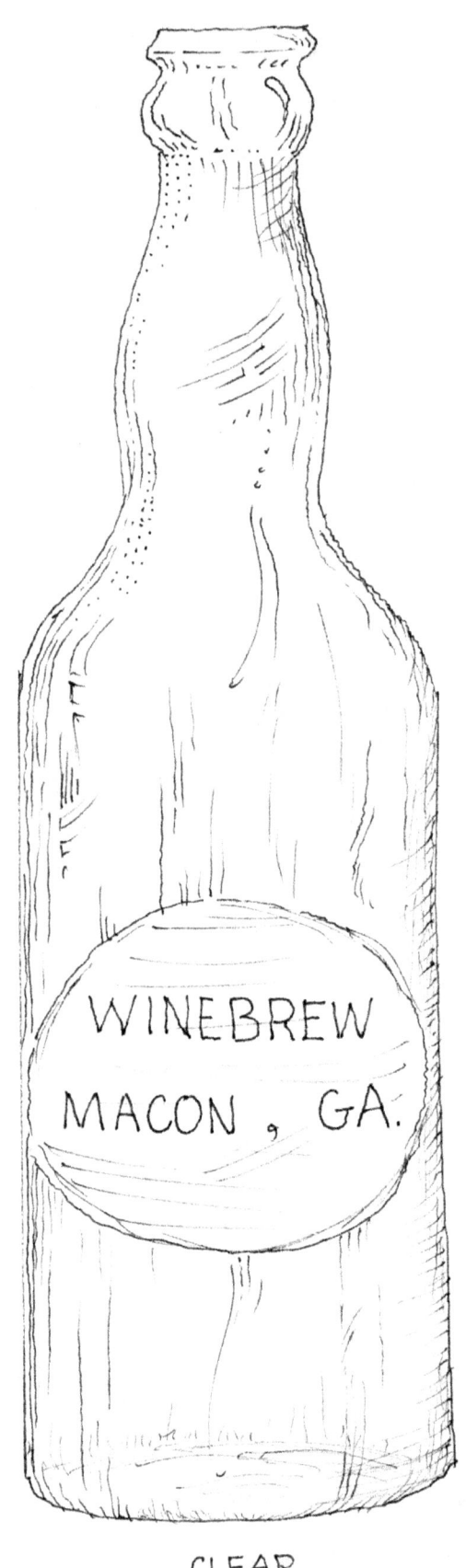

CLEAR

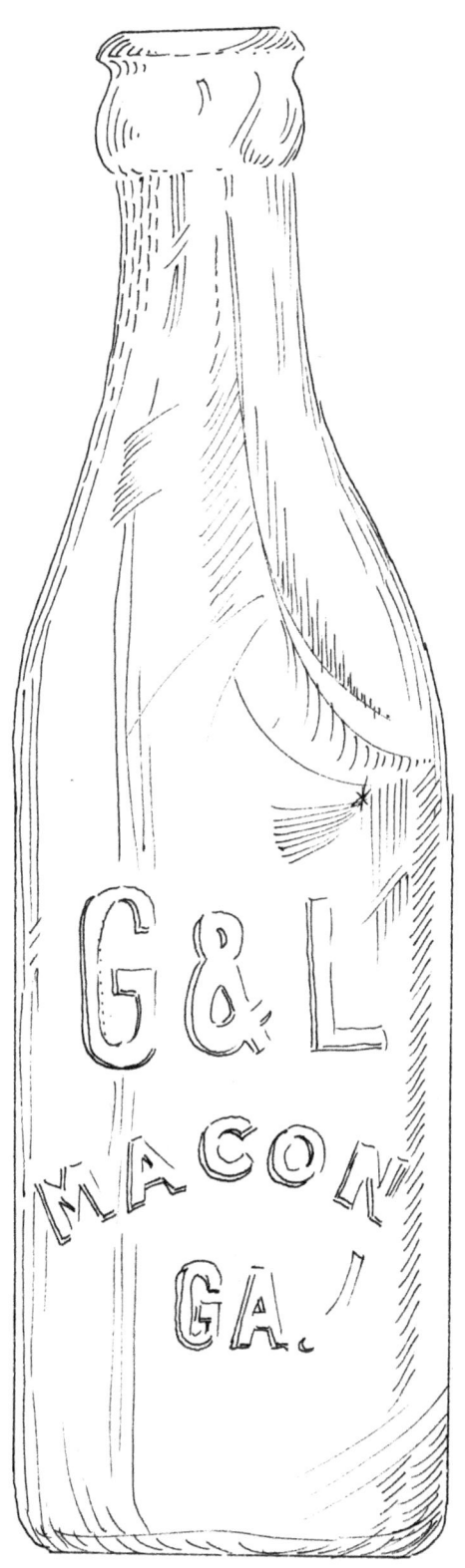
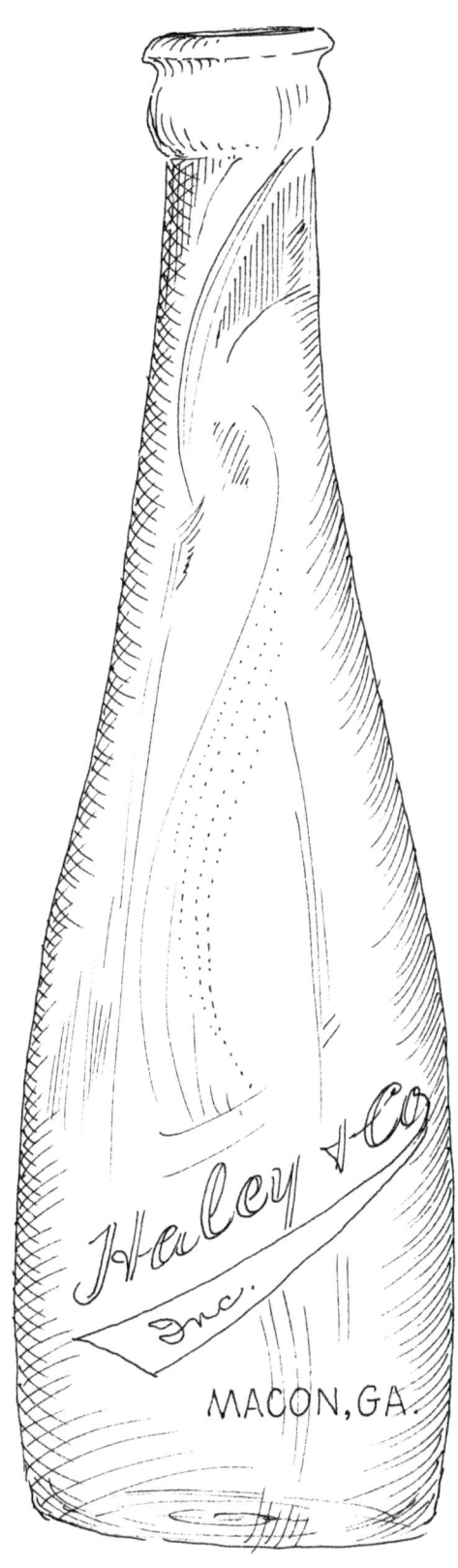

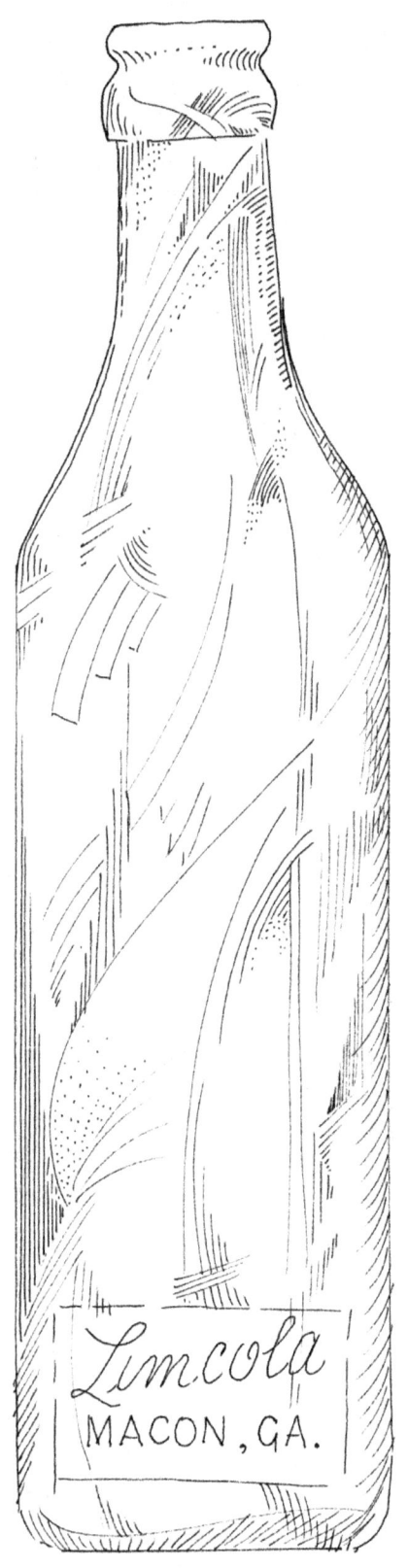

Limcola
MACON, GA.

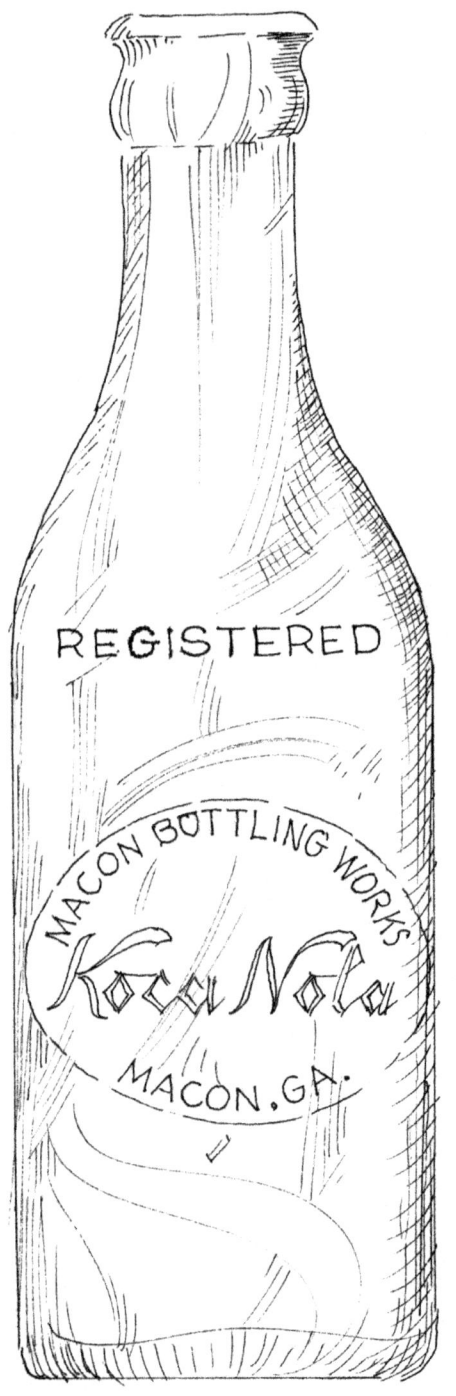

REGISTERED

MACON BOTTLING WORKS
Koca Nola
MACON, GA.

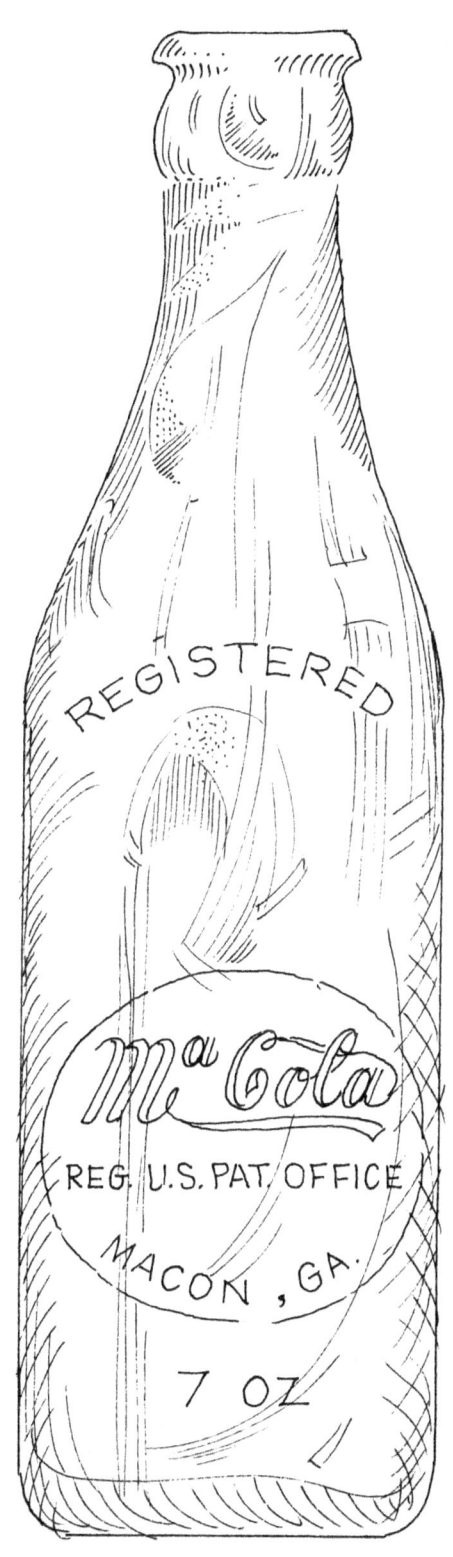

REVERSE-THIS BOTTLE NOT
TO BE SOLD

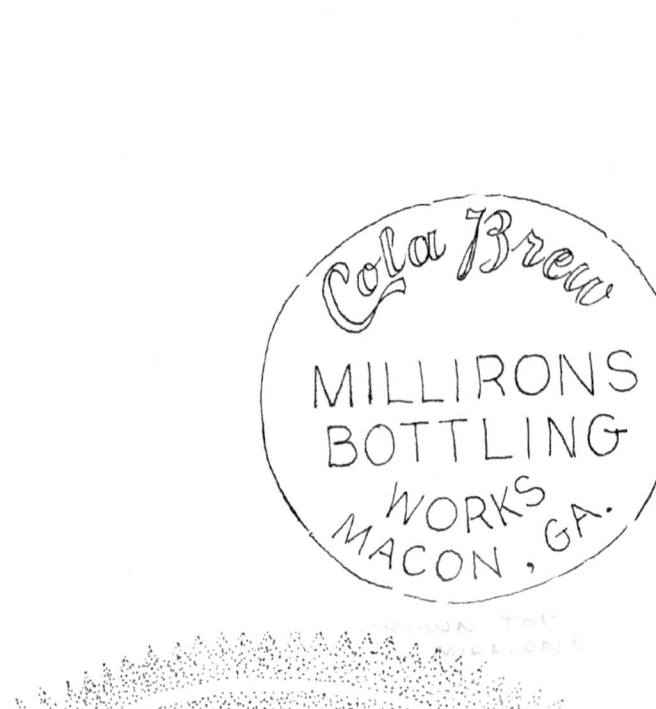

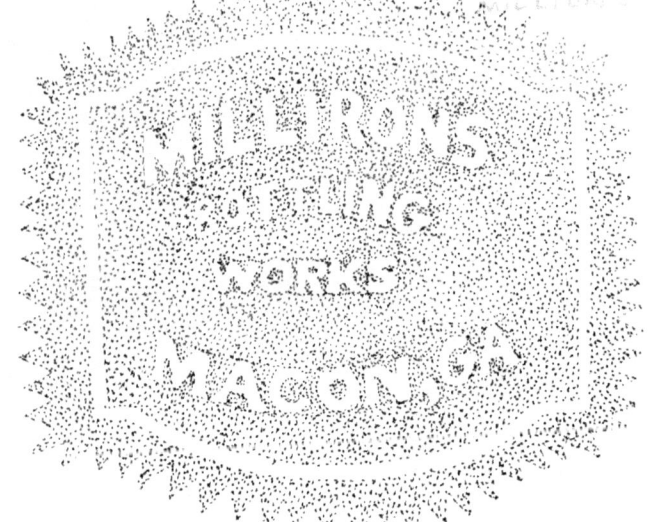

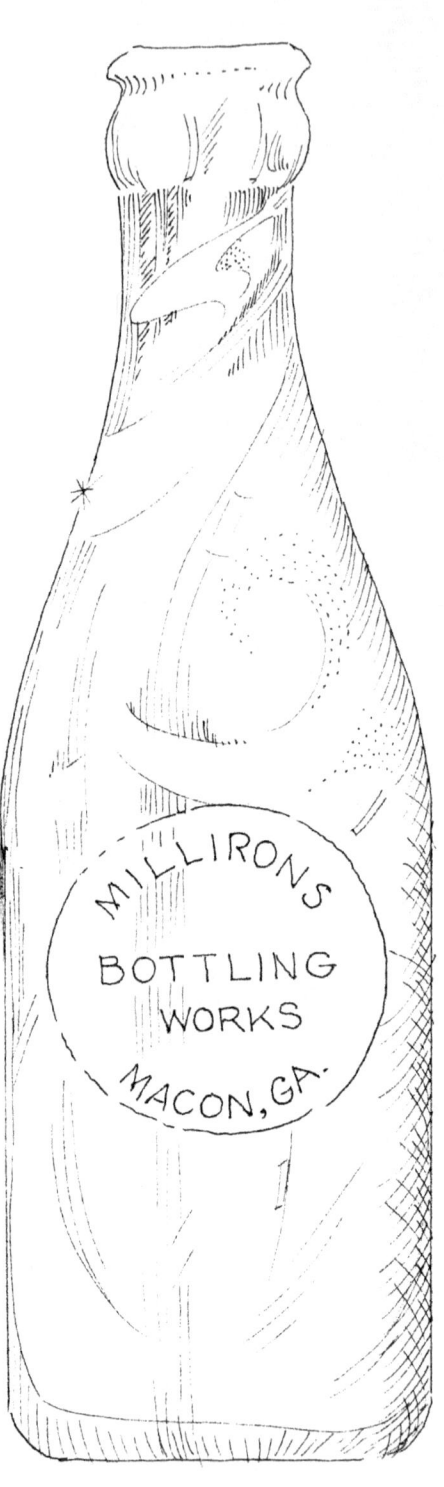

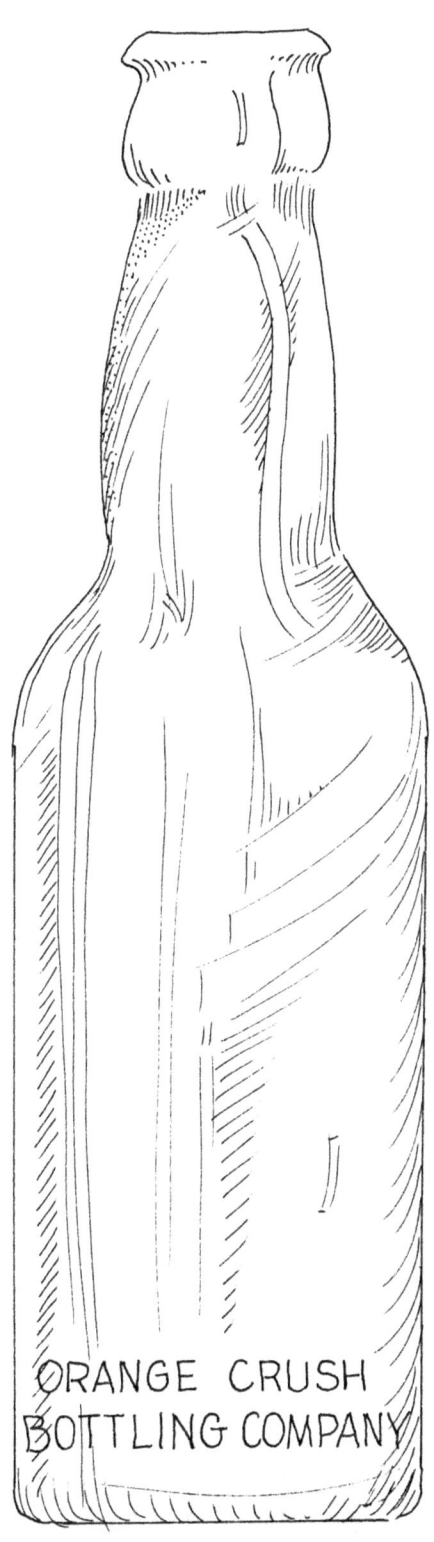

ORANGE CRUSH
BOTTLING COMPANY

BACK - MACON. GA.
CONTENTS 6 FLU. OZS.

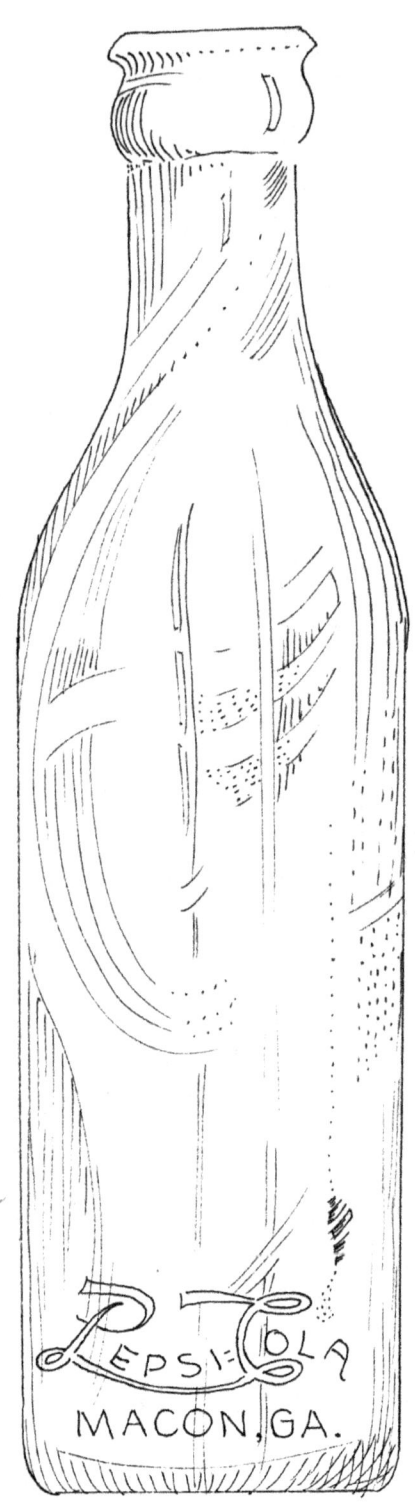

Pepsi-Cola
MACON, GA.

BACK - REGISTERED
8½ & 9 in. SIZES - ALSO HAS
MONERGRAM & BOTTLING CO.
MACON - CONTENT 6 FL. OZ
REGISTERED

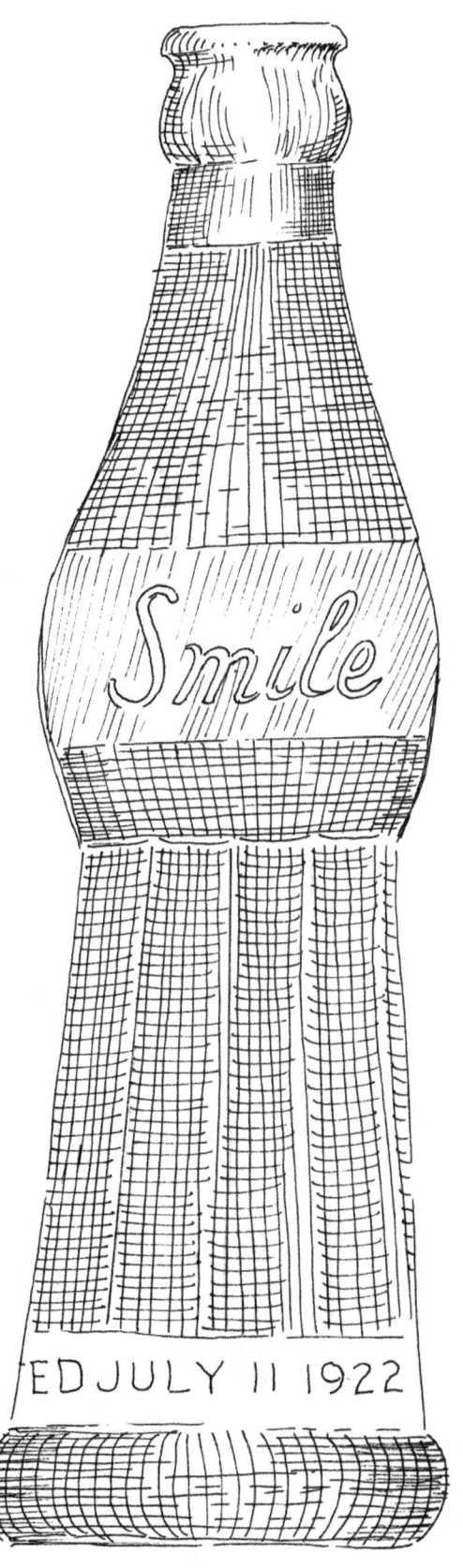

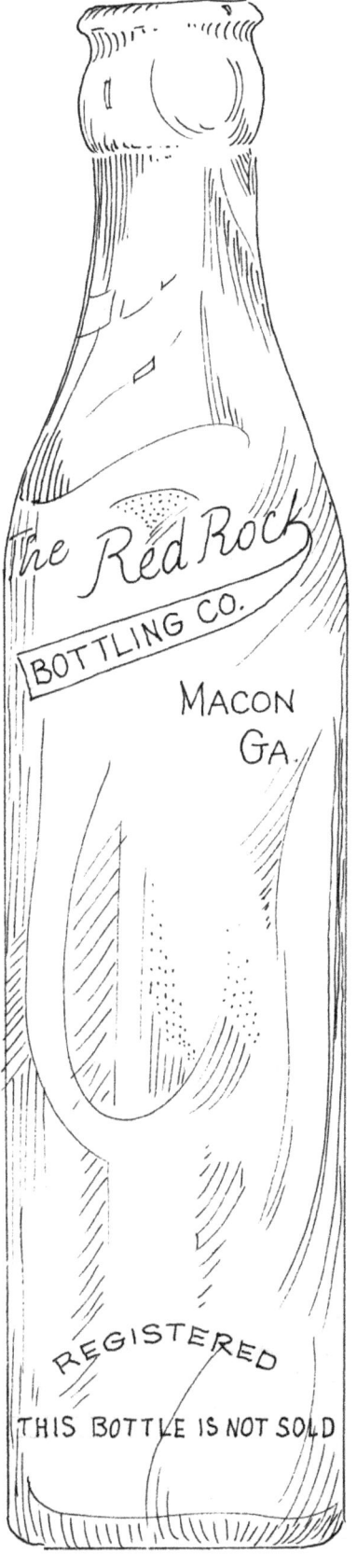

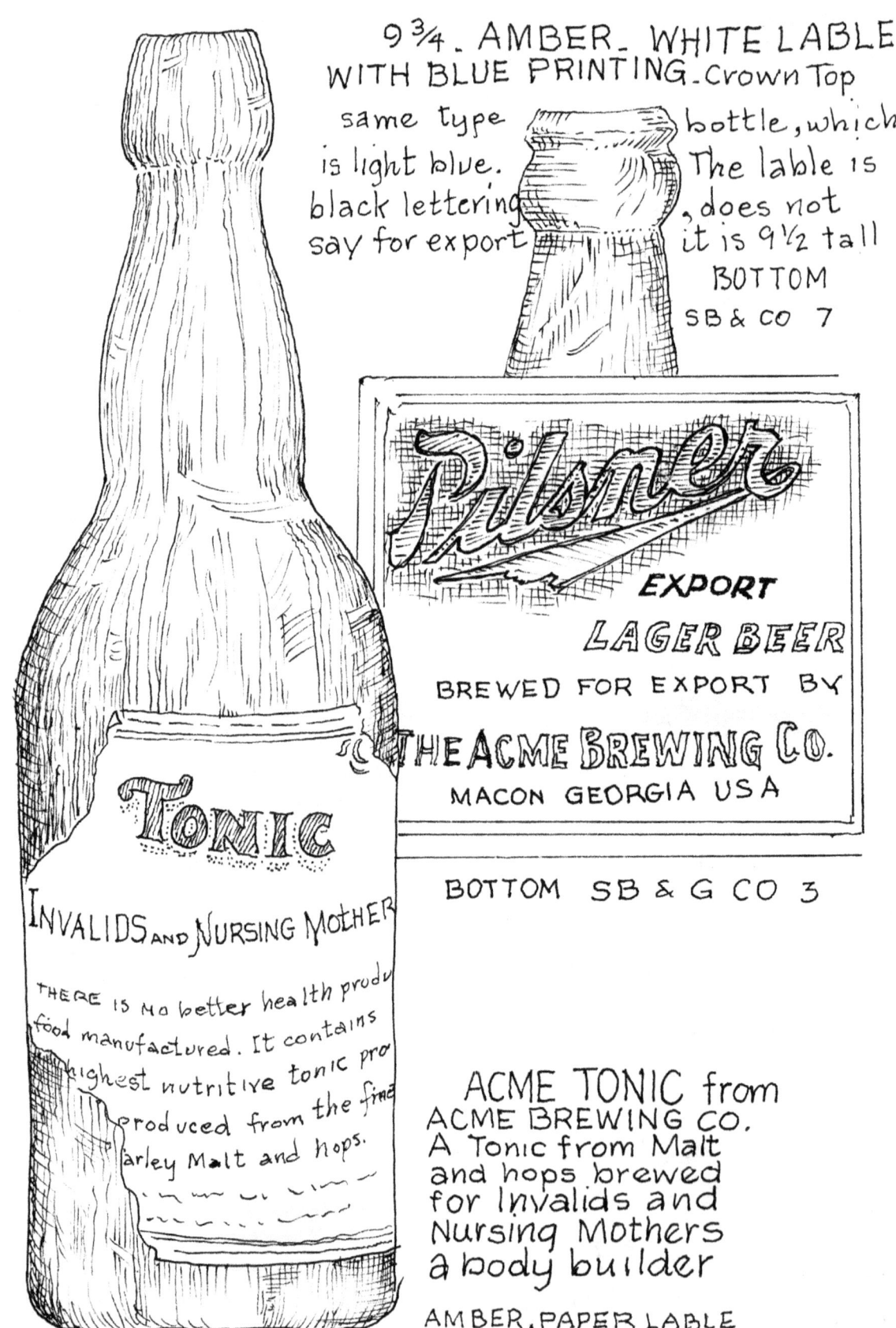

9¾ _ AMBER _ WHITE LABLE WITH BLUE PRINTING _ Crown Top

same type is light blue. black lettering say for export

bottle, which The lable is , does not it is 9½ tall BOTTOM SB & CO 7

Pilsner

EXPORT

LAGER BEER

BREWED FOR EXPORT BY

THE ACME BREWING CO.

MACON GEORGIA USA

BOTTOM SB & G CO 3

Tonic

INVALIDS AND NURSING MOTHER

THERE IS No better health produ food manufactured. It contains highest nutritive tonic pro produced from the fine arley Malt and hops.

ACME TONIC from ACME BREWING CO. A Tonic from Malt and hops brewed for Invalids and Nursing Mothers a body builder

AMBER, PAPER LABLE

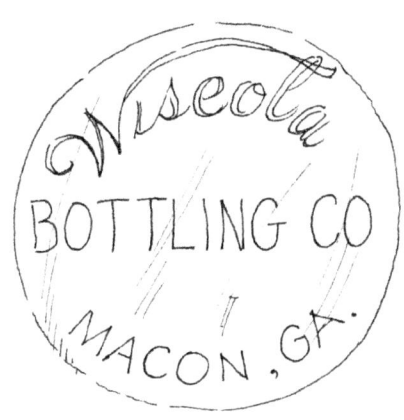

Wiscola
BOTTLING CO
MACON, GA.

G.B. WELLS
MACON. GA.
SELTZA WATER
ETCHED IN GLASS
TWO SIZES OF
PRINT
CLEAR GLASS

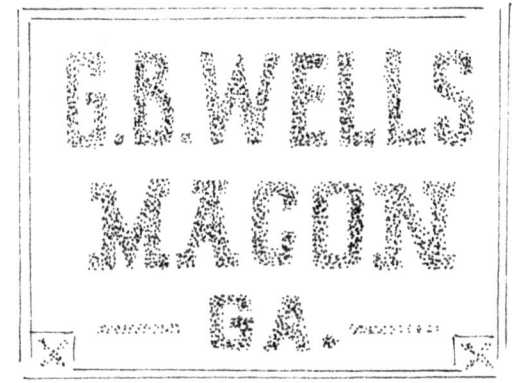

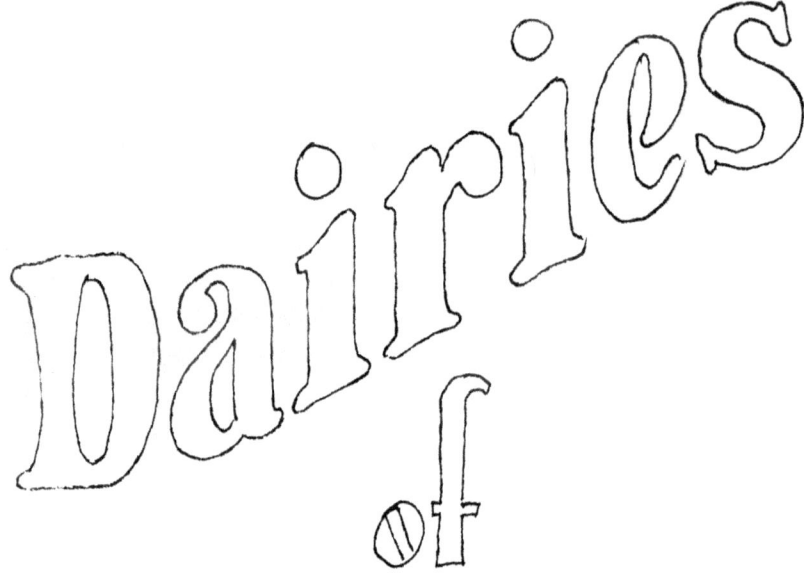

Dairies
of
BIBB CO.
MACON, GA.

CLEAR, QT. EMBOSSED & WHOLE BOTTLE IS FLUTED

ONE QUART
LIQUID

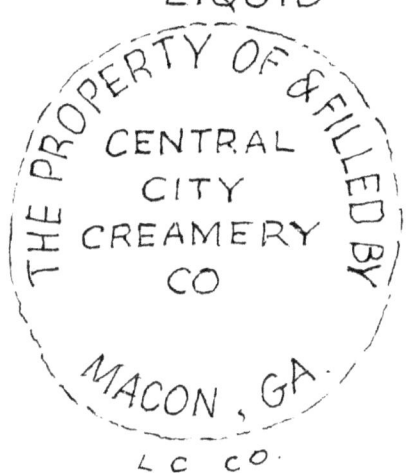

THE PROPERTY OF & FILLED BY
CENTRAL CITY CREAMERY CO
MACON, GA.
LC CO.

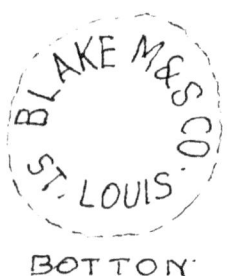

BLAKE M&S CO.
ST. LOUIS

BOTTON

CLEAR, QT. EMBOSSED

ONE QUART

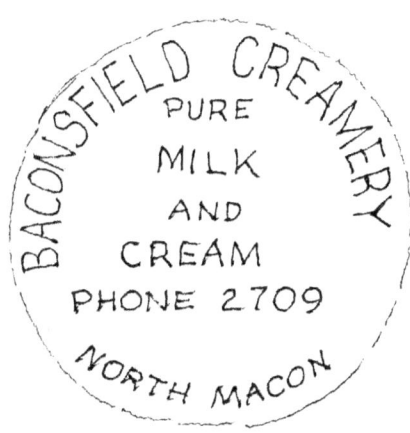

BACONSFIELD CREAMERY
PURE MILK AND CREAM
PHONE 2709
NORTH MACON

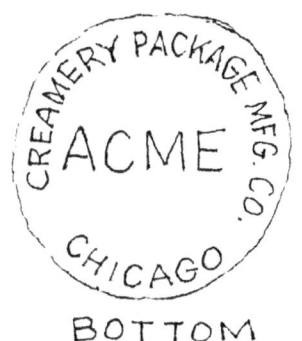

CREAMERY PACKAGE MFG. CO.
ACME
CHICAGO

BOTTOM

Pt. SIZE
silk screen
lettering

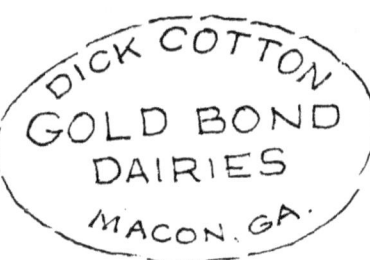

DICK COTTON
GOLD BOND
DAIRIES
MACON, GA.

EMBOSSED
REGISTERED
SEALED 11114.

There is listed in the 1922 Phone Directory
Hunter D. Cotton - 2334 Forsyth RD. Ph. 820-W

CHEROKEE FARMS DAIRY
L.M. SOLOMON JR.

There was all size bottles, embossed and
silk screen lettering. Listed in the 1922 &
1932 Ph. directory at Bellevue area Ph. 3800-J.
They also had milk cans, I had one about 3
gal. size. I got one in trade for painting, Ga Bulldogs
on two of them. One was owned by L. Gordon and
the other one owned by Charlie Ragen.
There was brown bottles, chocolate milk.

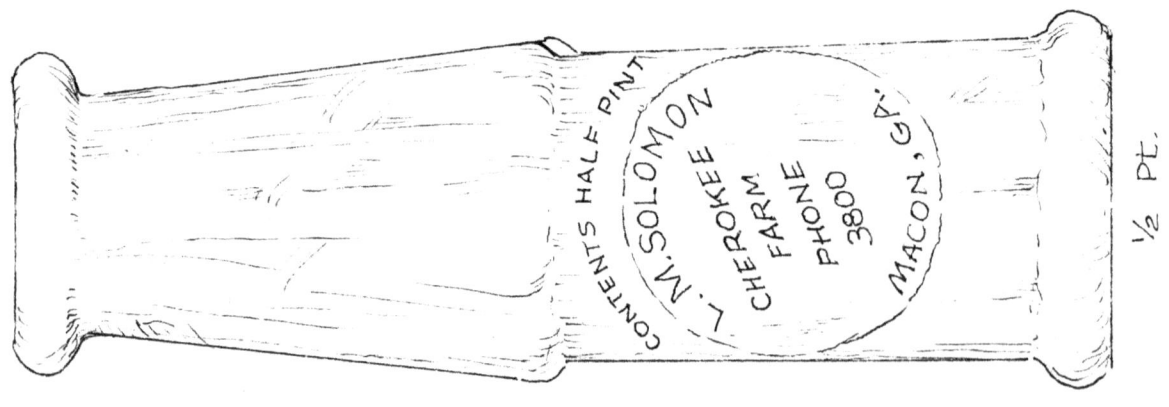

EMBOSSED, ON BOTTON   LMS MTC S 24

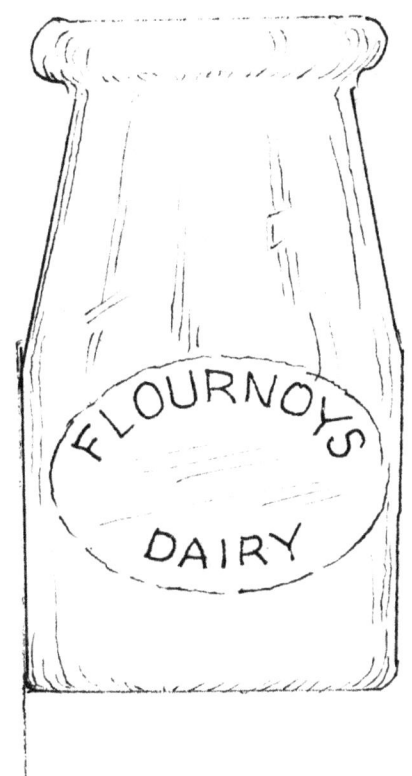

There is listed a
J. A. Flournoy at
RIVOLI area
Ph # 2957-J
Office 2893
in the 1922 Ph. directory

Embossed

not sure this a Macon Dairy
DUG on 8th Street.

Dixie Dairie

I remember this dairy as it was the largest (in 1940s) or equal the SunShine Dairy. They had all sizes of bottles, embossed as well as silk screen ones.

In 1922 Ph. directory there was a Dixie Ice Cream at 631 Cotton Ave. Then in 1932 Ph. directory the Dixie Ice Cream is at 658 Arch St. A 1949 City Directory list the Dixie Dairy and Ice Cream at the same number on Arch Street. They had bottles embossed and silk screen on same bottle.

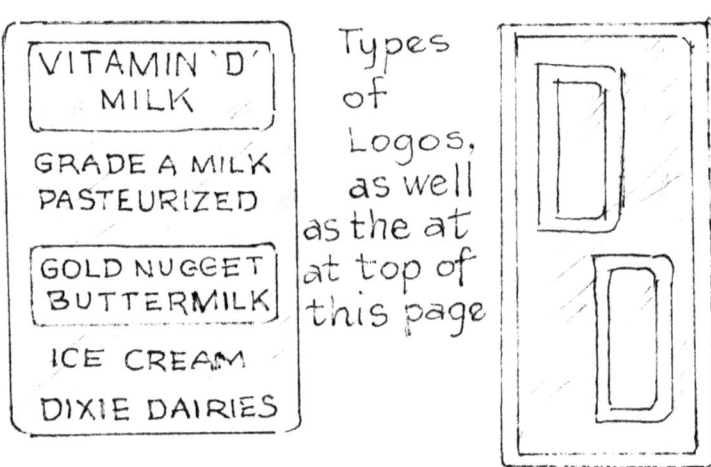

VITAMIN 'D' MILK

GRADE A MILK PASTEURIZED

GOLD NUGGET BUTTERMILK

ICE CREAM

DIXIE DAIRIES

Types of Logos, as well as the at at top of this page

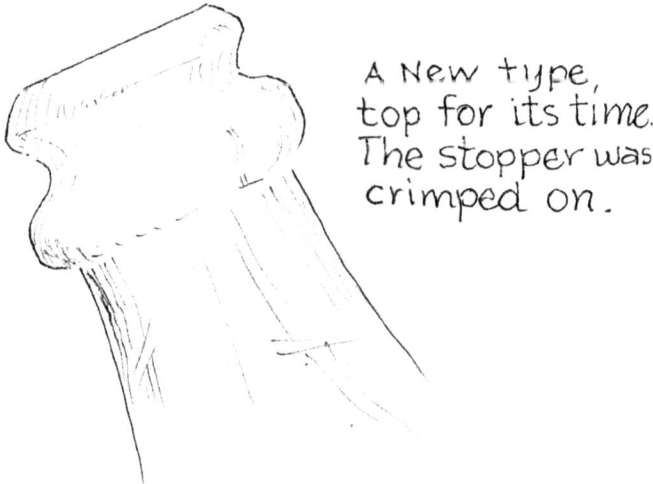

A New type, top for its time. The stopper was crimped on.

GRAY, BLUE
LETTERS
14 ¼ in. TALL

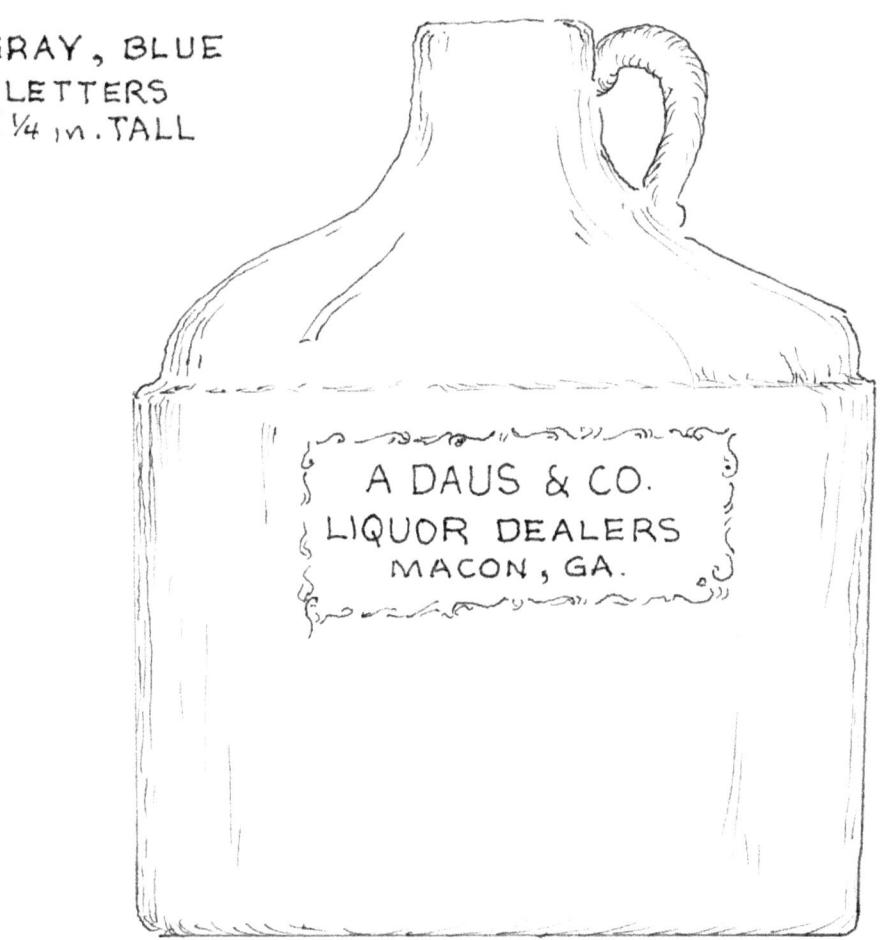

A DAUS & CO.
LIQUOR DEALERS
MACON, GA.

GRAY TOP
WHITE BOTTOM
& BLUE STRIP &
LETTERS
7 ¾ in. Tall
TWO KNOWN SIZES
THIS IS SMALL

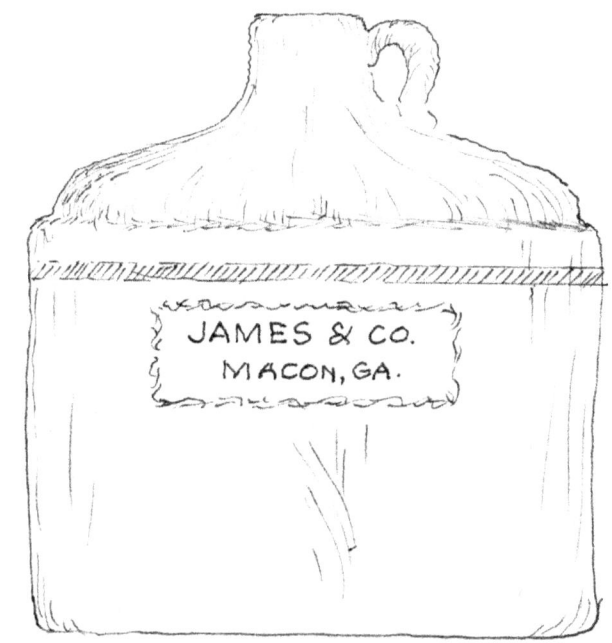

JAMES & CO.
MACON, GA.

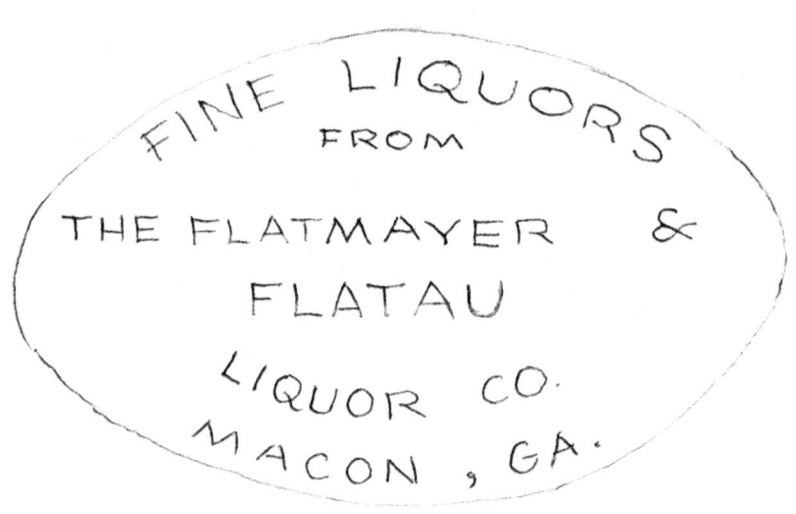

FINE LIQUORS
FROM
THE FLATMAYER &
FLATAU
LIQUOR CO.
MACON , GA.

Gal. Size
WHITE, BLUE LETTERING